THE IMPORTANCE OF WEARING CLOTHES

The artistic body painting and decoration which antedated clothing is shown in this fanciful portrait of ancient Britons published March 10, 1804, by J. Wilkes, London. The blue woad used as paint doubtless afforded little protection against the British climate.

THE
IMPORTANCE
OF
WEARING
CLOTHES

by LAWRENCE LANGNER

Revised & Updated in Color with a New Introduction
by International Fashion Authority

JULIAN ROBINSON DesRCA, FRSA

Published by

GROWTH PRESS
LOS ANGELES

Published by
ELYSIUM Growth Press
Los Angeles, CA 90027 USA

Hardcover: ISBN # 1-55599-039-8

Library of Congress Catalog Card Number: 91-070677

Bibliography: page 348

I. Social Sciences—the meaning and purpose of clothing in society

II. Psychology—the psychology of clothes   III. Art/Fashion—history

IV. History—clothing and costume

This book is dedicated to my friend,

John Steinbeck,

who encouraged me to write it.

—Lawrence Langner

Contents

Foreword

Why do we wear clothes in the broiling heat of summer? Why do women dress differently from men? Why do men wear such uncomfortable clothes? These and other questions perplexed me in my youth, and I sought the answers in such literature on clothing as existed at the time. Unsatisfied with the current explanations, I began to study the subject at first hand and learned that it embraced almost every aspect of human behavior. I also found that clothing, unlike beauty, was far deeper than skin-deep, and indeed had affected religion, morals, sex, marriage, and most of our social activities and institutions through the ages. After I had formulated some of my own answers to the questions I had raised, I wrote a play on the subject under the title *Lady Godiva, or The Importance of Wearing Clothes.*

My play was produced in due course at the Country Playhouse in Westport, Connecticut, with the charming actress Violet Heming in the title role. Supposedly riding naked on a wooden horse, Miss Heming portrayed the character of Lady Godiva with so much artificial hair covering her body that when she was drawn across the stage on the horse, her head emerged from her hair as from a bale of mattress stuffing. When the horse warned her of the immorality of riding naked through the town, the audience was utterly bewildered, for Peeping Tom would obviously have been the most disappointed man in Coventry had he seen her in these circumstances. The audience was even more bewildered when Lady Godiva was arrested and brought before Edward the Confessor on a charge of indecent exposure.

The same play was produced several years later in London at Bolton's Theatre under the title *The Importance of Wearing Clothes.* In due course I began to write a preface for the printed version. The preface grew longer and longer, and by the time I reached the end of it, there was no room for the play.

Hence this book!

I have been asked by many friends how I became especially interested in the subject of clothes and the reasons we wear them. In the course of a busy life extending into several different fields, there was one subject which I encountered in all of them, and this subject was clothing. I was therefore able to approach it from several viewpoints. These were based on my professional experience with new inventions relating to clothing; my experience with theatre and ballet costumes; my experience with the New York fashion industry in studying the protection of fashion designs as a member of the Patents Committee of the former Merchants Association of New York; my work with the U. S. Army, Navy and Air Force as Secretary of the National Inventors Council; and finally, from the viewpoint of some special studies I had made in the fields of psychology under Dr. Alfred Adler of Vienna, and sociology under Professor Thorsten Veblen at the New School of Social Research in New York. I might add that I have also had opportunities for firsthand observation on the subject, since my wife, my children and all my friends wear clothes, although few of them know why. As a result of my experiences and research, I reached a number of conclusions, some of which I believe to be new, based on the fact that all clothes were originally "inventions" and that the inferiority feelings of man have played a major role in ˙stimulating him to make these inventions. Some of these conclusions are new and startling, yet capable of substantiation, and have been italicized for emphasis. Since this book is written for the layman, as well as for the specialist, I have sometimes erred in the direction of oversimplification rather than attempt to furnish complex explanations according to existing and sometimes conflicting schools of psychology.

I take this opportunity to thank several friends for their assistance in giving me helpful information in preparing this book, and particularly the late Dr. Merrill Moore, psychiatrist, of the Massachusetts General Hospital of Boston; James Laver, the English authority on costume, of the Victoria and Albert Museum, London; J. P. Powell, anthropologist, Assistant Curator of the Department of Primitive Art, Brooklyn Museum; Lincoln Kirstein of the New York City Ballet; Lillian Moore and Gemze de Lappe, of New York, for information on ballet costumes; also Alice Raphael and Philip Nasta for their painstaking criticism of the manuscript; and last but not least, my editor, Henry Alsberg, for his excellent editorial suggestions. I am also indebted to James Laver and Clark Kinnaird for permitting me to use illustrations from their excellent collections of costume pictures; and to Macmillan & Co., Ltd., London, England, for the use of the pictures herein taken from *Across Australia* by Spencer and Gillen, and from *Melanesians and Polynesians*.

Finally, I express my special thanks and gratitude to my wife, Armina Marshall, who encouraged me to write this book and shouldered many of my burdens in other fields in order that I might do so.

LAWRENCE LANGNER

Introduction

by Julian Robinson
Designer of The Royal College of Art
Fellow of the Royal Society of Art, Great Britain

For thousands of years, men and women in many parts of the world have gone to enormous and often elaborate lengths to change their natural physical appearance—altering the look of their hair, ears, nose, teeth, eyes, skin, hands, lips, breasts, feet, genitals, neck, shoulders, rib-cage, legs, pubic region or silhouette, in order to conform to the prevailing mode of their particular cultural group, or to mark themselves as being different from their neighbors.

This desire to change our natural, naked bodies is so universal that it would appear to be an inborn trait which many people regard as an essential expression of our humanity. Yet few cultural groups agree as to which parts of our bodies should be covered and which parts should be openly displayed. Nor can they agree about which parts of the body they find sexually attractive.

Indeed, many people find it difficult to comprehend the logic behind any other mode of clothing and adornment than what they are currently wearing, finding them all unnatural or even uncivilized. The thought of exposing or viewing those parts of the body which they generally keep covered so frightens or disgusts them that they call upon their lawmakers to protect them from such a possibility.

Few contemporary authors have ever attempted to determine the motivations behind these prejudices, nor have they discussed, in any depth, the psychological reasons that have driven so many members of the human race to adorn and decorate their bodies in such diverse and wondrous ways. In short, they appear to believe that this extraordinary manifestation of human inventiveness is completely arbitrary and meaningless. They label it a universal "folly of fashion," not worthy of further discussion.

Lawrence Langner, the author of this important work, has attempted to unravel the complicated web of reasons that prompt us, and others, to wear the particular mode of clothing that we do. This book, in fact, is one of the most stimulating and interesting treatises written on the subject since Professor J. C. Flügel's *The Psychology of Clothes* (1930) which concludes with the Freudian assertation that: "clothing originated largely through the desire to enhance the sexual attractiveness of the wearer and to draw attention to the genital organs of the body."

In the original introduction to this book James Laver, a scholar of the Victoria and Albert Museum in London, pointed out that Langner proposed an distinctly new and different line of inquiry to that undertaken by Flügel. He noted that although Langner was not a professional psychologist, he was nevertheless fully acquainted with the psychoanalytical literature of the period and with the theories of Alfred Adler who proposed that a primary objective of the human psyche was to demonstrate superiority. Based on Adler's concept, Langner convincingly argued that a great deal of the development of civilization has been dependent on the efforts of the powerful ruling minority to display their authority and dominance by regulating their own as well as their subjects' mode of physical attire: from monks to merchants, from clerics to policemen, and from concubines to the royal family.

However, Langner's true avocation was the theatre. As director of The Theatre Guild and founder of The American Shakespeare Festival, he had ample opportunity to study both modern and historic costume, and to see how a change in clothing styles affected both the behavior of an actor, and the response of the audience. Much of the originality of Langner's ideas lies in the fact that he spent a good portion of his professional life involved in developing a varied array of inventions, many of them related to clothing and costume. He regarded clothes as inventions in and of themselves, created for definitive functional, social and psychological purposes. His duality of experience enabled him to draw some interesting and enlightening conclusions that have greatly increased our understanding of this broad and fascinating subject.

I was first made aware of Langner's book in 1959 when I was researching material for a series of lectures I planned to give on the varying ways that different cultural groups from around the world adorn and decorate their bodies—a study that continued for twenty-five years culminating in my book *Body Packaging: A Guide to Human Sexual Display*.

During my original research, James Laver introduced me to *The Importance of Wearing Clothes*, for which he had just written the introduction. He also drew my attention to Flügel's treatise, Hilaire Hiler's *From Nudity to Raiment*; Bernard Rudofsky's *Are Clothes Modern?*; Volume IV of Havelock Ellis' *Studies in the Psychology of Sex*, and Thorsten Veblen's *The Theory of the Leisure Classes*—all of which, together with Langner's work, now form an essential part of my personal research library.

During the intervening years, while working as a fashion designer, lecturer, design consultant, journalist and author, I had the good fortune to travel the world and see for myself many of the exotic modes of body decoration and adornments about which Langner wrote.

I also lived in such diverse communities as the East End of London, Beverly Hills, the aboriginal wilds of Central Australia, the tropics of Micronesia, Papua New Guinea, and in the center of the fashion world, Paris. Throughout these experiences I have had the opportunity to work with many of the world's most beautiful and talented individuals.

In these travels, though my attention was directed toward clothing and social interaction, I could not ignore the darker sides of life—the envy, the hate, the fear, the disenchantment, the greed and bigotry—which have plagued mankind since the beginning of time and which still exist in many places of the modern world. I have seen people killed by bombs, city centers destroyed by riots, countries devastated by famine, great opulance and thoughtless waste—all of which has greatly affected the way I, among many others, think about our current Western way of life.

As I compared new-developing civilizations and our own modern society, I noted how directly our clothing expresses the feelings we have about ourselves. It was clear to me that modern dress remains a function of our way of life as it has in the past, but because of accelerated development, the rate of change in styles of dress has increased greatly.

Many factors have impacted on our Western lifestyle since the beginning of the 1960s. International business has been affected by the boom of computerization in manufacturing and assemblyline technology. World-wide jet travel, the international spread of TV, the rise of popular music as an agent of social and political change, and the challenging of censorship and national boundaries have all contributed to a greater world homogeniety. Even the quality and selection of the food we eat and our concern for exercise and fitness reflects influences from cultures heretofore barely recognized by most of our society. Today, more than ever before, events and developments worldwide affect every aspect of living at all levels of our society.

All these changes have taken place since *The Importance of Wearing Clothes* was originally published and cannot be ignored in a re-issue of this important book. So, in addition to a revised introduction, a chapter dealing with how these changes effect the clothing styles we wear today has been added, entitled *Changing Influences and Changing Attitudes*, located in the Addendum at the rear of this book. Also, in the center of the book, is a selection of color illustrations aimed at enhancing those photos originally chosen by Langner.

I also have taken it upon myself to condense Langner's original notes which dealt with other aspects of dress not covered in the main body of the text. Everything else in the book, however, is exactly as published in the original edition, which on re-reading I found to be just as provocative and informative as it was when I first encountered it. Certainly, this book in its new form is a worthy addition to the library of all those interested in the subject of human clothing and adornment as sociological and psychological phenomena—a book to be placed alongside those of Flügel, Ellis, Veblen, Rudofsky and Hiler.

Los Angeles, California
Spring 1991

PART I

WHY

WE

WEAR

CLOTHES

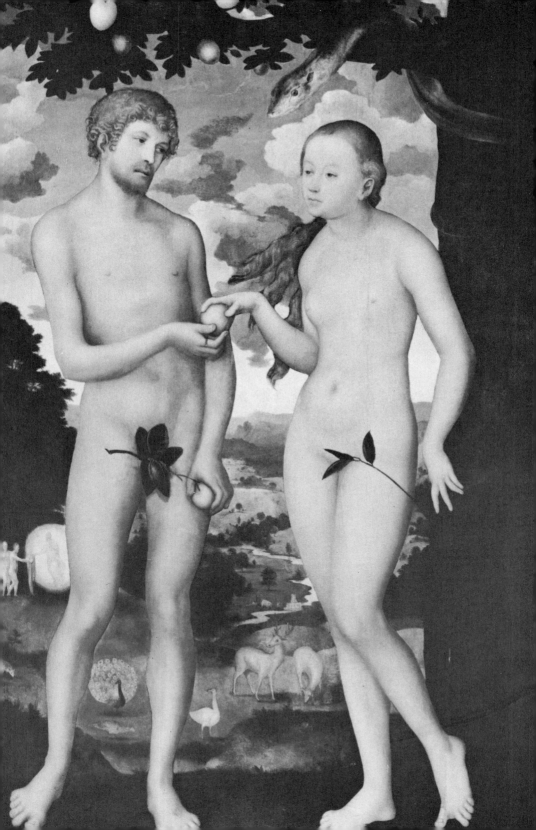

CHAPTER 1

Man, the Tailor-Made God

While Thomas Jefferson's immortal declaration that all men are born equal has been hotly disputed ever since the day it was defiantly hurled at an extremely class-conscious society, no one has ever disputed the fact that this equality extends at least to the condition of nakedness in which we emerge from the maternal womb. We may, therefore, confidently assert the "self-evident truth" that all men are born equally naked. But doubtless some voices will be raised against the validity of even this comparatively modest thesis, since there may be certain inequalities in the universal condition of nudity at birth. Man comes into the world covered with a skin that is either white (or as some sticklers for greater accuracy would have it, not white, but a sort of grayish-pink), or black, or brown, or yellow, according to the racial group to which his parents belong. In a world still largely dominated by Caucasians, to be born with a skin of any tint except grayish-pink implies a certain inferiority, at least in the opinion of some erstwhile discredited members of the "master breed."

At any rate, a man's skin is usually similar to that of the members of his family, or his neighbors, and so confers no distinction upon him in the immediate society in which he is born. His skin is a sort of equalitarian uniform which he seeks to negate as rapidly as possible. For, Mr. Jefferson notwithstanding, man constantly tries to escape from equality with his fellows and to achieve superiority over them. Body decoration, ornaments and clothes represent his early efforts to escape from the democracy of uniformity which nature

This picture, painted in Germany about 450 years ago, emphasizes the sexless innocence of Adam and Eve according to Genesis. Attributed to the workshop of Lucas Cranach the Elder. (The Isabella Stewart Gardner Museum, Boston, Mass.)

imposed upon him. The fact is that no group is known in which men are completely without clothes, ornaments or body decorations.

Man differs from all the other creatures which inhabit the earth by creating and wearing clothes. Why do we wear clothes? Ask this question of a fellow man, and he will regard you as a mild lunatic. "Obviously," he will reply, "to keep us warm in winter and cool in summer." If you point out that in some tropical countries the natives wear clothes despite torrid temperatures, he will reply that this is due to a feeling of modesty. But clothes are worn by savages who do not have any concept of modesty at all, and there are some aborigines who paint their bodies but wear no clothing whatsoever, even in cold climates, and others who dress themselves in order to become sexually excited, and still others who run around nearly nude in their ordinary daily pursuits, and only don clothes, of a highly decorative character, for religious dances and other rites. So much for the man-in-the-street's explanation of why people wear clothes. Should you go a step further and ask him why men and women dress differently, he is apt to meet such an inquiry with a blank stare and a facetious, "Well, I suppose it is to be able to tell one sex from the other, isn't it? But it's getting more difficult every day." The fact is that most of us accept our clothes as one of the simple facts of life, such as eating, drinking and having children.

But the whole subject of why men wear clothes deserves much more serious consideration than the average individual seems willing to give it. For clothes, as we shall learn as we investigate the matter more closely, have had a profound if not decisive influence on man's social evolution. As we look more deeply into the subject we will find that from the dawn of history until today, there is not a human institution which has not been importantly affected by the clothes we wear.

The first concept we must rid ourselves of is that of Naked Man, or Man-without-His-Clothes. Such a creature does not exist in our world of today, except for the short spaces of time when he removes his clothing, usually before going to bed or arising. The rest of his waking hours and his intervals of sleep are mostly spent hidden in his clothes. Clothes are an indispensable part of modern man. In a practical sense, there is therefore no such animal as Naked Man functioning in modern civilization, but only a composite creature who should be designated as Man-and-His-Clothes.

A bear or almost every other animal lives completely in its coat of fur or hair. In contrast, man, having been born naked, without any protective outer integument, has had to create for himself a second skin in which he lives and has his being from the day he is swaddled to the day he is laid out in "decent blacks," as completely as the grizzly bear in his shaggy coat. The leopard cannot change its spots. The power to change his skin at will is solely reserved to man. Although one wonders whether perhaps the leopardess doesn't sometimes grow weary of her resplendent coat and yearn to assume the fantastic feathered glory of the bird of paradise. She certainly would were she animated by emotions similar to those of the female of the human species.

Now what had at first appeared to be a dreadful, almost fatal handicap—man's unprotected nudity—turned out to be an unlimited blessing. Being a creature of infinite ingenuity and variety, man soon discovered that he could make himself not only one additional skin, but practically as many as he liked, an endless variety of them, to meet his every need and fancy. Hamlet hit the heart of the matter when he sneered at Ophelia, "God gave you one face and you make yourself another." Since the beginning of time man has been continually changing and disguising the skin he was born with. In the view of such philosophers as Jean Jacques Rousseau, who wanted man to revert to the Golden Age of unspoiled nature in which the Noble Savage flourished in a state of nudity mitigated only perhaps by a loin cloth, the sophistication of clothes was a curse rather than a blessing since it implied the vices of an effete society. But Rousseau and Hamlet notwithstanding, man has continually kept adapting his second skin so as to achieve an appearance that varied with his activities or social status, from king to beggar, from priest to warrior, or from business executive to ditch digger. There was just no limit to these chameleon possibilities.

It was as a consequence of their versatile adaptability that clothes came to play such an important role in the progress of civilization and all its cultural aspects; religion, government, sexual habits, social conduct and behavior, the performing and visual arts, and most other branches of human endeavor.

The reasons why men wear clothes are not the simple ones usually given by the unreflecting average citizen. Prehistoric man's original invention of clothing, which may have taken place over 75,000 to 100,000 years ago, or even earlier, did not necessarily arise from the need for protection against the elements, for he evolved in warmer climates where clothing was not needed. Climate played an important role only when man moved from the tropics into colder regions and needed body warmth. Then clothing became important for survival. But climate never has been the only important factor, for men can live in cold climates without wearing clothes, as witness many of the inhabitants of Tierra del Fuego who are completely naked and shield their painted bodies with screens against the bitter winds that blow furiously in that region. The tribes of Central Australia also paint their bodies, but wear no clothes, although they often suffer miserably from the cold. And early travellers in our West recorded that they saw young Indian braves playing a sort of lacrosse or hockey in the bitterest winter weather—as naked as when they were born; and civilized ladies in low-cut evening gowns sometimes evince a similar contempt for wintry climates, being presumably warmed by the admiration of their escorts.

What is the difference between body ornament, decorations worn on the body, and clothing? The answer would at first glance seem to be obvious. But on reflection, the query cannot be answered as simply as at first appeared possible. What one wears may have a mixed character. It may be both ornament and clothing. It may have been

Clothes are not actually necessary in order to live in cold climates. Left, some early inhabitants of Tierra del Fuego (Patagonia), who painted their bodies or ornamented them with feathers, but used screens to protect themselves against the wind. (Photo by Gusinde.) Right, Australian aborigines who are usually naked and ornament their bodies for corroborees or festivals.

Australian aborigines who usually wear no clothes: Left, *Arunta woman.*
(American Museum of Natural History.) Right, *old men who are the*
masters of ceremonials. (Australian Information Service.)

put on first as a mere ornament and then become a useful article of
clothing, or, *per contra,* an article of clothing may turn out to be pre-
dominantly decorative. The primitive hunter who proudly wears as
an ornamental trophy across his shoulders the pelt or fur of an animal he had killed, has also unwittingly provided himself with a
cloak. The aborigine who has entwined ornamental feathers together
to wear on his head so as to symbolize his relationship to the sun,
has also made himself a hat. *It is the nature of most materials from*
which clothing is made (such as furs, pelts, hide, the soft bark of
certain trees, and textile fibers of all kinds) that when worn on the
body for ornament or for any other reason, they inherently provide
physical protection for the wearer, and therefore constitute clothing.
But the reasons for wearing such clothing are not confined to the
protection of the body. Indeed, the hunter with his trophy-cloak
might well find it uncomfortable to wear in the heat of the tropics.
The nature of the material of which the clothing was made gave the
wearer some body protection, but from the beginning on, this was
often secondary to its decorative or ornamental effect.

It is amusing to note in passing that modern women for many
years have worn mink coats in America, providing decoration and

warmth, for much the same reasons as the primitive hunter wore his trophy. However, mink coats have become so commonplace during the past ten years that they are no longer regarded as symbols of distinction. Were the women and the fur dealers nonplussed? Not a bit of it. The mink breeders began to breed mink mutations—blue minks, silver minks, golden minks, pink minks and white minks—minks of every hue and shade, masked under such fancy names as Cerulian, Azurine, Lutetia and so forth. These new, highly colored skins restored the little animal to its position of distinction. The woman of fashion who wishes to appear superior to her sisters can now wear a superior mink by paying a superior price for it, and again triumph over the rest of the mink-wearing tribe.

One of the first writers to pay any attention to clothing from the point of view of sociology was the verbose Scots philosopher, Thomas Carlyle, who in *Sartor Resartus* (published in 1833) indulged in some vivid speculation as to the origins of clothes and their use. Carlyle, speaking of prehistoric man, stated that "the pains of hunger and revenge once satisfied, his next step was not comfort but decoration. Warmth he found in the toils of the chase; or amid dried leaves, in his hollow tree, in his bark shed, or natural grotto; but for decoration he must have clothes. The first spiritual want of a barbarous man is decoration, as indeed we still see among the barbarous classes in civilized countries." Curiously enough, although Carlyle poured out thousands of words on the subject, he failed to give any reasons for this spiritual want in mankind for body decoration. This spiritual want, in my opinion, is due to man's inherent feeling of inferiority.

It is generally recognized today that the feeling of inferiority and the goal of superiority which compensates for it are two of man's prime general motives for bettering himself or becoming a superior being. Dr. Alfred Adler, who originated the conception of the "inferiority complex," stated this in the following language: "I shall consequently speak of a general goal of man. A thoroughgoing study has taught us that we can best understand the manifold and diverse movements of the psyche (soul) as soon as our most general presupposition is recognized, viz.: that the psyche has as its objective the goal of superiority."

The good doctor goes on to state that great thinkers have given expression to much of this, and in part everyone knows it, and he adds that "Whether a person desires to be an artist, the first in his profession, or a tyrant in his home, to hold converse with God, or

*Wearing ornaments preceded wearing clothes. Shells provide both decora-
tion and protection to the aborigines of the Torricelli Mountains, New
Guinea. Many of the shells come from ancient times and are handed down
from father to son. (From* Softly, Wild Drums, *by Beth Dean and Victor
Carell, Sidney, Australia.)*

humiliate other people, whether he regards his suffering as the most
important thing in the world to which everyone must show obei-
sance, whether he is chasing after unattainable ideals or old deities,
overstepping all limits and norms, at every part of his way he is
guided and spurred on by his longing for superiority, the thought of
his godlikeness, the belief in his special magical power." Adler himself was a sickly child and overcame his feeling of inferiority by

becoming a doctor, while Eugene Sandow overcame his physical weakness as a youth and made himself one of the world's strongest men. Such examples could be multiplied a thousandfold, and are also recognized by disciples of Freud and Jung.

Prehistoric man's first spiritual want to compensate for his feelings of inadequacy and insecurity was both in relation to nature and to the creatures of the animal world. His need was subconscious but nonetheless potent. It also led him to desire to "belong" to a group or tribe which in turn led him to wish to feel superior to others of his fellow men and to win their admiration. The invention of body ornamentation or decoration began in the tropics where clothes were unnecessary, and enabled early man to meet his subconscious spiritual need and to demonstrate his superiority by decorating his body by painting or tattooing, or wearing ornaments such as feathers or jewels. Face and body markings and ornaments were designed for many purposes; to frighten the enemy, to propitiate the gods, to indicate the tribe to which he belonged and his rank in the tribe, to win admiration in sexual pursuits, to protect the wearer by magic, and to bolster his courage in facing the world. Body ornaments were made of skins, leaves and flowers, or circlets of animals' bones, claws, shells, stones and other natural objects strung together and attached to the body to produce the desired decorative effect.

Body ornamentation or decoration to demonstrate superiority is still common today as it was thousands of years ago. The soldier wearing his medals, the statesman his decorations, the lord mayor his chain of office, and the monarch his crown upon state occasions, are the modern counterparts of man's prehistoric usages of ornament and decoration to show superiority. The same holds true for the modern lady of fashion who bedecks herself with expensive jewelry, as did her remote barbarian ancestors.

Indeed the modern man of wealth finds a ready means of showing his marital love, and also advertising his fortune and superiority over other men, by making gifts of expensive jewels to his wife, who, by the time she has become a dowager, will have collected a large assortment of these tokens of his esteem. Where can she display all these glittering advertisements of his wealth and affection? Fortunately, nature has provided her with an excellent showcase. She can wear earrings in her ears, necklaces around her neck, a tiara on her head, bracelets on her arms and wrists, brooches on her bosom, and a jewelled belt around her waist.

Should a wealthy lady consider the display of jewelry possible in the Western manner to be insufficient, she can emulate the Hottentot women by wearing a jewelled stick in her nose; the Makonde women who live in Tanganyika by inserting an ivory labret into her lips to make them protrude; the high-caste East Indian women by setting jewels in the sides of her nostrils; and the Burmese women by providing gold rings under her neck to stretch it in an ecstasy of affluence; or as in ancient Rome, she could have her excess jewels worn by a special slave.

Of course she will do nothing of the sort. Being a lady of fashion, she will wear no more jewelry than is permitted by the bounds of good taste, which implies not wearing anything which is overostentatious. "Do you think my pearl necklace is too long?" a well-kept lady of dubious reputation is said to have asked Mme. Pompadour. "Not at all," was the reply, "it is merely attempting to get back to its source."

The desire to achieve superiority and to win the admiration of our fellow men and women is one of our deepest spiritual needs. It even extends to our poor relations, the monkeys, who when given pieces of ribbon with which to adorn themselves, do so with great delight, prancing up and down and preening themselves with conceit like some of our own better-known betters. As Professor Kohler has said, "The trotting about of apes with objects hanging around them not only looks funny, it also seems to give them naive pleasure." Nor is this desire for admiration limited to civilized society. "Great as is the vanity of the civilized," said Herbert Spencer, "it is exceeded by that of the uncivilized." According to Westermarck, "there are peoples destitute of almost everything which we regard as necessities of life, but there are no people so rude as not to take pleasure in ornaments."

We can gain some further insight into the reasons we wear clothes in the modern world by making an investigation among some of the men and women of our acquaintance.

You meet a handsome woman friend wearing a highly fashionable dress which suits her style of beauty. She looks adorable, and you tell her so. By her radiant expression you realize she has achieved a definite if transitory state of happiness. Why? Because her clothing has given her a feeling of superiority, which she enjoys to the utmost.

You know a woman friend who was feeling utterly dejected and depressed. She buys herself a new hat and dress. She feels happy again. Why? Her new clothes have given her a feeling of superiority and lifted her out of the doldrums.

You go to a party. Everyone is wearing evening dress except you. You are uncomfortable. Why? You are not conforming, and you feel inferior.

You go to business and absent-mindedly forget to wear a necktie. When you discover it, you feel uncomfortable, and rush out to buy one. Why? Because without it, you appear "undressed" and feel inferior.

You meet a man who is smartly dressed, or well dressed, or even overdressed. He wears his clothes with a self-confident manner. Why? They give him a feeling of superiority, or help him overcome a feeling of inferiority or insecurity.

Conversely, you meet a man wearing worn-out clothes due to poverty or lack of success in life. He has a hang-dog look. His clothes proclaim his failure and increase his feeling of inadequacy.

One of the most embarrassing accidents which can happen to a woman is to have her "panties" drop off in a public place. Her embarrassment is even greater than that of the man who discovers that his "fly" is conspicuously open in public. Why is this? The incidents have called attention to the more intimate parts and functions of the body, resulting in a loss of composure due to a feeling of inferiority on the part of the wearer. To be "caught with one's pants down" is a colloquialism commonly used today to mean one has been discovered in an embarrassing situation.

These examples, to which many more could easily be added, confirm the general principles already announced, that man from the earliest times has worn clothes to overcome his feeling of inferiority and to achieve a conviction of his superiority to the rest of creation, including members of his own family and tribe, and to win admiration and assure himself that he "belongs." This urge of wanting to "belong" is particularly strong among all classes, even among the humblest. Eugene O'Neill, in his *Hairy Ape,* has his hero, a tough stoker on an Atlantic liner, constantly reiterating his desire to "belong," which in his case was a desire to be a sufficiently tough member of the coal-heaving and dock-walloping fraternity. His sweat-stained shirt and oil-reeking trousers were the badge of his membership in the tough community of his choice. Actually, none of us is indifferent to the clothes he wears. Even those of us who seem not to care whether our garments are in fashion or not, or eccentric in style, really achieve a

Body painting, tattooing and scar patterns are still in use instead of clothes. Right, fashionable lady of Upper Congo wears ornaments and scar patterns. Above, tattooed marriageable girl of Koita, New Guinea. Below, South American Indian women with patterns painted on their bodies for dancing.

feeling of superiority because of the fact that they are shockingly unconventional. We get a thrill of satisfaction from the notice our "different" or slovenly clothes attract.

If man had not had certain capacities not possessed by other animals, capacities which enabled him to evolve toward what we perhaps conceitedly consider a higher civilization, he probably would never have evolved a cruder kind of protective body covering into sophisticated ornamental and decorative clothing. The mere feeling of inferiority and a desire to feel superior to his surroundings, animate and inanimate, would not have been enough. He needed to call into play the inventive faculty with which he was endowed, and which seems not to exist in any other living creature to any substantial extent. From this faculty sprang man's first great inventions; the edged tools, the wheel, the lever and the thousands of other devices which have evolved from them into our modern scientific civilization, so that today, like Jove, we can hurl our thunderbolts across the heavens. Probably among man's first inventions—and earlier than most of them—were clothes.

We are apt to overestimate the importance of what might be designated as his material inventions—the importance of his discovering that a branch of a tree might become useful in defending himself against his enemies or in killing other animals for his dinner, or his discovery that by rubbing two sticks together he could get fire with which to cook raw roots and wild vegetables and the meat of his animal victims. But the evidence seems to establish that probably almost his earliest invention, clothes, was motivated by other than material considerations, by considerations rooted in aesthetic and social yearnings. And in its effects on his later evolution, this invention was perhaps his most significant.

Whatever may have been the various reasons which led man to invent clothes, the results of wearing them soon began to appear. *One of these was the self-importance which clothing imparted to man in the wearing and the pleasure he derived from this, as well as from the admiration of his fellow men. Furthermore, he was enabled to cover his body and particularly his sexual and excretory organs for protection, and thus to hide these parts from himself and others.* His new skin gave him a sense of security and importance such as naked he had never felt. For most of his waking day he was able to travel over the face of the earth wearing his newly devised integument (which improved his appearance) buoyed up by the illusion that he was superior to members of his own and other tribes, whose admiration he craved, and also to the creatures of the animal world. If you wish to experience somewhat similar feelings of superiority, wear a new dress or suit for the first time, or put on your best and most appropriate clothes and join the admiring parade on Fifth Avenue on Easter Sunday, or imagine yourself dressing up for the fashionable enclosure at Ascot on Derby day! You, a creature of the animal world? Perish the thought!

When man began to seek explanations for the mysterious, unknown and frightening phenomena of nature, such as thunder, lightning, earthquakes, and especially nightmare, illness and death, he invented the answers in the form of ghosts or spirits and finally gods who appeared in dreams and often seemed to have powers greater than his own. He created these gods in his own images and endowed them with most of his virtues and many of his vices, as well as his clothing. For example, in ancient Greece his gods were not only godlike but also manlike, since Zeus was often promiscuous, Hera was jealous, and Hermes an occasional thief. *Then, paradoxically enough, man sought to propitiate or control these gods and to emulate their virtues. In this he was helped by the invention of clothes which covered his body, kept his higher centers plainly visible, but covered the lower centers which emphasized his kinship to the animal world. He no longer felt akin to this animal world, but to the world of gods or spirits.*

Man's desire to be godlike accounts for the belief in his divine origin in the folk myths of certain religions, and especially in the Hebraic-Christian religions. The association of this desire with clothes is symbolically recounted in the legend of Adam and Eve. We are all familiar with this story, but we tend to forget the details. After eating the fruit of the tree in order to become godlike ("Your eyes shall be opened and ye shall be as God, knowing good and evil," said the Serpent), Adam and Eve "knew they were naked, and they sewed fig leaves together and made themselves aprons." They hid themselves, Adam stating as the reason, "I was afraid because I was naked." Thus was sin first associated with nakedness, and a sense of shame thereafter associated with the uncovering of the sexual parts of the body. "Then the Lord God made for Adam and his wife coats of skin and clothed them."

These are the second articles of clothing mentioned in Genesis, and were made by God. Thereafter, all clothes were man-made miracles. It is amusing to note that according to Genesis, the humble apron was the first garment worn by man. It has since become a badge of servitude which is rapidly passing out of existence, since even waiters now refuse to wear them.

Whether the Bible story be regarded as gospel by the orthodox or folk myth by the scientist, it is a symbolic explanation of what occurred over a period of probably more than a million years. During this period, man, engaged in satisfying his daily needs for food, shelter and protection, and covering his body with clothes, *began to believe that he was created in the image of a Superior Being, as expressed in Genesis, "And God created Man in his own image." This belief by man that he is a superior being whose destiny is the concern of a Divine Father, God or gods is the basis of most of the Western religions. And it is his belief in his own godlike qualities which has made man seek ever more and more knowledge and dominion over the earth and the secrets of nature.*

What is the part played by clothes in the march of man's development from the primitive creature of a million years ago to the complex individual of modern civilization? *The answer would appear to be that man would not have developed as far as he has today without his invention of clothes, which enabled him to claim kinship with superior beings, deities or gods and, in the case of the Western religions, to believe that he was created in the image of God.* He could believe that he possessed an immortal soul, and he could acquire some of the qualities of the Deity among which are universal knowledge and eternal life. And this is the belief of a large part of mankind today.

Western man has arrived at his present world dominion through the practices which have developed from this belief for thousands of years. What matter if, along the wayside, a small band of atheists, agnostics, materialistic doctrinaires or certain scientists disavow these beliefs? Man will continue to progress so long as, with the aid of his clothing, he regards himself as a godlike creature. Should this belief ever fail universally, so that it is no longer an impelling force for civilization, man will need to create some new belief to give him the necessary feeling of superiority to aspire for dominion over the world of nature. Voltaire's saying that "If God did not exist, man would have to invent Him" can be paralleled by saying that *"If clothes had not been invented, man could never have believed that he was made in God's image and could therefore partake of His godlike attributes."*

That the majority of Western men universally believe that they are akin to a world of gods or spirits rather than animals can easily be proven. We have only to recall the irate hysteria into which Darwin plunged the religious world when he dared to assert that mankind was a member of the animal kingdom and related to the apes. Only a relatively few years ago, it was considered criminal in the deep South of the United States to teach evolution in the public schools, as witness the famous Scopes trial. Moreover, most of the important religions of the world, and many of the unimportant ones, teach the divine origins of mankind; and attempts on the part of governments, such as the Soviet government, to inhibit such beliefs have been only partially successful. We are not here concerned with what man is, but what he believes himself to be. And we know that countless millions of human beings do not regard themselves as animals, but are motivated by the belief that they possess an immortal soul and that the Kingdom of God is within them.

Margaret Mead gives the following amusing instance of men's behavior in the Western world, once released from the compelling desire to be godlike. "Long ago in a New England village one of the villagers received a revelation from God that everyone was to do exactly as he wished. Sadly, with exemplary rambunctiousness, the villagers took off their clothes and ran around on all fours like animals, making animal sounds. No one had a better idea." One can imagine some of them remarking, "If God doesn't care what we do, we might as well be animals."

We who call ourselves civilized men and women and wear clothes based on those worn by our primitive ancestors still feel ourselves godlike and superior to the animal world. We still refer to our sexual functions as "animal"—even though no normal animal except those debased by man for breeding purposes would ever dream of engaging in all-the-year-round sexual activity as we do. We still feel uneasy at the suggestion that we are somehow related to the monkey world—though no decent ape would slaughter his own fellow ape in the manner in which we kill our fellow man. We call these actions "animal" or "brutal" because we seek to blame the creatures of the animal world for our own shortcomings. And perhaps it is well that this is so, because by repudiating these as "human" actions, we seek everlastingly to find a higher sphere of moral and spiritual life in which to function.

The general theory of a relationship between clothes and the progress of civilization has been confirmed by various authorities in the past, but only in general terms. Thus Carlyle in *Sartor Resartus* pointed out what he called "the moral, political, even religious influence of clothes, and undertook to make manifest, in its thousandfold bearings, this grand proposition, that man's earthly interests are all hooked and buttoned together and held up by clothes." Also that "society is founded on clothes and sails through the infinitude on them, and without which it would sink to endless depths or mount to inane limboes, and in either case be no more."

Carlyle's conjectures were correct. Man's amazing aspirations and achievements are all held together by the clothing made by the tailor, the dressmaker, the *couturier* and the clothing manufacturer. For there would be precious little religion, government, society, law and order, morals and many of the other attributes of modern civilization were it not for the invention of clothes. Ridiculous? Well, let us embark on a voyage of discovery among our human institutions and the clothes on which they are so largely dependent. We shall find that Carlyle's surmises are actually understatements of the contributions made by clothing to the advancement of civilization in the past, and the progress of the human race to its high destiny in the future.

CHAPTER 2

Invention and the
Evolution of Clothes

Since all inventions represent attempts to improve on nature, the successful inventor achieves a certain superiority over his fellow men by his inventions. The Russians are now thrusting their collective chests forward with understandable pride because of their invention of the Sputnik. We Americans feel nationally inferior at the present moment because an American didn't invent it first. So it has probably always been with clothing. The man who first invented clothes was better adapted to his environment and felt superior to his naked fellow man, just as the man in the first motor car felt superior to a man on a bicycle, who in turn felt superior to a man riding on a donkey, or on foot. Thus inventions make superior beings of us all.

Of all living creatures, man is almost alone in being able to invent. Professor Wolfgang Kohler has described how a chimpanzee invented a way to reach a banana lying outside his cage beyond his reach. He seized a long stick and thrust it through the bars until it touched the banana, which he then dragged into the cage by manipulating the stick. The chimpanzee's problem was solved by using the stick to bring the banana into reach in order that he might fill his need to eat. When the stick was removed, the chimpanzee replaced it successfully with a tree branch. Apparently, after eating the banana, the chimpanzee felt no further urge to invent, for this is about as far as he has gone on his own initiative on the road to progress. Dogs are also capable of exercising some ingenuity in solving problems, yet there are no canine Edisons, for the inventive faculties of animals are strictly limited.

19

Among the first objects which met our remote ancestor's gaze as he descended from the trees and stood upon the ground was a stick and a stone. With the need to provide for his family, he used these as weapons to furnish them with food and to protect them against the onslaughts of wild animals. Then he contracted enemies of his own kind. He either hit them with the stick or he threw the stone at them, and he has been doing the same thing ever since, until he can now propel his missiles around the earth and beyond the moon. When he attached the stone to the stick, he made the first hafted tool, and when he pierced someone with a sharp stick or bone, he made the first spear. Thus armed, man faced the world and by improving on his simple tools and weapons, he ultimately conquered it. Man's ability to invent, therefore, enabled him to survive and become today's hero or monster, depending on how you happen to regard him. *His inherent sense of inferiority, as his brain developed, made him strive to walk upright with his chin up and his eyes gazing at the heavens in order to free his hands for useful work and increase his physical stature over the other four-legged creatures walking on the ground. It also made him dissatisfied with his new environment. It drove him on to develop his inventive faculties to improve his condition—for all invention, beginning with the most primitive, represents man's desire to improve on nature and to secure dominion over her.*

Man's ability to invent would have been of no use to him had he not possessed a tool or means for making his inventions work, or, as the patent lawyers say, "reducing them to practice." This he owned in the human hand, a marvellous device which developed during millions of years of living in the trees and holding onto them by his palms, fingers and thumbs. This hand was shared by him with all the tree-dwelling monkeys and apes, but with no other animal. With the aid of the human brain, however, these hands could grasp and make things and thus carry out man's imaginative ideas in the form of inventions. Tree dwelling made his hands particularly suited to holding needles, weaving fibres and doing other necessary work in the making of clothing. Man owes a great deal to his remote forefathers' habit of leaping from tree to tree.

What was the first garment invented by man? Experts appear to agree that our prehistoric ancestors ultimately came down from the trees and roamed the jungles and plains for perhaps a million years or more. Those with the shortest pelvic structure, which enabled them to stand upright and walk on two legs, were best fitted for survival, since this released their arms and hands to serve as tools. Erect posture in walking was possible only after a long series of adaptations, and was an enormous improvement on man's four-legged crawling or walking posture. But in one respect it was not. The male sex organs, which were protected by his back and the forepart of his body, as with all four-legged animals, were now thrust forward and exposed and without protection when he walked along the ground. Since he sometimes wrapped thongs, girdles and ornamental objects and material around his arms and legs for decoration, it was not beyond his power of invention, even in the early days of history, to hang similar material around his waist in the form of a small apron or flap of bark, matting, hide or fur hanging from a girdle of thongs around his middle, which also served to protect his sexual organs.

By placing this apron in a protective position over these, prehistoric man was at least partially protected, if not as well protected as the animals who walked on all fours. He was thereafter able to move around in the jungle or tall grass without hurting himself.

Evolution of male clothes: Man's first clothing was probably the apron which is still worn in primitive societies. Left, Hawaiian surf rider wearing small apron. Right, apron modified into loin cloth worn by native of Simbo Island, Australasia.

Thus the apron, originally deriving from body decoration and providing body protection, may well have been the first garment invented by man. This conjecture is partly confirmed by the fact that it is used in one form or other, with variations, among the almost naked aborigines all over the modern world. It also conforms with the Bible story of Adam and Eve. This conjecture should therefore please everybody, although it cannot be proven. The Scottish sporran is a lineal descendant of the first apron and serves substantially the same ornamental and useful purposes, besides containing a pocket for the frugal Highlanders to keep their money. This apron is also used as an ornament by certain savage tribes today, and by this I do not mean to insult the Scots!

One of our early ancestors with too large a piece of matted material or hide for his apron, probably conceived the idea of tucking it under his crotch and fastening it to the thong or cord at his back. This increased his body protection, but was less comfortable to wear. The natives of Melanesia to this day use such aprons made of highly colored straw, and this is true of natives in other tropical countries. Colored gourds, in the place of aprons, are worn today by the natives of the Upper Sepik region of New Guinea, the chief wearing the largest gourd to indicate his rank! And the male natives of Tanna, New Hebrides, wind enormous bundles of calico around their sexual organs, decorating the extremity with flowering grasses. This is said to protect them from the "Narak," or bewitching forces. Women, with less exposure, were often satisfied with a string of beads or shells worn over the pelvis, which probably was more effective in provoking attention than in providing protection.

Tracing the invention of clothing down the ages, prehistoric man's desire for decoration and to protect parts of the body was the primary impetus for the invention of clothing in the warmer climates, while in colder climates desire for warmth created an additional need and probably first resulted in the extensive use of fur for clothes. A large fur wrapped around the body served as a covering or cloak and provided some insulation against the cold. Since furs and hides were used for clothing before the invention of tanning, a means to soften the skins had to be devised. Skins were probably made pliable by biting them, a job which may have been performed by the wives who still do this today among the Eskimos. The bones and parts of skeletons unearthed in widely separated parts of the world testify to the great chronological age of man, but we have naturally found none

Evolution of male clothes: The apron became a male skirt which, when tucked under the crotch, made the early form of trousers. Upper left, male skirt of furs, Patagonian Indian. Upper right, skirt of flute player of New Caledonia. Lower left, trousers worn for many ages by the Kurds of north-west Persia. Lower right, medieval form of trousers still worn in Brittany.

of his early clothing. What we have found, however, are his orna-ments, and awls and needles of bone and ivory with which he made his clothes. Stone scraping tools of great antiquity have been found in prehistoric cave sites estimated to date from 75,000 years ago and these were probably used to scrape the hide and make it more flexible.

Evidence in the form of an amazing number of the skulls of the great cave bear has been found in the caves of southern France and Spain and indicates that these animals were dispossessed by prehis-toric man, who killed and ate them during their hibernating periods and transferred their fur to his own body for warmth. The tools used for this purpose have also been found in these caves and consist of rough skinning knives of stone, scrapers and awls of flint and pol-ished bone used to make holes in skins or furs and to insert thongs for making them into garments. Thus was invented the first winter clothing of a type which is still fashionable, and which enabled our cave-dwelling ancestors to survive the glacial cold.

Judging by modern standards, it may not seem to have called for much inventive ingenuity to cover the body with a cloak made of a large fur-bearing animal's skin, but to do this and attach the cloak to the body by thongs worn around the shoulders or neck so as to give freedom of movement without bodily discomfort, or to connect a series of pelts together and attach them to the body as a coat, re-quired ingenuity of a high order. When man realized that a quantity of small furs could also provide a covering, the tremendous inven-tion of sewing by a needle and thread to connect them together was made by these early peoples. A number of very fine Stone Age ivory and bone needles, with eyes suitable for thread, have been found in different parts of Western Europe. The sewing of the pelts was done with these fine bone needles with eyes, and sinews, thongs or vege-table fibres served as threads to join the pelts together or fasten them in position, or both. M. D. C. Crawford, in his *Philosophy in Cloth-ing,* states that "the oldest needles with eyes we know of were found in quantity in the upper Paleolithic caves, together with toggles and buttons. Needles were also known in Predynastic Badarian Egypt, in the silt of Neolithic Swiss Lake villages, and at least as early as the Shang period in China, traditionally 1766–1122 B.C." In modern times these primitive fastening means developed into steel needles and thread, hooks and eyes, suspenders, zippers, and all the other devices for attaching apparel so that it will cover the body or its parts and stay in position.

Evolution of clothes: Animal furs worn as cloaks. This fanciful print of albino Negroes by J. Wilkes, London, 1797, suggests the earliest type of fur garment, a cloak connected at the wearer's neck.

Some of the earliest drawings and paintings discovered in various caves inhabited by prehistoric man in the latter part of the Ice Age show him wearing ceremonial clothes in the form of animal skins and masks with animal horns. These Ice Age paintings may go back 20,000 years or more, although recent estimates date them at considerably later. Sculptures believed to antedate these drawings and paintings by perhaps 10,000 years indicate the use of ornaments before the use of clothing. One of the earliest known statuettes was named, by a scientist with a sense of humor, the Venus of Wellendorf, the latter being the name of the village in Austria where it was found. This little figure, believed to be a fertility amulet, depicts a woman with disproportionately huge breasts and buttocks; but what interests us most is that while she wears no clothes she wears ornamental bands around her wrists, and her hair is arranged in ornamental rows of curls which today would call for hours spent at a beauty parlor. Other somewhat similar statuettes have been found, such as the Venus of Laspugne and the Venuses of Grimaldi.

Some definite pictures of early man's clothing can be seen in the later prehistoric paintings of the Spanish Levant. Although emphasis is placed on the headdress, body ornaments or weapons of these tiny figures, it is possible to discern in them knee breeches, skirts, loin cloths, hats, and ornaments. *It would appear from these pictures that trousers and skirts were invented at least 10,000 to 12,000 years ago, or possibly earlier, to protect the wearer against cold, and even in those early times the male usually wore trousers for hunting while the female wore the ancient equivalent of a shirtwaist and skirt.* These were probably made of reindeer hide in the same way that the Eskimos make their clothes of skin today, despite their acquaintance with the Sears Roebuck catalogue. In considering these time periods, we must remember that they are in the nature of scientific guesses, and even now are being re-evaluated in accordance with new radioactive-carbon methods of testing age which were recently invented. Indeed, we must assume that in order to survive in the early glacial times, prehistoric man in Europe must have devised and worn clothing long before the periods of the cave paintings of southern France and the rock paintings of the Spanish Levant.

Let us imagine a fashion parade along the coastal regions of eastern Spain from Lérida in the north to Cádiz in the south about 10,000 to 12,000 years ago, and note what the well-dressed prehistoric men and women were wearing. Among the hunters of the

The earliest known pictures of men wearing clothes are found in the cave paintings of Southern France about 20,000 or more years old. These represent sorcerers or medicine men dressed as animals for animal food-hunting ceremonies. Center, the great sorcerer of Les Trois Frères with reindeer horns and hide, horse's tail and bear's paw. Upper left, dancing wizard, Les Trois Frères. Lower left, masked wizard with sleeves simulating mammoth's tusks. Upper right, sorcerer, Espélugues, near Lourdes. Lower left, wizard wearing animal mask and tail, from a rock painting, Spanish Levant, Gasulla Ravine of about 12,000 year ago. (Drawn by S. Schoenberg.)

The earliest "everyday" clothes, from rock paintings, Spanish Levant, of about 12,000 years ago: Upper left and right, *men in "shorts."* Center, *woman wearing loin cloth.*

period was illustrated a gentleman wearing Bermuda shorts or "running" trousers such as might be sold today by Brooks Brothers in New York or Simpson of Piccadilly, the trouser legs terminating just above his knees, which goes well with his bobbed haircut.

A woman from Miateda, Province of Albacete, is shown wearing a very handsome loin cloth tied in at the waist, with points extending along the bottom of the garment and probably made of reindeer hide. For the rest, she is naked, and shows substantial if pendulous breasts. However, a far more stylish woman is represented in another painting, also at Miateda. She wears a knee-length skirt pulled in at the waist and what appears to be a blouse or jacket. Indeed, it may be possible that she is wearing a complete robe drawn in at the middle with a belt around the waist. A frieze known as "The Dancing Women" at Cogul, Province of Lérida, shows several women wearing bell-shaped skirts which hang from the hips, as well as capes or cloaks over the shoulders.

As the hunting groups were largely superseded by agricultural communities living in villages and later on in towns, important improvements took place in the development of clothing. As the result of the domestication of sheep, the cultivation of flax in Egypt and cotton in India, and the invention of the distaff and, later on, the spinning wheel to transform animal or vegetable fibres into twisted thread, textile fabrics were produced by weaving these threads into cloth. A great improvement in the garments depicted in the Spanish rock paintings was therefore made possible by the invention of fabrics which, in their more advanced form, were probably first introduced during the upswing of civilization in the Middle East around 8,000 years ago. However, primitive peoples have independently invented the weaving of fabrics in widely separated parts of the world,

Left, *woman wearing earliest known blouse and skirt.* Right, *dancing women with bell-shaped skirts. All of these clothes were probably made of reindeer hide. (Drawn by J. Powell.)*

although most inventions throughout history have been made in the temperate or near-temperate zones, and not in the tropics where nature has been more bountiful in meeting man's primal demands.

At the end of the Ice Age, the so-called "cradle of civilization" in the Middle East areas possessed a climate much milder than Europe at that time, resulting in substantial tracts of fertile grassland, some of which are arid deserts today. With the growth of agriculture and villages in this area, many inventions relative to clothing were made. These included hand looms for weaving, devices for spinning, dyestuffs and methods of dyeing, and processes of tanning leather. A representation of a hand loom on a pottery dish found in Badaria, Egypt, is estimated to date back to about 4400 B.C. These devices and methods developed to such an extent that when the historical periods were reached, men were already in possession of two types of clothing which substantially covered all or most of the body. The first was made by weaving animal or vegetable fibres into fabric which was draped around the body, the second by cutting and sewing pieces of fabric or material together, such as sheepskin or fur. Peoples who make fabric have a reluctance to cut the fabric, and it is believed by Crawford and other authorities that the making of clothing from woven fabric by cutting and tailoring the fabric to the shape of the body was introduced to weaving peoples rather than developed by them.

Some of the most ancient costumes that have so far been discovered anywhere in the world are two of this latter type, and date from the Bronze Age graves of Denmark, approximately 2500 B.C. These costumes were miraculously preserved because the coffins were of hollow oak logs and the tannic acid acted as a preservative. These fabrics have been described as the original tweeds, and the

Evolution of women's clothes, from beads or ornaments: Left, *African Haviroudo girls completely attired in beads.* Right, *unmarried Telefolmin girl, New Guinea, wears a pelvic ornament, with boy also wearing standard head and pelvic decorations. (American Museum of Natural History.)*

costumes show some needle decoration. The man's costume consists of a loin cloth, a sort of a poncho tunic and a short cloak. The woman's costume has a sleeved bolero jacket and a skirt. Here we have what seems to be an early composite between the tailored fur costume of the north and the draped fabric garment from the weaving areas.

In the weaving areas of the Middle East, the clothes, draped or wound around the wearer's body or sewn together, formed tunics and robes. Wool, cotton and linen were the favorite textile materials, and these became more refined as the Assyrian, Babylonian, Egyptian and Persian civilizations developed. Linen for clothing became one of the principal manufactured products of ancient Egypt, while silk was developed in China and arrived much later from Persia via India.

In what order and where were the most important articles of clothing which we wear today invented? We have already mentioned the trousers, skirts and cloaks of fur or hides of the Spanish Levant of about 10,000 to 12,000 years ago; tunics corresponding to kilts or skirts of woven cloth were worn by the Sumerians, Assyrians, Baby-lonians and Persians 5,000 or more years ago, while the latter also invented the two-piece suit of textile fabrics consisting of coat and trousers, which, however, were probably not tightly fitted to the body. The woven bell-shaped skirt and the flounced skirt, and the corset or girdle, were invented by the Minoans of Crete between 4,000 and 5,000 years ago, and very attractive and modern their women looked in them, judging from the statuettes we have of them. Clothing with sleeves and trousers fitted to the body were probably first invented in northern climates, to provide warmth.

The cutting and sewing of woven fabrics into the form of tubes to make sleeves and trousers, while used in the East during these early historical periods, did not begin to be generally adopted in the Mediterranean areas until later, when they superseded the use of draped clothes. The designing and sewing of pieces of fabrics to form tubular sleeves and trousers was an invention which we still use after all these thousands of years, having invented nothing better!

Evolution of women's clothes: Left, *unmarried girls of Minj, New Cale-donia, wear grass aprons. (Courtesy of Dean and Carell.)* Right, *a grass skirt worn in the South Sea Islands. (American Museum of Natural History.)*

Evolution of women's clothes: Left, a Fiji woman with sarong tucked under crotch. Right, Solomon Islands belle wears a palm-leaf skirt.

Evolution of women's clothes: Left, Patagonian Indian wearing fur skirt similar to ancient Spanish rock painting dresses. Right, an Eskimo woman, (most of whom wear no clothes in their igloos) here dressed in trousers for outdoors. (American Museum of Natural History.)

Climate has obviously played an important role in determining the necessity for inventing the various kinds of clothing worn by humanity. The tropics were responsible for the most primitive kinds, the loin cloth and apron in all its forms which cover the middle of the body, and including its derivative, the primitive skirt hanging from the loins. The temperate zones are responsible for clothing which covers substantially the entire body, including draped robes, skirts, tunics, trousers, etc., and also including the enveloping desert clothing which protects the wearer against heat, cold and sand storms. The colder climates gave birth to clothing covering the entire body and fitted around the arms, legs and torso for greater warmth.

Flügel classified clothing into two classes: (a) the fixed and (b) the modish. The first are substantially permanent and are not subject to fashion changes, but vary with each locality; the second type

Evolution of women's clothes: The skirt develops more voluminously and ornamentally. Left, Kenyah (Borneo) woman in elaborate skirt. Right, Taupo girl, Samoa, in elaborate hat with skirt. (American Museum of Natural History.)

predominates in the Western countries and changes rapidly in point of time over all parts of the world which are subject to fashion changes. As Shakespeare states in *Much Ado About Nothing,* "Fashion wears out more apparel than the man." It is a *sine qua non* of fashion clothing that it exists only in countries where part of the population is generally wealthy enough to discard clothing before it is worn out in order to maintain its position of superiority in the community.

The division of Western people into classes wearing different kinds of clothing to denote each class developed as the ancient agricultural Mediterranean village communities began to use slave labor or other forms of labor, and the division was intensified when some of the villages grew into cities with a ruler or ruling class and a priesthood wearing special clothes to indicate their rank. The making of fabrics was at first the special province of the women (the reason we refer to them as "the distaff side,") but later on it also became a masculine occupation. Herodotus was surprised to find that in ancient Egypt weaving was done by forced laborers or slaves working at the

Evolution of women's clothes: Women are usually completely covered in India. Left, modern New Delhi woman wearing sari. (Information Service of India.) Right, Afghanistan woman with bejewelled nose wears trousers and veils.

Ancient costumes: Left, *the full skirt and blouse, Crete, about 1500 B.C.* *(Metropolitan Museum of Art.)* Right, *short skirt and robe, Egypt, about* *2500 B.C. (Louvre.)*

looms (about 447 B.C.). *With the advent of a middle class which included the lesser officials, the stratification of society into three classes, the aristocracy, the middle classes, and the workers and peasants, all distinguished by their own particular clothing, became an accomplished fact, and this still remains to a considerable extent the pattern of present-day society.*

The first fully dressed men and women of Egypt wore tunics which provided a knee-length skirt for the men, and an ankle-length skirt for the women similar to the modern sarong of the Malay states. For a full description of the elaborate costumes worn in the ancient world, the reader is referred to the many excellent illustrated histories of costumes such as that of Davenport or Gorsline. All of these show that as civilization progressed, the rulers and superior people usually wore the most elaborate costumes, while the middle classes wore simpler clothing; the slaves wore loin cloths and were often quite naked.

According to Werner Keller in *The Bible as History*, excavations at the ancient city of Ur of the Chaldees unearthed a clothing factory of about 4,000 years ago, where several dozen women worked and produced twelve different kinds of fashionable clothes. Clay tablets were also found on which were enumerated the names of the mill girls and the quota of rations. Even the weight of the wool given to each girl and the number of garments made from it was meticulously recorded.

The invention of dyeing fabric followed that of weaving. Over 4,000 years ago the early Semites enjoyed an excellent business in selling the rare purple dye which was extracted from the shellfish murex and was the sign of high rank or royalty. In fact the name "Canaan" means "Land of Purple." The long and arduous voyages which the ancients undertook to secure this purple dye for a symbol of superiority show how strongly ancient man relied on clothes to indicate the importance of rank and authority. Egyptian wall paintings of Israelites show that they were expert in dyeing and weaving fabrics, so that Joseph's coat of many colors, one of the early garments mentioned in the Bible, is substantiated by the evidence of these paintings.

As clothes developed from prehistoric to historic times, as shown in paintings and statuary, man began to use his ingenuity to impart different functions to his clothing and to combine these in one and the same garment. *As a result, almost every article of clothing from ancient times down to today performs the following functions: (a) It is useful, as for instance in protecting the body, (b) it is ornamental or possesses aesthetic qualities, (c) it indicates the superior rank, or lack of rank, of the wearer, or his calling, (d) and it has qualities which tend to stimulate sexual interest.* While all of these functions may not appear in each and every garment, most of them do, man being loath to wear clothes for utility alone.

Most of the succeeding improvements in the manufacture of fabrics, such as spinning, weaving, embroidering and dyeing, gave men and women increased opportunities for making clothes which enabled their wearers to emphasize their superior power, beauty, attractiveness, or rank, as well as overcoming physical deficiencies and protecting them from sun, rain and cold. The inventions which have been made in this field for thousands of years are continuing at an accelerated rate as new fibers, new fabrics and new fashions are generated by the rapidly increasing family of mankind. And the end is not in sight, nor is it likely ever to be reached so long as man continues to press on towards goals which are yet to be attained.

PART II

CLOTHES

AND

SEX

Ambivalent clothing which conceals and reveals: Compare the seductive gown worn by Gypsy Rose Lee, author and actress, with the less seductive appearance of the scantily clad girl at the left.

CHAPTER 3

Clothes and Sexual Stimulation

Man's unconscious desire to feel superior by covering his body with clothing produced an unexpected result. *Instead of reducing man's sexual desires, it actually increased them. Mankind, striving to rise above the call of the flesh, became one of the most erotic of all living creatures because of his clothing.* This posed a neat problem which has been with us for thousands of years—how to control our interest in sex so that despite this increased stimulation due to clothing, we may enjoy an orderly society based upon a firm foundation of family life. Man has largely solved this problem of control by inventing clothes which in their usage either inhibit or stimulate sexual desire.

Does the wearing of clothing actually stimulate increased sexual interest? The answer will become apparent when we compare the sexual habits of many civilized peoples with those of many naked or almost naked peoples. Another question to be considered is the service performed by clothing in controlling eroticism to enable man to apply his major efforts to mastering his occupational environment. Modern man has also, in part by means of his clothing, succeeded in the main in adjusting to living in two worlds, the one of the spirit and the other of the senses. The role played by clothing in regulating sexual interest has also been of importance in maintaining marriage as a stable institution. We shall now discuss all these questions with reference to the use of clothing to maintain the illusion that men are more godlike than animal, and also with special reference to the use of clothes to hide certain basic physical sexual phenomena of both the male and female which create embarrassment or shame.

Man appears to be the only creature among the higher mammals

39

of which the female, as well as the male, for better or for worse, maintains an interest in sexual activity, spring, summer, fall and winter, and morning, noon and night. Among mammals, mating is usually a seasonal affair, related to the ovulation of the female. With most higher mammals this takes place in the spring and only during the limited period that fertile mating and therefore reproduction of the species is possible. During all other stages of the female's reproductive cycle, she is infertile and usually will not permit mating. (Exceptions to the above are found in connection with some primates, usually when living in captivity.) This is not true of humans, in which the sexual interest of most females is far from being limited to thirteen short periods annually, as would be the case were sexual interest to exist only during ovulation.

What part have clothes played in imparting to men and women these sexual attributes which make them differ from most of the creatures of the animal world? As the result of inventing and wearing clothes (and undoubtedly an unexpected result), man has been able to impart an important stimulus to the mating instinct which has helped to make this all-the-year-round mating continuously interesting, usually with the coexistence of the emotion of love, but by no means necessarily so. *This stimulus resides in (a) the curiosity which is aroused by the habitual wearing of clothes which keep the naked body from becoming commonplace, and (b) the erotic impulse which comes into play with the removal of these clothes.* It is important to emphasize these two factors for a proper understanding of the effect of clothing on human eroticism, for while primitive naked peoples are just as much interested in sex, *they lack the immediate sexual stimulus due to the uncovering of the body.*

Modern man's curiosity about a woman's body, no matter how well her charms are hidden by her clothes, is perennial and insistent. "That's a sexy-looking girl walking behind us," remarked one man on the street to his companion. "How can you tell without looking behind you?" asked his friend. "By the expression on the faces of the men coming our way," was the answer. Women have a similar curiosity which, however, is often limited by the role played by love and marriage.

Thus we find that the curiosity aroused by wearing clothes and the stimulus due to their removal is part and parcel of our all-the-year-round sexual life. This is merciful, for if we had a spring mating season like most other mammals, our babies would all be born around

Christmas time, and we would never be able to find sufficient obstetricians, midwives, or hospital beds to bring them all into the world at once. Moreover, during the spring, mankind would have to cease most of its other activities, and concentrate on mating. We therefore should be grateful for the role played by clothing in helping to spread our sexual activities over all four seasons of the year!

If increased sexual activity in men and women is due to the wearing of clothes, we should logically expect to find this activity affected among primitive peoples who are habitually naked. And indeed, according to some authorities, among habitually naked primitive peoples, eroticism due to viewing the opposite sex in the nude is less aroused as compared with the sexual stimulus due to the nakedness of people who habitually wear clothes. For example, the men of Pongo, French West Africa, refused to allow their women to wear any kind of clothes because, if they did, the women would become more beautiful and be desired by the men of other villages. With some habitually naked tribes, clothes are worn on special occasions for the express purpose of provoking sexual excitation, as in sexual rites and dances. In some other instances certain clothes are worn only by prostitutes. The custom of both sexes bathing together in the nude which existed in some parts of Japan, and in nudist colonies in this country and Europe, is not usually accompanied by increased sexual stimulation, but the reverse.

The effect of trying to inhibit the sexual activities of people by forcing them to wear clothes is often quite the opposite of what might be expected. Hurlock states: "When primitive peoples are unaccustomed to wearing clothing, putting it on for the first time does not decrease their immorality, as the ladies of missionary societies think it will. It has just the opposite effect. It draws attention to the body, especially to those parts of it which are covered for the first time." Arthur Grimble, Research Commissioner of Gilbert and Ellice Islands in the South Pacific Ocean, expressed his views in regard to this matter as follows: "Clothes may have originated in the Garden of Eden but they have spoiled a Pacific paradise. Clothes covering bodies which once went naked, have contributed to the natives' moral decadence by stimulating a nasty curiosity which never before existed." In this connection, an art teacher informed me that a completely nude female model produced no disturbing effect on his male students. However, when the same naked girl appeared wearing either a hat or a pair of stockings, an unrest appeared through the classroom which he felt was entirely due to the erotic feelings aroused by the partly clad model.

The eroticism of modern society due to wearing clothing, resulting in an increase of curiosity and fantasy in relation to sex, has had a profound effect on man's creative functions, especially in the arts and music. Sigmund Freud confirms this in the following: "Covering of the body, which keeps abreast with civilization, continuously arouses sexual curiosity and serves to supplement the sexual object by uncovering the hidden parts. This can be turned into the artistic 'sublimation' if the interest is turned from the genitals to the form of the body. The tendency to linger at this intermediary sexual aim of the sexually accentuated 'looking,' is found to a certain degree in most normals; indeed, it gives them the possibility of directing a certain amount of their libido to a higher artistic aim."

But clothing plays an even more important role in relation to sex than mere stimulation. With clothes man has invented a regulating mechanism by which sexual interest can be turned on or off almost at will, like an electric current, a function not only valuable for marriage but for all forms of social contact between men and women. This is accomplished (as all my readers must know, even if they may not have considered it in this light) by wearing two kinds of clothing *(1) work clothing, or clothing which is used for occasions where one or the other or both sexes desire to inhibit sexual interest; and (2) leisure clothes, which also conceal the wearers' bodies to the extent desired for purposes of public decency, but also reveal the charms of the wearer and exercise a seductive influence on the male or female beholder.* Among these latter clothes for women are included all kinds of gowns such as afternoon and décolleté evening gowns designed to arouse erotic interest; while for men there are included athletic clothing, evening dress (to a limited extent only), and all the different kinds of sportswear from Bermuda shorts and Hawaiian shirts to swim suits.

Because of the use of suitably plain work clothes, we can usually enter an office or workroom where men and women work side by side without arousing more than casual curiosity. There is of course the flirtatious minx who wears dresses or blouses to business which reveal as much or even more than they conceal. The men who work in the same office with her usually recognize the fact and are on guard, since if she "dresses to kill" in business hours, her mind may not be primarily on her work.

Ambivalent clothing which, like hypocrites, pretends to conceal the wearer, but fails successfully: Prominent actresses, left, Eartha Kitt, upper right, Sophia Loren, below, Gina Lollobrigida. (Photos on the right by Ormond Gigli.)

Quite different is the effect of wearing seductive clothing designed for leisure hours, one of the main purposes of which is to gain the attention of the opposite sex. Here the control changes as the occasion changes, and clothing which conforms to the proper standards of concealment can cross all the permissible boundaries when it comes to revealment.

Flügel in his book, *The Psychology of Clothing*, has well described this role played by clothes in revealing and concealing as "ambivalent," as the term is used today in psychiatry. A perfect example of this ambivalence is found in the décolleté evening dress which goes back historically to the end of the Middle Ages. So long as only the upper parts of the breasts are exposed, and the balance hidden, no undue sexual excitement is produced and no shock is administered to modern morality. But let the nipples fall out and panic ensues! Ambivalence no longer exists. Our motion-picture Solons have even measured the amount of cleavage between the breasts a woman can expose on the screen without breaking the rules of decency. It is approximately two inches! Such squeamishness would not have been understood by the Minoan women of Crete 2,000 years ago who displayed their breasts and gilded their nipples, in a décolleté which left nothing to the imagination, nor by the society women of the Napoleonic era who shamelessly exposed their breasts.

This ambivalence of women's clothes is also a thoroughly useful invention for the practical purposes of love and marriage. By revealing a certain amount of the body, much may be promised. By hiding even more, the wearer's ability to come up to expectations cannot be challenged. The more the body is covered, the greater can be the promise, and sometimes the less the performance.

It is superfluous to consider the many ways in which clothes help to stimulate men to respond to the sexual attraction of women. Yet there is very little in the male's work-a-day or business clothes of the West today to enhance his physical charms. Since men have discarded ornamental clothes (other than uniforms or traditional robes) as effeminate in the Western world, laces, frills and furbelows now symbolize the female sex only. Therefore the absence of any seductive or ornamental frippery in men's clothes today usually conveys an impression of plain masculinity and solid security to the female—something which she values in the father of her children. Not that men's clothes do not often indicate masculine charm—to

Ambivalent clothing which both conceals and reveals: Prominent American actresses, left, *June Havoc,* right, *Marilyn Monroe.*

their wearers and women. The fastidiousness of the young American man, his insistence on the long coat or the short coat, or the Continental cut or the English shoulders, all indicate that he is greatly interested in his clothes and their effect on the opposite sex. He has yet to learn that however much women may flatter him on his taste in clothes, their erotic interest is generally aroused not by what he wears, but by what he says, does and is. A wise man once said, "Men love with the eyes, women with the ears." Speaking generally, most women would far prefer a clean-cut masculine man with a sense of humor, a not-too-handsome face, with a feeling of independence, to any foppish dandy who is absorbed in the effect produced by his clothing, no matter how subtle or expensive, on the fair sex. Yet there are articles of masculine attire to which women often respond; the white shirt open at the neck, the Byronic cloak, the hat worn at a jaunty angle, the smoking jacket and pipe, the silken pajamas and dressing gown—all these play a subtle role in the game of clothes and sex. Many young college men feel they are at their sexiest wearing sweaters and slacks, and there is evidence that many young college girls feel the same way.

Woman, on the other hand, having sensibly appropriated all beauty and ornament in clothes to herself, uses her clothing to compose an alluring picture of outer manifestations of inner delights. At their best, her clothes supply a discreet invitation to indiscretion. At their worst, they represent a vulgar display of her wares like an overcrowded shop window. The low-cut gown must not be cut too low, the tight-fitting skirt must not fit too tightly, the bosom may protrude but not obtrude, and the dividing line is always set by the good taste of the wearer. Thus dress is woman's subtle invention to tempt, but not to insist on, masculine admiration. The color, the materials, the texture, the softness, the lines, the fit, all these conspire in a good costume to set off the wearer in the same way that an appropriate frame sets off an exquisite picture. And if she possesses money enough, woman, unlike the picture, can move from frame to frame, as her mood or the occasion demands. Thus she becomes queen over all other creatures, for she can change the color of her skin with more variety than the chameleon, outdo the animal kingdom in the richness of her furs, and vie with the birds of paradise in the glory of her jewels. And, for most women, the purpose behind all this enchantment is to capture the male she wants as her own and hold him with the superiority of her beauty and raiment. For woman, like the male himself, is a servant of the life force and her primary purpose is to procreate. And if she is not interested in this primary purpose, as many women are not, she will still find in her clothes a source of security in whatever walk of life she has chosen.

What part do clothes play in stabilizing marriage and the family in Western society? At the very outset, the bridal costume and the wedding ring symbolize the alleged purity of the bride and the avowed intention to hold marriage vows sacred, an important necessity when it takes seventeen to twenty years to bring up a child to the point where it can fend for itself. And during this period of family life, the wife must continue to make herself attractive to her husband, and *vice versa,* in order that they can express their mutual love in terms of sexual satisfaction so that it need not be sought disruptively outside the home. And it is here that clothes play an important role in helping to maintain the marriage. Clothes enable the wife to supply herself every so often with "a new skin" to break the monotony of married life. The husband, to a lesser extent, is able to do the same. The result is stimulation of sexual interest which might otherwise wane.

Wives will agree with me that the role played by clothes in support of family life has never been given sufficient importance. A wife must be able to defend herself against the use of attractive clothes by the seductress who wears her finery to aid her in breaking up another's home. So, if you are a wife, never hesitate to buy yourself new dresses if you feel the slightest chance of your home being threatened! And make your husband pay for them, for you are on the side of the angels.

Another sound reason for covering our bodies is because they are so often unattractive physically. *With clothes, many such individuals appear to be more interesting sexually and, consequently, superior beings.* If you doubt the truth of this, regard the people you meet everywhere and imagine them all "as naked as jay birds." For every beautiful body, you will probably encounter at least a dozen ugly ones. Nor is this to be explained by the sedentary lives so many people lead today. Examine the pictures of naked savages from the jungles of Africa, Asia and Australia, and you will find that potbellies and pendulous breasts predominate. Rousseau's beautiful savage existed more in literature than in life. And while we often observe magnificent specimens of males and females among both primitive and civilized peoples, these are in the minority. The gradual deterioration of the body as we grow older is another potent reason for hiding ourselves in our clothes. Thus clothes have often greatly improved on nature's handiwork in adding to sexual attraction. Many a man whose superior position in modern society is due to intellect rather than to brawn, can thank his lucky stars for the invention of clothing which enables him to appear sexually attractive by covering his meager body. The same is even more true for women. But of course, clothing also causes the deterioration of the body by permitting the lazy wearer to hide the effects of his lack of exercise. We shall deal with this more fully when discussing nudism in Chapter 6.

Prehistoric man living in a state of nudity had another cogent reason based on sex for inventing clothes. Man's external sex organs may, by visible distention, involuntarily indicate interest in the presence of a sexually attractive woman. The inventions of the apron, the loin cloth and, eventually, trousers or other garments capable of hiding this, made it possible for groups of people to live peaceably together without arousing the disruptive suspicions and jealousies of the males in a community. On the other hand, it has been noted in certain primitive groups, for example the American Indians, that no one pays attention to the appearance of a man in public in this, to us, embarrassing condition.

The need of clothing to hide the effects of sexual excitation among certain groups of men found its counterpart in the need of clothing to hide the menstrual period in women. Men, associating

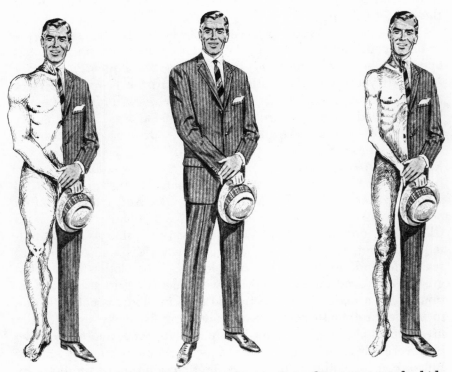

Men, what are you hiding? The attractive male in the center may be hiding the Herculean muscles of the man on the left, or the "skin and bones" of the man on the right. (Suit from an advertisement of Botany "500"; additional drawings by S. Schoenberg.)

Women, what are you hiding? The full skirt solves two of women's biggest problems—hiding what they have too much of, right, or hiding what they don't have enough of, left. (Dress, center, from an advertisement of Jeane Scott; additional drawings by S. Schoenberg.)

the sight of blood with painful wounds or death, experienced a feeling of revulsion against the menstrually bleeding woman and often treated her abominably. Tribal customs among most primitive people to this day include the isolation of women during menstruation. The virtual imprisonment of girls undergoing their first menstrual period is often cruel in the extreme. The belief in the uncleanliness of women during this period was also expressed in the Old Testament. It became desirable for women to hide the effects of menstruation and this, too, was a contributing factor in the invention of clothes.

Another sexual factor responsible for the wearing of clothes was the appearance of pubic hair in children as they approached the period of puberty. Society permits children to run naked on the beaches of Europe and some parts of America up to a certain age, but with the appearance of budding breasts on the girls and pubic hair on both boys and girls, we hasten to cover them with clothes. (In Mexico even the smallest girl child may not appear naked in public.) Pubic hair on children announces that they are fast ripening for procreation. By keeping the girl child covered with clothes, (a) she is protected from family interest in her (incest inhibition), (b) her curiosity about the naked body is inhibited, and (c) she is able to ripen sexually and yet be shielded from the premature advances and intentions of the male. Children's clothes mean "hands off." Children are protected by society against sexual aggression, and the sign identifying the child is often the style of her dress. Thus, the wearing of overly mature clothes by a young girl on the street is both dangerous for her and for the male who may be deceived by her appearance into believing she is past the so-called "age of consent."

The growth of pubic hair which marks the beginning of puberty also notifies the world that man appears to be related to the fur-bearing animals, a fact which does not please him. He hastens to hide his ignominy beneath a garment which covers his middle, although curiously enough, pubic hair (which is rare with many Orientals) does not usually exist in the animal world. It is odd that through the ages Western man has usually tried to deceive himself in paintings and sculptures as to the existence of this small patch of pubic hair. This will be discussed further in Chapter 18 dealing with the arts.

Photographic and nudist magazines published in the United States are not allowed to picture nudes with pubic hair in certain states under penalty of being considered obscene and unfit for transmission through the mails. So they remove the hair from the photographs, which look more obscene than ever. (The United States Supreme Court recently handed down a decision which may possibly change this.) And if we are unwilling to admit the existence of pubic hair in photographs, how much less willing are we to admit its existence in real life? We hide it beneath our clothes, and thus avoid being reminded of our relationship to the rabbits.

Finally, it is the contention of many writers that natural "modesty" plays a leading role in inhibiting the full exposure of the human body. It is my opinion, however, that modesty is far less likely to have played this role than our basic sense of inferiority. The desire to separate ourselves from the animal world remains one of the most potent reasons for wearing clothes, and one of the consequences is the phenomenon of modesty which will be discussed later.

CHAPTER 4

Clothes to Distinguish the Sexes

Why do men's and women's clothes differ? "To distinguish between the sexes" is the obvious answer, but it is only superficially correct. Another frequent answer is that women, by wearing different and more ornamental clothes, make themselves appear more beautiful in order to attract the males. But if this were so, why do women not wear attractive men's clothes, such as were worn by King Charles II or Beau Brummel?

Nature at the outset ordained that men and women should differ in appearance by providing their bodies with distinctive physical characteristics. Yet, despite nature's clearly defined differences, man insisted on emphasizing them by inventing different clothes for men and women. We have dressed our men in clothes labeled "male" and women in clothes labeled "female" for thousands of years, and utility, ornament and sexual attraction initially had little to do with it.

Contrary to established beliefs, the differentiation in clothing between men and women arose from the male's desire to assert superiority over the female and to hold her to his service. This he accomplished through the ages by means of special clothing which hampered or handicapped the female in her movements. Then men prohibited one sex from wearing the clothing of the other, in order to maintain this differentiation. There is a question as to whether this sex differentiation by clothing will continue in the world of the future, especially in view of the change which is now taking place in the economic position and power of women.

In order to maintain his masculine domination as head of the family and food provider, man invented "man-clothes" which were

51

Hobbling Western women: All skirts are encumbering, some more than others. From left to right, hobble skirt, Paris, 1914; afternoon gown, Berlin, about 1870; walking costume, Paris, about 1878; sheath skirt, Jacques Fath, Paris, 1955.

the exclusive property of the male sex, gave him complete mobility and made him feel superior to his woman. He also devised "woman-clothes" for the female which made it difficult for her to wander far from the camp fire and the children. He also found in these "man-clothes" a bond with the other males in his group and this gave him even greater security since he was not equated with the women and children of the group. As a result of the female's dependence on the male, her apparel became a badge of servitude. It also served to announce certain other facts; as a female, she was entitled to the protection of the males of the tribe; in war, she did not participate as a warrior and was exempt from slaughter, thus assuring the continuity of the race, an exemption which no longer applies under our so-called civilization of today.

How were men able to use clothing to demonstrate the male's

superiority over the female, giving him greater mobility while hampering her in her movements? This was accomplished in Western civilization by providing divided garments such as trousers, knickerbockers and so forth, or pleated kilts, or tunics, which permitted free movement for the male, while the female was forced to wear hampering skirts and dresses which impeded her movements. *In this way the male covered her and hobbled her at the same time.* Later on he handicapped her still further in other ways, such as by dresses with hampering trains, and by high-heeled shoes which made walking a kind of acrobatic feat. Nor was this handicapping limited to Western women. In the East the sexes often reversed their clothes. The woman usually wore trousers or pantaloons, but to prevent her free movement, her feet were bound and crippled, as in old China, or her steps were limited by her kimono in Japan, or her ankles

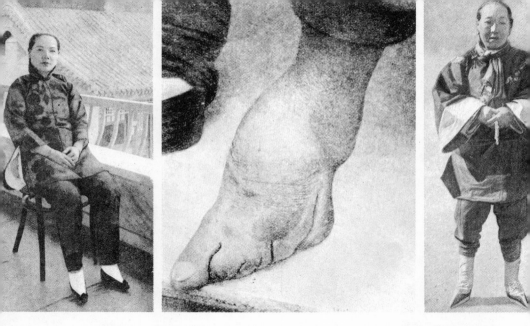

Hobbling Eastern women: Left and right, *women of Old China wore trousers but were hobbled by the binding of their feet from about the age of eight.* Center, *shoe and foot of upper-class woman deformed by binding in childhood.*

were shackled, or her sandals were provided with stilts, or her face and body were heavily veiled, as in Arab countries. And the main purpose of all these costumes and customs was to make it difficult for her to run away. *Thus, by imposing confining garments on woman, or by otherwise hobbling her, man was enabled almost universally to keep her in a state of inferiority and subjugation to him as a personal possession.*

How far back in history does this differentiation in clothes between the sexes go? The Spanish Levant rock paintings dating from about 10,000 B.C. reveal prehistoric male hunters wearing short trousers and women wearing long skirts, probably of unwieldy fur or hides, which undoubtedly handicapped them in their movements.

The hobbling of Western women by skirts has been a universal custom through the ages. In the days of the Egyptians, Greeks, Romans and other Mediterranean peoples, both men and women wore robes, but the men and warriors generally wore the short knee-length tunic or kilt, usually with folds or pleats which did not hamper movement (the ancestors of the modern Highland kilt). Their ceremonial robes were longer. The women usually wore long encumbering robes which reached to or below the ankles. The early Sumerian male (2700 B.C.) wore a long robe with pleats ingeniously placed around the lowest part to give him freedom of movement, while the Amazons were distinguished by wearing short knee-length skirts, like the modern girls of the 1920's, which enabled them to battle with the males on more or less equal terms.

Special hobbling devices have also been invented for upper-class women. In Venice, from the fourteenth to the sixteenth centuries, women wore a stilt under each shoe called a "champiny," many of which were a yard high and "All their gentlewomen and most of their wives that are of any wealth, are assisted and supported either by men or women as they walk abroad, to the end they may not fall." The custom of wearing "chapins" or "chopines" spread through all Europe. Rudofsky notes that the Queen of Spain, wife of Philip V, had to rely on the support of two pages when she walked on her chapins. (Filthy streets may have been a secondary reason for wearing these.) In Palestine, women's ankles were connected together by chains to which bells were attached that would tinkle if they tried to run away. A bell is also used today for the same purpose with cats, cows and sheep. Arabian women wore high sandals on stilts or pedestals held to the foot by a knob passing between the toes. Large anklets, weighing from a pound to two pounds, helped further to cripple the feet. The Koran says of women, alluding to

Hobbling Eastern women: Left, *Arab women, Tunis.* Right, *Arab woman, Damascus.*

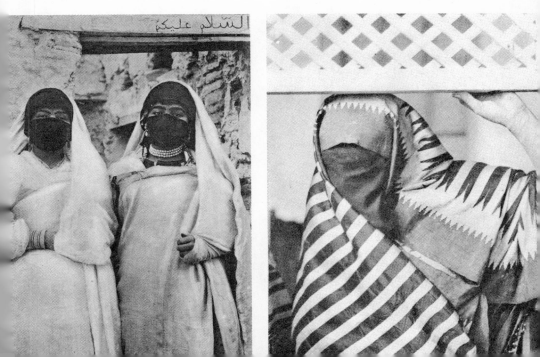

these anklets, "Let them not make a noise with their feet, that the ornaments which they hide may thereby be discovered." In Central Africa, the wives of some of the wealthy tribesmen carry close upon half a hundredweight of iron ornaments, and the rings with which they load their wrists and ankles clank and resound like the fetters of slaves.

Women's inferior position and the jealousy of the male also accounts for the hampering half or full veil or hood which Arab women wear over their faces. Some of these costumes resemble tents in which the women are completely enveloped. In modern Iran, the Moslem women of the unemancipated classes wrap themselves in a large shawl which is held by the teeth to cover the lower part of the face. This shawl successfully hampers walking, although the women wear trousers beneath it. The Purdah, or complete seclusion of woman, is still practiced by most of the Moslems of Pakistan.

But we do not have to travel to the Middle East to find further evidence of the male desire to hamper the female by her clothing. Why was it that until recently most women rode horseback pillion-fashion or sidesaddle? The conventional male answer is that since women wore skirts, it was only natural for them to ride in skirts; moreover, their child-bearing and sexual parts were said to be protected in this way. But since the pressure of the knees against the flanks of the horse is a considerable factor of safety in riding, one

Hobbling Western women: Left, twentieth-century high heels, by Andrew Geller, New York, 1959. Right, sixteenth-century chapins, worn by fashionable Venetian women, a fashion which spread to many other countries.

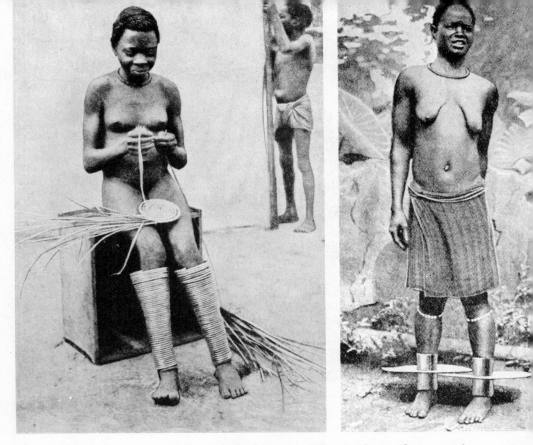

Hobbling women: An African method was to apply weights to the women's legs. Left, Nigerian woman with brass rods weighing about fifteen pounds coiled around her legs. Right, Congo woman with regulation metal ankle discs to impede movement.

of the real reasons begins to appear. Don't make it too easy for the little darlings to ride away from home. You may lose them!

The main exceptions to the rule that it pays to hobble women are found usually among nomadic peoples where the women must walk alongside the men in the seasonal migrations of the tribes. There the women often act as porters and trudge along with the animals, so that it is easy for the tribesmen to keep a watchful eye on both. In general, primitive agricultural peoples have been more indulgent on the subject, especially when hobbling the females interfered too greatly with their capacity for work. But even in primitive societies where women do most of the work in the fields, hobbling has still been practiced almost continuously.

If any man reading this feels I have been unfair to his sex regarding the hampering purpose of women's dresses, let him essay a

Hobbling Eastern women: Shrouded women of Isfahan, Persia.

little adventure by his own fireside which I tried myself—but let him not go out on the streets where he may be committing a misdemeanor. Experiment with wearing women's clothes, and see if you do not experience a feeling of embarrassment and restraint. The embarrassment comes from a disdain for the finery, the laces and what not, which give us mere men a feeling of foolishness in wearing such useless fripperies. But try to walk freely in the skirt and you will find that each step forward requires you to move a load of the material with your knees. The skirt also limits your stride and forces you to walk with a shorter step. You cannot open your knees freely when sitting down, as you are sharply restrained by the width of the skirt. This limiting factor is not present in all skirts, but it exists in most of those which lack excessive fullness. But try wearing a very full skirt. You will experience the feeling of walking around inside a large textile bag or tent. Your women friends will tell you that they become used to this, but if they are truthful they will

*Hobbling Eastern women: Raised sandals which effectively impede move-
ment are worn by women of different countries. Left, Arab harem costume.
Right, Japanese woman in tight kimono. (Traphagen School of Design.)*

agree that long skirts are not the best garments for working in, or
running up and down stairs, or walking in the woods. Assuredly the
skirt is not a very good invention for woman's comfort, but an
excellent one for keeping her "in her place."

A woman wearing male clothes suffers none of the above disadvantages. Male garments may not be "pretty," but they do not hamper free movement. And they protect the parts of the wearer's body
which, when wearing skirts, are exposed under the dress. But when
a woman wears men's clothes, she also wears a happy feeling of
equality with men which gives her a sense of freedom that is bound
to have a striking effect on the achievements of women in the future.

Women have always been confronted with a problem in clothes
which does not exist for the opposite sex—that of accommodating to
an expanding body to house the oncoming child. This called for the

Sturdy males who wear skirts: Left, *Hungarian peasants, Mezökövesd section.* Right, *Guatamalan Indians, descendants of the ancient Mayans.*

invention of dresses or skirts which could adjust to this change in size during pregnancy, something which could not be easily accomplished with trousers. Down through the ages some women have felt inferior because of their bulging bodies and have sought to hide their pregnancy, the classic example being the invention of the crinoline which disguised expectant mothers by making every fashionable woman appear to be pregnant, a condition which appeared to be repeating itself in the so-called "chemise" or "sack" dress which recently became fashionable, but has now disappeared. For many years, maternity-clothing manufacturers specialized in making maternity clothes the main object of which was to hide the appearance of pregnancy for as long as possible. Today young women no longer appear to be ashamed of maternity and derive a feeling of superiority from it. They reveal their condition to the world by wearing comfortable blouses or dresses which hang from the shoulders and are free from any obstruction at the waistline which would affect circulation. As with the women in Botticelli's paintings, pregnancy has taken on a new form of beauty which, during the season of 1957-58, was briefly expressed in bulging clothing.

Sturdy males who wear skirts: Left, *Pipe Major Angus McLeod. (British Travel Association.)* Right, *Greek native of modern Thebes.*

So strong is our determination to differentiate between the sexes by means of clothes that savage laws still exist in many countries branding, under the name of transvestitism, as a serious offence punishable with imprisonment the wearing of women's clothes by men in public places, and *vice versa*. These laws will be dealt with in detail in Chapter 12. The Old Testament was quite definite on this same subject. Moses, in Deuteronomy 22:5, thundered: "A woman shall not wear that which pertaineth unto a man, neither shall a man put on a woman's garment; for whosoever doeth these things is an abomination unto Jehovah thy God." Philip Stubbes in *The Anatomie of Abuses*, written in 1585, went even further than the Bible: "Our apparell was giuen as a signe distinctiue to discerne betwixt sexe and sexe; and, therefore, one to weare the apparell of another sexe is to participate with the same, and to adulterate the veritie of his owne kinde. Wherefore, these women may not improperly bee called hermaphroditi, that is, monsters of both kindes, halfe women, halfe men; who, if they were naturall women, and honest matrones, would blush to goe in such wanton and lewd attire, as is properly onely to man."

Male influence in women's clothes goes back to Elizabethan days. Left, *female bowler hat and tweed coat, about 1883.* Right, *female straw hat and tailored costume with pleated skirt, about 1883.*

We shall here discuss some of the reasons for the persistent desire on the part of some individuals to wear garments of the opposite sex. The interest may be primarily in the apparel itself, but often the clothing has enough erotic value to facilitate the wearer's sexual arousal. Dr. George W. Henry, a leading authority on the subject, in his book *All the Sexes,* states: "Interest displayed in dressing as a member of the opposite sex is most frequently noted in childhood. This interest is often fostered, or at least condoned, by adults. Although indications of transvestitism may be evident in childhood, anomaly in dress is not given serious consideration unless it persists after puberty."

Dr. Henry gives the following characteristic case histories of transvestitism: "At the age of nineteen, Abraham's major sexual desire was for intimacies with men, and he preferred to wear women's dresses and shoes. He was not interested in feminine underclothing. At the home of some of his friends he would dress as a girl, and he liked to be one of the belles at a 'drag'—a ball at which male homosexuals appear in female apparel. His interest in women's clothing closely resembled that of the 'fairy'—an effeminate homosexual who dresses as a girl."

The following was written by a male with a habitual desire to dress as a girl: "Girls' clothing gives them freedom. The little ones are expansive, joyous and free. When they grow up a little, they begin thinking of themselves. They relinquish their freedom and develop a slave psychology. The putting on of long skirts, a tight corset, a skirt with a belt, is curtailment. They develop an inferiority complex which they attempt to assuage in exhibitionistic ways. Feelings of inferiority are shown by tight lacing or by pinning on bows, or other meaningless ornaments."

In contrast, a masculine woman's attitude toward clothes was expressed by Dr. Henry as follows: "Male dress gave her a sense of freedom and enhanced the fantasy of her masculinity while she was making love to boys or girls. When she wished to look feminine, she borrowed the dresses of an effeminate homosexual with whom she was living. 'I'm not interested in feminine clothes. I rebelled in high school because my mother made me wear them. I hate hats and

Women's revolt against hobbling: Left, *the Bloomer costume, about 1851.* Right, *Dr. Mary Walker dressed in tunic and trousers similar to the Oneida costume designed by John Humphrey Noyes, Oneida, New York, about 1860. Note her abundant hair.*

gloves—anything that is uncomfortable. I have a regular obsession
against high heels. They are uncomfortable and fragile. I don't like
to wear stockings, but I always do except when I'm in the country.
I like underclothing to be comfortable. I've never had on a girdle or
a brassière. I always wear flat heels, shirts and tailored suits. I have
tailored slacks because I think it's pathetic to run around in pants
with a fly. It looks like a sad imitation. I can be a masculine girl, but
not a man.' "

Further consideration of the reasons for requiring differentiation
in dress between the sexes leads directly into the problems of the
homosexuality which might arise were men permitted to wear
women's clothes indiscriminately and *vice versa*. (a) Many male
homosexuals like to dress in women's clothes and the public display

Women's revolt against hobbling: The Rational Dress movement. Left,
Mrs. Marie Reideselle, prize winner, New York Herald, *for best bicycle
costume for ladies, 1892. Right, Miss Margaret Connolly in Boston Rational
costume with divided skirt, 1893. (From* The Arena, *1893.)*

of men so dressed would undoubtedly lead to an increase in sex deviation; (b) when parents dress in clothes which do not differentiate between the sexes, this confuses the children and may cause psychiatric upsets in later life; it may also give the child a tendency towards homosexuality. Modern psychologists warn us of the damage which is sometimes done to the children in families in which the wife plays the aggressive, masculine role; her "wearing the trousers," literally as well as figuratively speaking, often makes this worse. Women who dress and behave in such a way that their bewildered small children have grave difficulty in determining who is their father and who is their mother, or believe that both parents are mothers, should realize that this may affect their children's sexual orientation, which in turn may be passed on from generation to

Women serving as soldiers tend to modify their feminine dress. Left, Emilie Plater, Polish heroine of the insurrection of 1831. She is credited with causing the Russian forces to retreat at Dünaberg. Right, Philis de la Charce, who protected Provence, France, from invasion by the Duc de Savoie, 1692.

generation. Men are often to blame for this condition, for when they
fail to live up to their responsibilities as husbands and fathers, the
mothers are forced to take over the male role in the family.

*The history of civilization has many examples of great nations
which became effeminate and were destroyed by more virile but less
civilized races which conquered and overran them. In all such effem-
inacy, clothes played a leading role. Thus the wisdom of the ages,
which is on the side of sex differentiation in clothes, is based on
realities of which most of us do not actually become aware in the
short experience of our life span.*

Despite all past prohibitions, women have continued to rebel
against what they regard as the injustice of being required to wear
skirts. During the last century they have sought to remedy this by
the invention of the divided skirt, by the bloomers invented by Mrs.
Bloomer in the 1870's, and by the modern slacks which so resemble
men's trousers that in certain parts of this country it has become
increasingly difficult to distinguish the sexes from one another by
their clothes. As a result, it is not hard today to imagine a world in
which both sexes will wear exactly the same clothes. Indeed, to some
extent this already exists in Red China where both men and women
wear quilted blue shirts and trousers. We seem to be rapidly drifting
into this condition in the West. Many problems are arising because
of this, not the least of these being that women, no longer having to
wear the badge of the so-called inferior sex, are becoming rivals
to men in most of men's habitual pursuits and are possibly too successful for male comfort. The first request Joan of Arc made of the
Dauphin was that she be permitted to wear male clothing. She was
thus freed from the inhibitions which accompany the wearing of
skirts, and ultimately made herself the supreme commander of the
French forces.

As far back as the year 1850 Helen Marie Weber, a feminist of
the time, wrote to the Woman's Rights Convention at Worcester,
Massachusetts: "In ten years' time male attire will be generally worn
by women of most civilized countries." These words were written
over a hundred years ago, and women for the most part still do not
wear male trousers, or wear them only for special occasions. Does
anyone doubt that our wives and mothers, those strong, fierce creatures who have borne the burden of child-bearing and stood behind

*Women's revolt against hobbling: "A Bride in Breeches." This picture of
the wedding of a pioneer "New Woman" in New Zealand photographed
by Standish and Preece, Christchurch, N. Z., 1894, shows the beginning of
a war which has since been largely won by women.*

their men in so many brutal wars, are incapable of doing away entirely with dresses and wearing only male trousers if they want to? The answer is that they recognize a value in covering their bodies with dresses, especially if they are overweight or ungainly, while the slender misses who look well in trousers will doubtless continue to wear them at times as long as it pleases them. Most women will therefore continue to favor dresses, not as the badge of inferiority which men have placed on them, but as a means for achieving an aesthetic perfection which does not exist with the display of potbellies, thick or skinny trunks, and ungainly legs revealed in their males by their trousers.

What we men can expect from trousered women was put very bluntly recently by their eloquent spokeswoman, Elizabeth Hawes. "People who argue against the equal right of females to take part in any activity they care to, and dress for it as they please, are waging a losing battle the world over. Free women who wear 'men's' clothes at times are merely increasing their efficiency just as they did when they dropped their crinolines, loosened and lightened their 'women's' clothes in every way. Their femaleness is in no way impaired by all this. They remain as sexually attractive to males and as able to bear children as females ever were. It's their 'womanliness,' their right only to keep house and raise children that's going by the boards, not their femaleness.

"However, American men now cook, clean, wash clothes, take care of children and otherwise enter freely into household and family activities in a way unheard of even a couple of generations ago. Men's clothes will really be revolutionized when the male asserts his right to be considered as alluring and decorative and beautiful as women." Men, brace yourselves, the worst is yet to come!

How are men reacting against the present female invasion into the masculine territory of trousers which have contributed to their feeling of male superiority for so many centuries? Men have retaliated by invading the field of feminine attire, though I doubt we will ever take to wearing dresses. Led by that dashing ex-haberdasher, the former President Harry Truman, men are wearing gaudily colored shirts and neckties during their leisure hours which equal or exceed in loudness the colored blouses worn by women. But modern men are unlikely to return to the old days of male finery. There has therefore begun a new vogue for men, who now sport bushy masculine beards. These beards, after an absence of seventy years, can

Modern women's victory against hobbling: Left, *combination feminine short tunic and tight trousers, by Gino Paoli, New York and Milan, 1959.* Right, *masculine-style outfit—turtle-neck shirt, sports jacket and cotton knit pants—showing women's final victory. Outfit by Aileen, New York, 1959.*

be seen in increasing numbers on the streets and represent an impregnable position of male superiority from which the women will never be able to dislodge them.

Is there any ultimate solution to this woman's trouser-and-skirt problem? Perhaps the answer lies in the wearing of two kinds of clothes, (a) female work clothes and sports clothes, which will include masculine- or feminine-looking trousers, if that is the way the individual woman wants it, and (b) leisure clothes, which will be skirts or dresses, unless the women wish to throw away the advantage of hundreds of years of developing beauty of line and form in dress. In this way our women will be able to straddle two worlds in more ways than one. Already, according to Cheryl Crawford, one of the heads of the Actors Studio, the wardrobe of many young New York actresses consists only of blue jeans or slacks for work, and party dresses for leisure and pleasure. In most parts of this country today, many wives wear slacks during the day and put on dresses when their husbands return home from work.

Perhaps the final solution to this problem lies in the invention of clothing which will give women all the liberating advantages of trousers, while maintaining sex differentiation by giving her clothes ornamental feminine attributes not present in those worn by the men. One of the most brilliant dress reformers for women was the late John Humphrey Noyes of the Oneida Community, who over a hundred years ago dressed the females of his community in men's peg-top pants of the period, but by a stroke of genius also provided a knee-length tunic which was as dainty, seductive and feminine as the trousers were masculine. Costumes of this kind, which are not to be confused with bloomers, were used in a play on the subject written by myself and Armina Marshall which was produced in New York under the title *Suzanna and the Elders.* They proved both beautiful, feminine and practical. As a work costume for women, worn with tunics or smocks, this may be the ultimate answer to sex differentiation in modern clothes which will enable women to wear practical trousers, and also enable their small children to know which of their parents is the mother and which is the father.

In conclusion, the invention of the trouser and the skirt has enabled Western men and women to achieve a balanced social and sexual relationship over the centuries which, if greatly disturbed, may produce some highly unexpected results. Not the least of these may be the male's loss of his dominating position in most of the fields where he now holds sway. For watch out for women! In our modern civilization some of them make far better men than we men do. And men, hold on to your trousers, or you may end up wearing skirts!

CHAPTER 5

Clothes and Modesty

Having attained a feeling of superiority by covering his body, man at an early date began to set standards of behavior regarding the permissible uncovering of his body. This behavior he called modesty, and those who live up to these standards in their communities or groups have generally been regarded as superior to those who do not.

The true origin and nature of modesty becomes apparent when we relate it to the circumstance of Western man's illusion that he is a godlike creature, an illusion he maintains by covering his sexual parts with clothing. When a Western man takes off his hat in public, he is not immodest. When he takes off his trousers, he is. In the first instance he is uncovering his head, the seat of his intellect, of which he is inordinately proud; in the second instance, he is uncovering the seat of his basic shame and inferiority. He is exposing the fallacy of his illusion, and the police must be called in to stop him, lest he expose the fallacy of our own illusion and that of most of mankind as well. *Stated in general terms, in my opinion the main purpose of modesty is to enable us to maintain our belief in our godlike attributes by inhibiting the removal of garments or clothing which expose our lower centers in public.* Modesty therefore probably began when society by its laws and religions made the public uncovering of the human body a criminal offense, calling for first aid for the observers and jail for the offender. However, as explained later, other parts of the body which are given an erotic significance are also subject to similar prohibitions as regards uncovering in public.

Many writers have speculated on the origins of modesty, and most of them have been incorrect. Certain authorities, including Havelock Ellis, regard it as innate in humanity. So does the Catholic

71

Church, which associates it with original sin. Flügel regards modesty as one reason for the invention of clothes. Another writer (in the *Encyclopaedia Britannica*) states that "Modesty is a feeling merely of acute self-consciousness due to appearing unusual, and is the result of clothing rather than the cause." *I agree with this, and believe that modesty came into being only after the invention of clothes, which resulted in sexual stimulation due to the simple uncovering of the body—a form of stimulation which does not exist in the animal world.* The Biblical explanation of the origin of modesty as being due to shame is based on an early association of shame with nakedness. However, as a general explanation of the origin of modesty, it does not hold water when we realize that most primitive peoples who are accustomed to nakedness usually have no sense of shame about it.

The subject of women's clothing and the question of whether or not they are modest or seductive has been the subject of fierce arguments by the moralists through the ages. One man's idea of modesty may well lead to another man's seduction. Bernard Shaw made the following remarks to me on the subject of modesty and seductive clothes in a discussion regarding the Roman Catholic interdiction forbidding Italian women to enter churches in sleeveless dresses or skirts which did not cover the ankles. "What on earth do priests know about the morality of clothing?" Shaw asked impatiently. "The trouble with these men who try to adjudicate upon what is moral or immoral in dress is that they really know nothing about the subject. Any man who attempts to decide that one style of clothing is seductive while another style of clothing is not, must know something about the art of being seductive, and priests who rail about women's costumes are obviously the very last persons to be in a position to express an opinion on the subject. I remember in my young days when women dressed in accordance with the dictates of the clergy, they were literally swathed in clothing so that they resembled feather mattresses more than anything else, and I may add the women who wore these clothes looked considerably more seductive than the half-clad girls of today. There are really only two competent judges of what is seductive in women's clothing, and they are the women who make it their business to be seductive, because they study it, and playwrights like myself, because it is our business to *know* what women must wear in order to be seductive."

C. Willett Cunnington expresses the same view quite amusingly in another way: "We have to thank the Early Fathers for having, albeit perhaps unwittingly, established a mode of thinking from which men and women have developed an art which has supplied them with so much agreeable entertainment, so many satisfying substitutes for Nature's omissions, and so many novel means of exciting the sexual appetite. Prudery, it seems, provides mankind with endless aphrodisiacs; hence, no doubt the reluctance to abandon it."

Modesty in the present era assumes different forms in different parts of the world, and even in different parts of our own country, and at different times of day. The Arab woman who takes for granted a display of her breasts so long as her face is covered, would be shocked by the customary exposure of naked shoulders, faces, arms and legs of Western women at dances or on the beach. The American or Englishman who would regard the same display of nakedness by women as immodest in the office, factory or on the street, will think nothing of it if it takes place after seven at a dinner party or dance, or in sun-bathing on the beach. Indeed, the Bikini bathing suit, which can be described as two narrow bands, one passed across the breasts and the other across and enclosing the pelvis, would have shocked our grandparents out of their senses. It may well have the same effect on our grandchildren. In old China, exposure of the upper-class women's tiny feet was regarded as most indecent. Chinese women's feet were even unmentionable in polite society because they were considered the most sexually stimulating parts of the body. The same was true of the back of a woman's neck in Japan. In parts of the Dutch East Indies, where women customarily displayed their breasts without the least sense of immodesty, a Dutch governor some years ago ordered the women to cover them on the streets. The women complied with the law by lifting up their skirts and draping them over their breasts when they saw a Dutch official coming their way, thus displaying an area of nakedness which was considerably more embarrassing to the Dutch. In certain other countries, the knees, the navel, the fingertips and other seemingly innocent parts of the female body must still be kept covered for modesty's sweet sake.

Why is the revealing of such relatively innocent or even non-sexual parts of the body regarded as immodest? The reason is because they are given either a secondary erotic significance, or serve as sexual fetishes, and act as surrogates or substitutes for the exposure of the more sexual parts of the body. Since these also arouse our erotic feelings, their exposure represents a symbolic exposure of our lower centers in public, and hence hinder us in maintaining our god-like attributes.

Among persons of the same sex, modesty, insofar as uncovering the body is concerned, is not generally a factor today, although girls frequently hesitate to appear naked before other girls because of their early training or some bodily defect. Nor is modesty usually involved in uncovering the body among men in private groups, as witness the unashamed nakedness which exists in men's locker rooms in the present clothes-conscious era of mankind. However, place the same group of naked men on exhibition on a public stage, with or without women present, and consternation would ensue; the place and the purpose make all the difference. In certain instances, however, men display modesty among themselves, as evidenced by the primitive Brazilian Indians, described by Francis Huxley, who feel ashamed when in the presence of other men they remove a string which ties the prepuce (foreskin) over the end of the penis.

Immodesty is seldom attributed to the male. He can display torso, arms, legs, and indeed practically every part of his body except one. Indeed, man has never imposed on himself such stringent rules of modesty as he has imposed on his females. In some ancient civilized societies, such as in Crete, and during the Middle Ages when he dressed in skin-fitting hose or tights, he wore what was known as a "cod-piece" which covered his sexual organs in a kind of package, the size of which was often exaggerated. This article of clothing which appears and disappears down the ages, was the occasion of much rough humor on the part of Shakespeare and Rabelais, and must have had the obvious effect of drawing attention to what it was supposed to hide, or conversely pretending to hide what it intended to reveal. Male ballet dancers and swimmers encounter the same problem today and it is solved to some extent by the use of supporters known as "jock straps."

A further examination of present-day modesty confirms its artificial rather than its natural origin. A group of seminude dancing girls will appear on the stage as part of their job and think nothing of it. Let a blundering male like myself open their dressing-room door while they are fully covered by their underwear, and they will scream and drape their shoulders with towels. They learned this kind

The relative nature of modesty: Left, *chorus girls for the French edition of the motion picture, "Folies Bergère." Center, dressed for English ideas of modesty.* Right, *dressed for U.S. ideas of modesty. (Photos by* Realities Magazine, *Paris, June, 1956.) Below, dancers in the night-club number of the musical play,* Bells Are Ringing, *screamed with embarrassment when seen in their dressing room completely covered by their underwear.*

of "modesty" at their mothers' knees, and will doubtless teach it to their children and grandchildren.

What is the history of modesty? In the pagan world of the Greeks, modesty in the modern sense of the word did not exist for the male. The invitation of Lysistrata to her guests, as expounded in the last act of the play of that name, if staged with the original wording and actions in New York and London, would result in the police pouring in and arresting all the actors. The Mosaic law was full of prohibitions against immodesty, and especially exposing the nakedness of a man's immediate family, but these were also due to a desire to inhibit incest as well as to modesty in the modern sense. In Europe during the periods dominated by the Roman Catholic Church, modesty was (and still is) strictly demanded of the female in her attire, although these demands were sometimes more honored in the breach than in the observance. Protestantism which opposed so much of the Roman Catholic Church's teachings, went even further in demanding modesty in dress, as did the Puritan religions which came to dominate the middle and lower classes in England, Middle Europe and the United States. Until the 1920's in the Western world, the exposure of women's legs up to the knees was the height of immodesty for literally thousands of years. Suddenly this taboo went out of fashion and legs came into view without explosive results. Female legs are now largely uncovered, and the sight of ankles no longer produces violent indignation or shock as in our grandmothers' day.

What is the generally recognized purpose behind all these rules of modesty? Marriage? The churches, with their insistence on modesty as a virtue (generally for the female), recognize the need to stimulate the appetite for marriage by limiting public sex excitation by modest clothing. But they do not carry this insistence on modesty to the point where it interferes with private excitation between married couples for the purpose of procreation. Even more basic in the game of marriage is the idea that there must be some parts with which the male is not overly familiar, so that his curiosity will be aroused and his interest stimulated to the point of betrothal and marriage. *In all conditions where sexual modesty comes into play, something is revealed in public, and something is covered up. Uncover that which is usually covered up in public, and you become immodest.* This is well illustrated by the riddle asked during the "flapper" era of the twenties. "Why do the debutantes wear their hair pulled down over their ears?" To which the ribald answer was,

The relative nature of modesty: Modest Victorian bathing costumes. Left, *designed by Maury, Paris, 1873.* Right, *by Sylvia, London, 1885.*

"So that they will have something left to show their husbands after they are married!"

Even with the violent reaction by the public against the old-fashioned Victorian clothing which has now taken place in the Western world, this reaction does not go so far as to call for total removal of clothing except in the case of the nudists who will be dealt with in the next chapter. Our change of attitude towards earlier and stricter rules of modesty in clothing during the past twenty-five years has been largely due to the healthful practice of sun-bathing which has spread all over the United States and elsewhere where the climate permits. The modern cult of sun-bathing originated in Leysin, Switzerland, where Dr. Charles Rollier effected cures in the treatment of tuberculosis and other diseases by subjecting his patients to beneficent doses of the sun's rays.

The healing effect of sunlight and air without the presence of clothing was well-known in antiquity. Hippocrates' prescription for good health was for the patient to wash himself in a little water and

The relative nature of modesty: From bikini to bikini in 1500 years. Left, *Roman girl exercising, from mosaics in Sicily, about 400 A.D.* Right, *modest girl wearing bikini swim suit by Cole of California, 1958.*

then warm himself in the sun; while Herodotus states that "Exposure to the sun is eminently necessary for people who need to recuperate and take on flesh." As a substitute for eating, this prescription is highly questionable. Roman houses of the upper classes boasted a solarium, a special room for taking sun baths without clothing.

Benjamin Franklin stated he was in the habit of rising every morning and reading or writing in his chamber without any clothes on for one half to one hour, according to the season, so as to get the benefit of a cold air bath. In this practice he was followed by Thoreau. As long ago as 1835, sun baths were successfully prescribed for rickets and scrofula. Downes and Blunt in 1876 proved that sunlight killed bacteria.

In order to obtain the maximum benefits from exposure to the sun, the bathing suits worn at beaches, which in our grandmothers' days covered the entire body from head to toe, have been increasingly abbreviated until they have reached a minimum. Women of all ages disport themselves on the beaches of Florida and California, some wearing an apology for a "bra" across their breasts and the Bikini already mentioned, which, by the way, was a standard bathing suit in the days of the fourth-century Romans. But since the Bikini went a little too far in exhibiting the female body, somewhat greater coverage is now more usually acceptable at public beaches in the United States. Men and women have come a long way, however, since the days when mixed bathing was prohibited.

Public sun-bathing in abbreviated costumes has brought about a new form of modesty for the innocent sun worshipper in this country. When approaching or leaving the beach through the public streets, some sort of covering for the greater part of the body is now usually required by our up-to-date Mrs. Grundy, with whom almost everything is now permissible so long as it is done in the right place at the right time.

The relative nature of modesty: Left, Annette Kellerman, American swimmer who shocked the world by appearing in this swimming suit which completely revolutionized the style. (U.P.I. Photo.) Right, conventional modest swimming suit of today, which shocks no one, by Cole of California, 1959.

In conclusion, it is interesting to speculate as to how our views of modesty are likely to change in the future. Modesty has never obeyed fixed rules. The lack of reticence which is characteristic of the novels and plays of today, the free discussion of the sexual functions which are commonplace in our thinking and conversation since the discoveries of Freud and his disciples, lead one to believe that modesty in the old-fashioned sense of the word is disappearing for good in the Western world. Yet in priest-ridden Ireland and anti-priest-ridden Russia, modesty is still enforced with almost puritanical fanaticism. And since civilization progresses by waves or cycles, we or our children may live to see the day when the present era is referred to as one of the most immodest periods of human history, followed by a reaction during which Western men and women are again swathed from head to foot in voluminous Victorian clothing. Women's legs will be completely covered again and our grandsons may experience the same thrills our grandfathers did when they caught a glimpse of an attractive female ankle. But enough of prophecy. Since modesty is a child of fashion and morality, neither of which is notably stable, its manifestations in the future are entirely unpredictable.

CHAPTER 6

Clothes and Nudism

The legally regulated amount of permissible nudity does not satisfy a growing group of amiable innovators in the United States and Europe—the nudists. While they wear clothes, they believe in coming together from time to time, stripping off everything and sporting joyously in the sun. *Just as most people achieve superiority by putting on their clothes, the nudists achieve it by taking them off.*

Since we are conducting an inquiry into the importance of wearing clothes, the nudists who believe in the importance of not wearing clothes must be given full consideration, for if they are correct, then the premise on which this book is based—the *importance* of wearing clothes—must surely be incorrect. We shall therefore give them their day in court, and finally have our say as to why we believe them to be mistaken in some of their basic assumptions.

Formerly, in the United States and elsewhere, attempts by nudists to practice their beliefs in a puritanical society which by and large was either hostile, skeptical, or sniffing for scandal often resulted in their being attacked as indecent or immoral. Although their views are now given greater credence by press and pulpit, they are still often on the defensive and justify their principles on the basis of health and morality, rather than sheer *joie de vivre* which would not be understood by their detractors. As compared with normal sun bathers who do not practice nudism, the nudists point to the experience of a French physician, Dr. Lastours, who made extensive experiments in exposing patients—men, women, and children—to the sun for fifteen days entirely naked and for fifteen days wearing drawers of fine white linen. His records reveal a greater rise in the weight graph and improved morale corresponding to the periods of complete nudity. Other examples have been given indicating a physical improvement arising from sun-bathing in complete nudity as compared with the almost complete nudity which exists on our beaches today. However, there is reason for doubt as to whether these physical benefits are sufficient in themselves to justify removing all our clothes in public before taking the sun.

A more important reason for nudism in the opinion of those who advocate it, is found in the following statement: "Many people have discovered that they enjoy being naked without really knowing why, except that they feel freer, more alive. Man has a deep-seated impulse to be naked. Most of us do not recognize this impulse because of our training and traditions. It is suppressed from early childhood and if we feel it, we consider it as evil. We all know the delight of children at being undressed, a perfectly natural delight."

One of the most important arguments in favor of nudism is its value in proper sex education for children. Dr. H. Forel, the famous Swiss psychiatrist, stated that prudery can be created or cured by

Nudists are usually healthy, happy, family people. A family scene at Sunny Haven Camp, Granger, Indiana. (Photo by Ed Lange.)

Nudism for joie de vivre: *Swimming is fun at nudist bathing beach, Los Angeles, California. (Photo by Ed Lange.)*

education in childhood. It may be cured by mixed bathing, by accustoming the child to consider the human body in all parts and functions as something of which one need not be ashamed. Gauguin, in his book, *Noa Noa,* stated in effect that the continued nakedness of the Polynesians had kept their minds free from preoccupation with the mystery of sex and has given their manners "a natural innocence, a perfect purity."

It is often assumed that if we lived in a nudist world, our nakedness would produce such excessive sexual stimulation that we would all rush to cover our bodies in order to survive. Hence the widely held but mistaken belief that the effect of wearing clothes is to inhibit sexual stimulation. It is now well established that the contrary is true. This is humorously recognized in the story of the two young men who visited a nudist camp and were introduced to a beautiful girl in the nude. On her departure one young man remarked to the other, "Can you imagine how exciting she would look in a sweater!"

The nudists are entitled to credit, if they desire it in an indifferent world, for reducing sexual activity by their mode of living, rather than increasing it. This may make such camps popular or unpopular according to the point of view of the visitor. And since obscenity dwells in the eyes of the beholder, the Pecksniffs in our midst have often hauled the nudists to court for indecent exposure when they should more properly have brought the members of their own congregations to court for indecent thinking, or for wearing clothes which were sexually overstimulating.

Let us hear the nudists on the subject. According to them, the unclothed body rapidly becomes commonplace, neither shameful nor erotic, and the prudery and curiosity fostered by the training of a lifetime vanish in a few hours. The modest are surprised that they are not shocked, and those seeking pornographic excitement are disappointed. Furthermore, nudists allege that their creed promotes the perfection of the human body, and those who practice it attempt to improve their bodies while those who hide their bodies in clothes make no such effort. Thus they conclude that a nudist society promotes health, morality and a healthy mind in a healthy body. They also argue that the ancient Greek devotion to physical perfection did not impair the artistic and intellectual achievements of the people. While these arguments in favor of nudism had merit when they were originally stated, most of them no longer have exclusive validity since nine tenths of the benefits claimed for nudism are now enjoyed today by millions who have become sun-bathing devotees. The nudists claim that the present cult of sun-bathing in abbreviated bathing suits is largely due to their propaganda, and for this reason alone we should all feel indebted to them, even if our gratitude does not take the form of removing all our clothes and joining them.

Nudists are an extremely vocal group in this country and abroad. They publish a number of magazines in the United States, Canada and many European countries. These publications are filled with pictures of beautiful and not-so-beautiful nudes, and they proselytize for their cause with a fervor which almost touches on the religious.

According to information gathered from various sources, in the year 1957 there were approximately 30,000 registered nudists in this country who belong to private clubs where they spend a good part

To promote "healthy minds in healthy bodies," outdoor sports are a major activity in nudist camps. Above, a volley ball game, Sunny Palms Lodge, Homestead, Florida. (Photo by Jim Hadley.) Below, canoeing at Squaw Mountain Ranch, Portland, Oregon. (Photo by Ed Lange.)

of their time in favorable as well as unfavorable weather. There are estimated to be about twice that number who are unregistered, and many thousands more who practice nudity in their family life. There are ninety-six of these nudist clubs in the United States listed in the magazine *American Sunbather and Nudist Leader* and thirteen in Canada as registered with the American Sunbathing Association. Regional and national conventions are held periodically, with the delegates attending in the nude under the auspices of this association. In England there are said to be between 5,000 to 10,000 nudists in more than fifty clubs. In Germany there are far more. There were at one time estimated to be between 200,000 to 300,000 members of the "Friends of Nature" who practiced nudism. The number in France is estimated to be smaller than in England. In most countries, devotees who gather together in the nude are subject to police action, even when their meetings and sports assemblies take place in private parks screened from the public. In Germany, however, there are public nudist beaches which are visited by thousands of men, women and children. Chief among them is Abersiwien, on the island of Sylt near the Danish-German frontier. In France there are several places

International Naturist Federation (I.N.F.) Convention in Vienna, 1954, attended by delegates from nudist organizations in Australia, Austria, Belgium, Canada, Denmark, France, Germany, Great Britain, Holland, Switzerland, United States. (Helios Magazine, Copenhagen, 1955.)

Nudists select convention queens. Winner, Mary Anne Mason, elected Queen of the American Sunbathing Association, Lupin Lodge near San Francisco, 1957. (Photo by Ed Lange, Swallows Club.)

where nudism is legally permitted, such as the famous Isle de Levant, sometimes called "The Island of Naked Women" off the Mediterranean coast. Sun- and sea-bathing in the nude is relatively common in Scandinavian countries and Russia.

How do people feel about joining a nudist camp? Mrs. Ruth B. Kirk has expressed herself as a wife and mother quite eloquently in a pamphlet recently published by the American Sun Bathing Association. After explaining how she and her husband became interested in nudism, she describes her first visit to a nudist camp.

"You round a bend in the road, through a gate, and suddenly you are there. You see a nude man chopping wood. There is a spirited game of volleyball going on. People down by the pool—children running back and forth . . . you sit in the car a minute taking it all in.

Before you can make up your minds to get out of the car you are greeted cordially by one of the members and invited to get out and walk around the camp and see what is there.

"You are taken here and there and introduced to some of the members by their, and your first names. You look at the inviting pool, the green lawn—and the sun is warm. The children are tugging at your hand, begging to go to the pool, and can't we take our clothes off, Mommy? And suddenly you feel so conspicuous with your clothes on and you want to enjoy the sunshine and fresh air with the relaxed freedom these other people seem to have. You go to your car and disrobe, and the first step has been taken. The biggest step.

"You find that the moral standard is very high in a nudist camp. There is no liquor allowed, either on the premises or on the individual. There are no smutty stories told—no overdisplay of affection. Folks conduct themselves the same as on any public beach—in fact the conduct is better. You find there is no sex stimulation brought on by lack of clothing of anyone present.

"There is almost always a game of some kind going on—volleyball is the universal nudist sport; there is usually work to be done to improve or beautify the grounds.

"As for the children—they are so healthy, living in the fresh air and sunlight in this way, learning new and interesting things about the outdoors. They do not have the ingrained inhibitions you had to overcome. To go without clothes is a perfectly natural thing for them. It is easy for them to understand that here they can go nude but in town they can't because everyone doesn't believe as they do at camp.

"They are not interested in sneaking down on burlesque row or reading books that have to be sneaked behind the barn or looking at obscene pictures. The facts of life are known to them and there is no vicarious thrill in those things." She adds that after continued visits "you remember wondering why nudists have to take everything off— why not leave something on. You have found out why—because you have overcome the shame of the body, of certain parts of the body. You have found that one part is as beautiful as the other and each has its own natural function to do. There is nothing to be hidden— no reason for wearing 'some little thing.'

"You go home rejuvenated not only in body but in mind. You get the feeling as you stand by your car and disrobe that with your clothes you strip off the ugly, dirty world and here alone is peace and brotherhood with your fellow man. Here you find friendly, cordial people, broad of mind, tolerant, respectful of persons. And when you do finally reach the understanding of the philosophy of nudism, you find your horizons unlimited, a great peace of mind, a richness in your enjoyment of life. You have found that freedom. And you bless the day you agreed to go to the nudist camp."

On the effects of nudist upbringing on children, Mervin Mounce, editor of *American Sunbather and Nudist Leader,* states in comparing them with other children that "In all fairness, we must make note of the high degree of selectivity practiced in the selection of nudist members. Nudist parents have universally been chosen for membership on the basis of high moral character, congeniality, and the fact that their children are, in general, well-behaved. Thus in the very beginning, many who might be inclined to delinquency are weeded out. The claim that nudist society has no delinquency problem is entirely accurate. Were we to apply the national average, the nudists would be entitled to more than three hundred delinquency arrests a year, and still be no worse off than the general public. The nudist record, however, is much better than that. As a matter of fact, it is near perfect. A number of nudist juveniles, over the years, have been guilty of such offenses as joy-riding, or petty theft. The number of these might be two dozen in the past twenty years. In the matter of sexual delinquency on the other hand, not a single case has ever come to my attention in all my experience, and believe me, I have my ear to the ground."

On the aesthetic side, there is much to be said in favor of nudism. The sense of shame which now prevents our wholehearted admiration of the naked human body has inhibited much painting and sculpture in the Western world. The ancient Greeks, living in the great period of their history, regarded the human body in terms of beauty and were entirely divorced from the sense of sin which inhibits enjoyment of human nakedness from the aesthetic point of view in our present puritan civilization. Consequently, the Greeks produced the greatest statues of all time, and while there are no traces left of their paintings, except on vases or pottery, it would be safe to guess that these were the equal of their works in marble. But more than this, the partly hedonistic spirit of Greek civilization, with its joy expressed in the divinity of the human form, resulted in a desire for physical perfection in the bodies of its population, notwithstanding the fact that the men and women were as fully clothed as the Israelites and equally desirous of being godlike. The Olympic games, in which all the participants competed with one another in the nude, serve as a reminder that physical health is a desideratum in modern as well as ancient times. And the fact that by the use of double-breasted suits, padded shoulders, corsets, brassières and the like, we lazy moderns can pretend by our clothes to a physical perfection which we do not actually possess, should make the arguments of the nudists even more potent.

Indeed, if so many favorable results are due to nudism, why don't we all become nudists? The answer is that modern man is a puritan and not a pagan, and by his clothing has been able to overcome his feeling of shame in relation to his sex organs in public, in mixed company. He has done this by transforming his basic inferiority into a feeling of superiority, *by relating himself to God in whose sexless image he claims to be made. But take all his clothes off, and it is plain to see that he is half-god, half-animal. He is playing two opposing roles which contradict one another, and the result is confusion.* In the Greek Pantheon the gods usually wore clothes (although some were naked), so that without any sense of sin or shame the men of that period could regard themselves as related to the gods without having to overcome a feeling of inferiority as regards their sexual parts. We could behave as the ancient Greeks did only if we followed their religion and way of life, which is impossible today. The modern nudist trying to forget or overcome his sense of shame while displaying his naked body in public, has no relation to the fifth-century Greek who never felt such shame and had no feelings of impropriety in joyously displaying his nudity. And we must always remember that among the Greeks female nudity was the exception and not the rule, either in life or in art.

Other reasons exist for believing that nudism is unlikely to spread as a way of life under modern conditions. Some of these follow from the amusing account of nakedness in the mass which was given me by an impartial observer, although the incident did not take place in a nudist camp but at a bathing beach in Soviet Russia. Dudley Nichols, author, critic, and motion-picture director, recounts the following experience when he and his wife Esta decided to go swimming at the seaside resort of Yalta in the year 1936. Nichols states:

"Innocently I asked the hotel desk clerk where I might find a bathing suit. She stared at me and said, 'Isn't there a towel in your room? That's all you need.' My wife and I gathered our towels and went down to the beach gate where an attendant was collecting a few

While conflict between nudists and the law still takes place at local levels, recent rulings of the U.S. courts have upheld private nudist camps and nudist magazines. Police officer visits nudist camp in Indiana. (Photo by Len Camp.)

kopecks per person. We took along with us a young girl, Cynthia, from New York, whom we had met on the train from Moscow. Cynthia was in constant dismay; when we parted at the beach gate, Esta and Cynthia going to one side, I to the other, she found herself in the midst of a thousand naked women sporting on the sand and in the water. Esta did as the Romans do (or as the Russians did in this case) and stripped off, but Cynthia shrank with modesty and donned her bathing suit. At first, only at first. She looked so shocking, clothed in the midst of all that nudity, that she soon cast off her swim suit which for some reason she had carried along all the way from New York.

"I, on my side, found myself amongst half a thousand stripped men. There were benches on which to lie or place your clothes. Deciding I'd never again see a thousand nude women, I took a bench right next to the three-foot fence which divided the sexes. On my side, the male side, women attendants were going around collecting or furnishing towels and indulging in vigorous conversations with the men on the benches. Watching one of these women talking with a man lying on his back on the next bench, the first thing that struck me was that there was no sense of sex differentiation, no apparent awareness of it on the part of anyone in sight; in fact there seemed to be no sense of sex at all.

"The women seemed equally unaware of my watching. And I must say that all awareness of sex began to leave me too. We were all a crowd of neuter animals enjoying the sun, the shingle and the sea. It was relaxed, easing, peaceful . . . and yet I found it in some curious way disturbing. It was as if sex had been abolished. I think I'm a fairly healthy, normal, moral man and I hold with D. H. Lawrence that 'sex in the head' is a vice, but my qualms didn't come from sex in the mind; rather, I felt that to have a complete sense of personal, individual existence we need to be aware of the opposite sex; and that should go for women as well as men. This was too impersonal for me; it seemed a negation of one's individuality. Perhaps I analyze it wrongly, but I felt that day as if Adam must have only begun to live completely when he discovered that Eve was a fascinating creature very unlike himself—rib be damned!

"I put on my clothes and went back to the hotel, having come to the conclusion that the day the human race stops wearing clothes, or the day that men and women dress precisely alike, wearing the same uniform, life will have lost much of its glory."

Most of us will agree with Dudley Nichols' conclusions. *Groups of men and women without clothing appear to lose their individuality and become merely a herd, like any other herd of animals.* The brilliant stage director Philip Moeller expressed a similar point wittily after seeing a revue at the Folies Bergère in which more than fifty naked women took part. He remarked, "A display of this character reminds me of nothing so vividly as mothers' milk!"

Another of the effects of nudism is, in the opinion of this writer, to rob human beings of their dignity of office and the authority which is imparted to them by their clothes. Carlyle in *Sartor Resartus* remarks humorously on the lack of dignity or authority of a naked House of Lords. The same thought applies to a naked Senate, or a meeting of a naked chamber of commerce, or a naked bankers' convention. One of the most disillusioning experiences in my memory was to meet a distinguished judge of the Supreme Court stark naked in a steam bath. The dignity of the law was left high and dry in the locker room along with his clothes.

Hundreds of the fanatic Russian Doukhobor nudist sect, the Sons of Freedom, march naked in western Canada to provoke arrest in protest against obeying the laws. (American Museum of Natural History.)

An instance of nudity which is practiced as a religious form is found among the Doukhobors, an anarchistic sect of Russian extremists who were banished from Russia to Asiatic Georgia and thereafter moved to western Canada in the spring of 1898. They now number over 15,000 and are in constant conflict with the government because of their refusal to conform to local laws and customs. The year 1903 saw the first of a series of nude parades by a group which was the forerunner of the Sons of Freedom, the troublesome extremists who not only deny smoking, alcohol and meat, but also formal education and clothing. The first parade of protest resulted in twenty-nine Doukhobors being sentenced to three months in jail. However, independents among the sect now accept education and Canadian standards and are likely to become assimilated.

Theoretical nudists such as Langdon-Davies and Maurice Parmalee have written books suggesting the adoption of nudism as a design for living. Davies visualized nudes walking up and down Fifth Avenue. I wonder why he selected this particular avenue which has the most fashionable clothing stores. I can imagine the sun-scorched or frozen nudes looking into the shop windows with longing envy. Parmalee envisioned a nudist state with a kind of skin-deep equality. The actual nudists of this country, as one of them reminded me, wear just as many clothes as anyone else. They differ from us mainly in that they are periodically given to removing more of them more publicly than the rest of us.

What are the results of all these efforts to cast off clothes? The inevitable workings of man's quest for superiority places the cult of body beauty and athletic prowess as one of the most important of the unconscious goals of such nudist organizations—which is nothing to be apologetic about. The moment groups foregather in the nude and after the first embarrassment of the newcomer is overcome, the exercises and games begin, and he or she who is the superior athlete often becomes an unconscious ideal for the group, just as the greatest hunter was the ideal for the primitive tribe thousands of years earlier. Indeed, the very great interest which nudists take in athletics, as well as the cult of the body beautiful, may well contribute to mankind's physical improvement in the future. *In my opinion, nudism mainly emphasizes the importance for the cultural progress of mankind of our continuing to wear clothes. To this we should add that we are also indebted to the nudists for emphasizing the importance of removing them from time to time for our physical and spiritual well-being.*

PART III

CLOTHES

AND

CIVILIZATION

CHAPTER 7

Clothes and Evolution

"Clothes make the man" is an old saying which we accept as a truism without giving it much thought. By this expression, simplified from Shakespeare's "for the apparel doth proclaim the man," we refer to the effect of clothing on man's outward appearance, position or character, rather than on his face and physique. Yet it would equally be correct to say that clothes not only "make the man," but have also affected his facial features and the build of his body.

It is a startling probability that clothing has altered the direction of man's more recent evolution, and that the human race, as it now exists in countries where clothing has been worn for many thousands of years, has been modified to some extent in both its physical and mental characteristics by wearing clothing. This is not surprising when we remember that "naked man" as such disappeared from the colder climates thousands of years ago and was replaced by the composite creature who can only be described as "man-and-his-clothes" and who remains with us today. And it is the breeding habits of this composite creature which have affected the later evolution of the race, since this creature has been affected for thousands of years by what is revealed and what is covered by clothing in the selection of a mate. Furthermore, it would appear that sexual selection has operated to favor the higher or more mental types of man at the expense of the lower or more physical.

Clothing, by focusing attention on the face, shoulders and breasts, resulted in a change in the later evolution of mankind from the ugliness of the Venus of Brassempouy to the beauty of the Venus de Milo. Earliest figurines of women, thought to be fertility amulets, are between twenty and thirty thousand years old. Upper left, *Venus of Lespugue;* center, *Venus of Brassempouy;* right, *Venus of Willendorf.* Lower left, *Venus of Serpenine;* right, *Venus of Dólni;* center, *Venus de Milo.*

A discussion of this subject leads us not only to an examination of the evidence on which our new explanations are based, but also invites us to consider clothing in relation to the modification and disappearance of racial types and physical characteristics; and also to consider race-building and the geographical dispersal of peoples as a result of clothing.

Standards of beauty in sexual selection over the centuries have undeniably been influenced by clothes. Professor J. B. S. Haldane states in *Daedalus* that "of the biological inventions of the past, four were made before history, the domestication of animals, plants, fungi for the production of alcohol, and a fourth invention," clothing, which he believed was of more ultimate and far-reaching importance than any of the others, "since it altered the path of sexual selection, focused the attention of man as a lover upon woman's face and breasts, and changed our idea of beauty from the steatopygous Hottentot to the modern European, from the Venus of Brassempouy to the Venus of Milo."

Since the steatopygous Hottentot lady had a rear protuberance shaped like a bustle, and the Venus of Brassempouy (about 30,000 B.C.) had a broad flat face and no visible chin, we have reason to be grateful for the part played by clothing in improving the beauty of the human face, shoulders and breasts. When the body is covered, attention is mainly focused on the face and the upper part of the body, and a pretty face, attractive hair and beautiful breasts become the first objects to attract the attention of the male. As a result, Darwin's law of sexual selection has operated for thousands of years to provide pretty girls, even when they lacked doweries, with husbands and children.

Not only were the women affected in this way, but also the men, so that because of the emphasis on beauty in sexual selection due to the wearing of clothes, the racial strain itself was improved in appearance. Thus Haldane suggests the important fact that clothes actually affect both physique and physiognomy, resulting in the refinement of the breed of civilized man with the passage of time.

Thanks to sexual selection as influenced by the wearing of clothes, we can look forward to our men and women becoming progressively more beautiful, according to our own standards of facial beauty, as the generations follow one another into the future.

But the progressively increasing beauty of the female was only one of the results of wearing clothes. *In my opinion, of far more im-*

portance for civilization and racial improvement was the progres-sively increasing emphasis which the wearing of clothes removed from the physical to the mental in man—from brawn to brains.

As a result of wearing clothing in the cooler climates, two important things have happened through the ages. First, in addition to the sexual parts being hidden, the torso and muscles of the body were also largely covered. Therefore the man who was the stronger or more muscular, being covered with clothes which hid or partly hid his body, no longer presented an outward appearance of physical strength as a dominant characteristic. Consequently, mere muscle was no longer the main attribute of male superiority in winning the admiration and submission of the female, but weaker men now stood some chance of being eligible as breeders. Secondly, the covering of the body emphasized mental attributes, and hid the lower centers. *As a result, the man with the superior mind and inferior body which was covered from view could be regarded as the equal of the man with a superior body and inferior mind, and could eventually surpass him in the struggle for survival and the selection of a mate.*

Brains eventually triumphed over brawn, and he who could ultimately contribute most to the material advancement and culture of the community or group by his mental attainments commanded more respect than the less capable but physically stronger man. Moreover, he represented a goal of superiority for others to emulate.

Clothing which covered most of the body therefore affected selection in breeding by focusing the attention in the choice of men as husbands and fathers not merely on their physique, but also on their superior mental attributes. This in turn has contributed to a profound change in the mental development of the human race. Man as he is today has emerged as a thinker with the help of clothing, as compared with what would have happened had the muscular strength of the naked male mainly influenced the selection of mates. With the development of man's mental centers, he acquired increasing self-confidence in his powers of reason, imagination and invention. Because his body was covered, his mind included different levels of values, and he focused as much or more on the spiritual and mental as on the physical. Therefore men whose physical attainments were overshadowed by their mental ability became more desirable as husbands than gladiators, wrestlers or prize fighters. The modern woman who is attracted to an Einstein or a Stravinsky is generally not too concerned with his muscles!

Thanks to clothing, when emphasis was placed on man's more intellectual qualities, Western culture took a jump forward with the rapid development of the civilizations which began in the grasslands of the Middle Eastern countries. As soon as spiritual and mental attainments were highly regarded, they became important factors in sexual selection and the later evolution of the human race. It is significant that this rapid development of Western culture began after the invention of clothes.

In considering these conclusions, it is not intended to indicate that because of early men's use of clothing, women were no longer interested in their muscle or brawn. On the contrary, clothes have never been entirely successful in hiding the wearer's body. In many periods of history, men's clothing emphasized manly beauty, for example in the tight trousers of the Napoleonic age and the "fine leg" of the eighteenth century. Brains attracted women largely because their possessors could conquer brawn, but doubtless untold millions of women would have preferred to mate with the man with the strong muscular body had he but possessed the requisite brains as well. And even under modern conditions, in which men have often used their clothes to hide their bodies, women are usually smart enough to find out what is hidden under the charcoal-grey or blue uniform of the present day businessman, and to be guided accordingly.

For those who fear that we have gone too far in preserving feeble physical types whose children will weaken the race, a hopeful sign is found in the present-day display of the nearly naked bodies of young men and women at bathing beaches. This rapidly growing custom enables the lovers of today to base their mutual admiration on the possession of attractive bodies as well as other attributes. This is something their grandmothers and grandfathers generally did not experience before marriage. Since we have now reached a stage in civilization when we place an extremely high regard on mental attainments, perhaps a swing in the opposite direction towards the physical may have a balancing effect.

In my opinion it is also possible that due to clothing, some of modern men's more brutish relatives, such as the Neanderthal man, may have disappeared or become amalgamated with Homo sapiens. R. Moore, in *Man, Time and Fossils,* speaking of Dr. Sherwood L. Washburn's recent contributions to the subject of evolution, remarks that "despite his forbidding appearance, Neanderthal man had a brain of near-human size. Washburn likes to say jokingly that if he had been enrolled in college today he might have done well, and probably would have been considered an invaluable asset to the football team. Since the Neanderthal man, almost the only important change in man has been a *decrease in the size of the features . . .* In the long range of evolution such changes are minor; they are only

Left, *the hairy Ainus of Japan are said to be the hairiest people in the world, yet are not hairy enough to keep warm in winter without clothes, as animals do.* Right, *restoration of a Neanderthal man, by Frederick Blaschke. (Field Museum of Natural History, Chicago.)*

the finishing touches, the top dressing. Just less face, less teeth, less bones, less muscle will account for these changes."

It is amusing to speculate more or less fantastically as to how man came by "this decrease in the size of the features." How did nature's potential gifts to Harvard or Yale disappear from the face of the earth, leaving it to Homo sapiens to provide football players through the ages? If, as Haldane stated, clothing resulted in focusing attention on the beauty of the female features and breasts, producing an improvement in the beauty of the race, it may have also resulted in the startling and unexplained disappearance of the Neanderthal man as a race as the outcome of many thousands of years of sexual selection. The Neanderthal man, with his huge brow ridges, heavy cheeks and massive jaws, apparently wore clothes of hide or fur which covered his body during the glacial periods. Neanderthal women were no doubt equally brutish in appearance. *As a result, Neanderthal man may have been partly bred out of existence by the preference in mating for the more delicate features of the less apelike types of Homo sapiens. As these latter were probably also the higher mental types, they were also better fitted for survival.* This, of course, is in the nature of guesswork. Carleton S. Coon has pictured a reconstructed Neanderthal man wearing a Homburg hat and coat. He could pass anywhere today as a modern New York gangster.

Clothing has also played a part in social evolution and in the stratification of a race or a people into different groups, such as the aristocracy and the peasantry, with somewhat different physical characteristics. The clothing which marked the difference between the various groups in the past helped to produce the social inhibition against intermarriage between individuals of one group with the other. While this intermarriage sometimes took place, it was the exception rather than the rule. With the emergence of the middle classes in Europe, wearing their own distinctive clothing, a third group was formed which was less strongly separated from the other two. In the United States, the differentiation of the classes is based primarily on standards of wealth and position rather than aristocracy and peasantry. *Inasmuch as almost similar clothing is worn throughout the country, differentiations between the groups are not too strongly indicated by their clothes, and intermarriage of the descendants of various European types and classes takes place fairly freely.* Thus the "melting pot" has become a racial reality from which a distinctive American type of much taller men and women is emerging, a mixture of the descendants of European aristocrat, middle class and peasant. A similar situation may ultimately develop in Europe with the decline of the aristocracy, the levelling of class distinctions and greater uniformity of clothing. In Soviet Russia a levelling of this type has already taken place with the emergence of a new class, the executive and intellectual class drawn from an admixture of the middle class and peasant stock.

Clothing has not only played a part in the amalgamation of selected groups of Europeans to build an American race, but has played a similar role in the early racial history of the Old World. However, we must bear in mind that clothing, in some of its earlier manifestations, tended to emphasize racial and class differences and thus to impede intermarriage, while today it tends to emphasize similarities between races and classes. *The role played by clothing in race building in the past will undoubtedly be accelerated in the future as all peoples and classes tend to wear the same kind of clothing all over the world. If this happens, we shall gradually drift into a new era of race building.* A process of this sort which is now proceeding in the British West Indies may well produce a new racial type within the next hundred years, known as the Bee Wee! This may set the pattern for the entire world a few hundred years hence!

While we are on the present subject, we may note that clothing has played a far more important part in the geographical dispersion and development of races than is generally recognized. *For example, without the invention of clothing it is highly improbable that the American continent would have been peopled at the time it was (about 25,000 years ago) by what are now the American Indian races, nor the northern parts of Europe by the racial mixtures found in the Nordics, Celts and so forth.* Because of the invention of warm clothes, man was able to survive the various periods of glacial ice and to cross the barrier of the Arctic ice region into America. Different species of man amalgamated and, as stated by Coon, "passed over the Bering Straits in early post-glacial times, if not earlier, to provide the basic genetic stock from which the American Indian developed, in combination with later arrivals. From a branch of this hyperboreal group there evolved in Northern Asia the ancestral strain of the entire specialized mongoloid family."

Early man, enabled to travel by means of his clothes in spite of adverse climates, and to hunt and feed on the bodies of fur-bearing animals which could live in such climates, settled down in segregated communities and introduced agriculture as the climates became warmer. Some of these groups developed over a period of thousands of years into the various branches of the white races which now people Europe. Without the invention of clothing, the story might be quite different. *When we realize that the very existence of the present racial mixtures which now inhabit Europe and America (other than the Negroids) was due to their ancestors' ability to survive by wearing clothing, the importance of wearing clothes is brought home to us with dramatic emphasis.*

The part played by clothing in affecting the more recent evolution of man leads us to consider some other pertinent questions. Why did man's body, almost alone of the larger mammals, develop neither a hide like the rhinoceros nor hair like the reindeer or horse? And yet all of us are familiar with the hair growing on our own bodies. Some men are covered with it. Is this hair a "throw-back"? Was prehistoric man once covered with hair like the apes, and if so, how and why did he get rid of it?

It may well be asked why, in a book about clothing, should we concern ourselves with hair on the human body? The answer is obvious. If our bodies were covered with a thick coat of hair, fur or wool, we should not have needed clothing to keep warm in colder climates, and the book of human history would have been written quite differently. And this book would not have been written at all.

That many of our male friends are almost as shaggy as a shaggy dog, and grow an abundant crop of hair not only on their chests, but all over their bodies, makes us wonder why we are not all equally hairy? We wonder even more when we learn that heavy growth of hair on the body is a characteristic of the European white peoples, and does not exist to any great extent among the Negroes and Mongolians, which latter include the Chinese, Japanese, Eskimos and American Indians. But of course, whenever we make a generalization about humanity, we always find some apparent exceptions. The hairy Ainus of northern Japan grow more body hair, as well as luxurious manes and beards, than any other race. How do we account for this? According to Boas they are "descendants of a European group that migrated to the Pacific." In spite of their luxurious body crop, the hairy Ainus still wear clothes to keep warm. Among the Negroids, the Ashantis, Congo Pygmies and Austroloids are quite hairy.

As to the quantities of body hair of various peoples, Coon states that this is "closely correlated with the amount of beard, and both are linked with age, for a hairy man grows hairier as he becomes older. At the same time, baldness is most frequent among those with the heaviest body hair and heaviest beards. Brow ridges and other bony excrescences of a hypermasculine nature, are closely linked with excessive pilous development of the body and beard, and with a tendency to baldness."

Some scientists believe that our progenitors were completely covered with hair at one time, and that we discarded it as useless in the march of evolution. They point, as evidence, to the existence of hair on the embryo in the womb, and the fact that both male and female bodies are covered with a fine or minute down. Boas states that "deficiency of the adrenals which control hairiness (and pigmentation) may be responsible for the meager growth of body hair of the Mongol and Negro as against its abundance in the European and Australian." He also thinks that "changes due to environment may well have been caused by a slight modification in chemical activity of the body. Thus environment may have increased the activity of the adrenals, causing growth of body hair on Europeans."

Boas also remarks that "most wild animals have straight hair and all parts of the body are well covered—except among anthropoid apes. The development of long hair of man is inconceivable in a wild species. It would make the arboreal life of man's predecessor impossible and would equally be a hindrance in life in the open unless man learned to dress it." Of course man ultimately did learn to dress it. He also invented the haircut.

Jacobs and Stern note that "heavy hair is apelike, but those people having heavy hair have several features which are further removed from the ape than equivalent features in populations which have little hair." Hairy men can derive some comfort from this statement, and also from the fact that gorillas, at least the ones with which I am acquainted, have no hair at all on their chests!

That many men's bodies are heavily covered with hair in the present day, cannot, in my opinion, be taken as satisfactory evidence that in prehistoric times body hair or fur was an attribute of the entire human race, including both men and women. Unlike the sparse hair on the anthropoid apes, human body hair appears to be a male sexual characteristic similar to the beard, and it is the exception for women to have body hair to anything like the same extent as men. Moreover, such body hair does not appear in childhood, but begins to grow only during and after puberty and usually considerably later. Contrast this with most animals, including the apes, irrespective of whether the young are or are not born naked, or bear "baby hair." There is usually no difference between the hair or fur coat of the male or female animal except with respect to such male characteristics as the mane, present in the male lion but not in the female.

The evidence is therefore against those who argue that the bodies of the human race, both male and female, were at one time thickly covered with hair or fur like most animals which was bred out by natural selection. Even if some of man's remote ancestors were hairy (and especially the remote ancestors of the Caucasians), it is certain that our present condition of nakedness has been with us for a long, long time. And it is man's natural nakedness which, in association with his inadequacy or inferiority, led him into the invention of clothing in order to cover and protect his body, just as his other physical inadequacies caused him to invent other ways and means to overcome them.

Finally, if a man feels inferior today because of the amount of hair on his body (and many do), he covers it with his clothes, or with a one-piece bathing suit when swimming. That such excessive apelike hairiness is repellant to some women is counteracted by the fact that it is generally believed that abundance of body hair is a sign of masculine virility. It therefore does not necessarily affect sexual selection as might otherwise be the case, or if we lived in a state of nudity. "If you love a man," a young woman once confessed to me, "you love his hairiness too!"

The savants of Hollywood feel differently. Actors who display their naked chests in motion pictures are required to shave them forthwith if they are hairy!

CHAPTER 8

Clothes, Religions and Cultures

That there is a relationship between religion and clothing has already been explained in Chapter 1 with reference to man's belief in himself as a godlike creature, usually claiming a divine origin or relationship to the spirits or gods. We shall now examine this relationship between clothing and religion in more detail, *particularly with reference to the novel proposition that the more fully peoples are clothed, the more advanced their religions, while the nearer they approach nakedness, the more primitive is their religion, though by no means the less complex. We shall also note that in the most advanced religions, most of the gods wear clothes.* Moreover, we will consider the manner in which religions and clothing have influenced cultures down the ages.

We shall begin by examining the earliest evidences of the religions of prehistoric man and attempt to fill in the gaps by referring to the practices and beliefs of primitive peoples or aborigines of modern times. *We shall note that as man became more fully clad in historical times, the more he believed in gods or deities who were concerned with his own behavior or welfare. Finally, before discussing the clothing worn by the priesthoods of various religions to indicate their closeness to the gods, we shall inquire into the fact that no great civilizations have existed in the world without the co-action of clothing and religion.*

The earliest evidence we have that prehistoric man believed he possessed a soul also shows that he possessed clothes as well. This evidence is based on the scrapers, awls and (later on) needles buried in Neanderthal graves along with the owner, probably for use by the spirit to make its clothing in the afterlife. *Over 75,000 years ago, and probably much earlier, evidence points to the fact that man wore clothes and believed he possessed a spirit which lived on after death.*

We can surmise from the paintings on the walls of the caves in southern France that the cave dwellers believed in spirits which could be influenced to aid them in securing food. The tools left by these peoples indicate that they were clothed, probably in the skins of cave bears, and later on reindeer. The form of their religion, so far as it can be surmised, was similar to many of the primitive religions of many of the aborigines of today, and their priests or wizards wore ceremonial robes and animal masks.

A study of many primitive peoples who wear little or no clothes indicates that they seldom believe in a Supreme Being but participate in an animistic type of religion or believe in totemism; and, according to Radin in *Primitive Religion,* where they have such beliefs the Supreme Being or Mana is a philosophical rather than a religious concept. Certain animals are still regarded as sacred in some religions. The cow which feeds the multitudes with milk is sacred in India because, as Mahatma Ghandi said, "The cow is a poem of pity. She is mother to millions of Indian mankind." And all who kill cows "rot in hell for so many years as there are hairs on the cow's body." A greedy Brahmin may drop to the inferior status of a lowly pig in his next reincarnation, thus showing the Hindu belief in the inferiority of animals, although respecting them as containing the souls of humans. Indeed, man's belief in his superiority over animals is emphasized in the Hindu religion by the fact that the soul of the unworthy upon death enters the body of an animal, while the superior soul enters into union with Brahmin or God.

As we pass from the primitive animistic religions to the higher anthropomorphic religions of the ancient Egyptian, Greek and Hindu types of polytheism, in which there is a belief in a family of gods with a superior god or gods, we find that the worshippers are substantially clothed, except for those classes which are unable to be so because of serfdom, poverty or climate. The gods were usually created in man's image and possessed to a magnified extent man's good and evil qualities. The grandiose conception of man being created in God's image was introduced by the Hebrews, and it spread through the Western world as a result of the introduction by Christianity of the Jewish conception of Jehovah or God as a Supreme Being. In the case of the Hebrew, Christian and Moslem religions, the con-

The Greek gods and goddesses usually wore clothing, some more, some less. Above, Zeus and Hera. Below, Hercules (naked) and an Amazon. (Museo Nazionale, Palermo.)

ception that men were created by God in His own image was accompanied by a sense of shame at exhibiting nakedness. The prohibitions of Moses against nakedness in family life made the use of clothing to cover the body in public substantially compulsory for both moral and religious reasons. Thus were created the world's first puritans, the Israelites, who looked upon their nakedness as something sinful, and hid their sexual and excretory parts which showed their affiliation with the animal world. No statues or pictures could be made by

Aphrodite (Venus) and Artemis (Diana), while they usually wore drapes, were sometimes naked. (Louvre.)

the Jews of men or women, either naked or clothed, for fear of idolatry, and the Jews were therefore strictly prohibited from artistic creation in these fields. Neither could statues nor pictures be made of Jehovah; and notwithstanding the fact that the Israelites believed they were created in His image, the idea that He might be possessed of the same organs of procreation and excretion that they were was unthinkable and even sacrilegious. Moslem civilization followed suit, and although ornate artistic tile work, pottery and architecture flourished, the human form was prohibited except among certain sects, such as the Shiite Moslems of Persia.

On the other hand, in ancient Greek civilization the gods were created in man's image, and partook of all the bodily functions of men and women. While the Greeks concealed their bodies with clothing, this was not done from a sense of sin, but for all the purposes of attaining superiority which have already been described, as well as for protection from the elements. Moreover, they invented the most beautiful clothing ever to be worn by man, and while there is plenty of evidence that nakedness was common among the men and women on athletic occasions, it would appear that women were usually clothed in voluminous draperies. This custom was probably a continuation of earlier Oriental influences as regards the covering up and hobbling of women who occupied a well-defined inferior position to the Greek men. Since there was no sense of shame attached to male nakedness, there was no feeling of disgust or inferiority at the existence of the procreative and excretory parts of the body, and no prohibition against making "graven images." The Greeks gloried in bodily beauty, and in their statues and pictorial pottery showed their admiration for the human body by creating the most beautiful nudes ever to grace the Western world. Indeed, so beautiful were their statues, statuettes and vases as works of art, that when they and their Roman copies were rediscovered in the fourteenth and fifteenth centuries, they inspired the Renaissance, the revival of art and learning that lifted the Western world out of the rut of the Middle Ages.

Did the gods dress, and if so, why? *Most of the Greek gods and goddesses are depicted in statues, statuettes and pottery as wearing clothes, some more, some less.* Apollo is usually shown in the nude, as might be expected, since he embodies the perfection of manly beauty. Aphrodite (Venus), however, is sometimes shown entirely nude, and sometimes with the lower part of her body draped, as with the Venus de Milo. This draping is the rule with almost all the other Greek goddesses with the exception of Artemis (Diana), who is sometimes shown naked. Hermes (Mercury) and Poseidon (Neptune) usually wear but little clothing so that they can travel fast, but they carry insignia such as the winged helmet and winged sandals of the former and the seaweed and triton of the latter. Hercules was usually unclothed, and so was Zeus on occasion, especially when he took the form of a man. Pallas Athena (later Minerva) is usually shown in statues as fully covered almost to her neck. Is it a mere coincidence that the wisest goddess has her body fully concealed as do many of the learned women of today, who despise the display of charms favored by their more feminine sisters?

An examination of the pictures and statues of the ancient Egyptian gods and the gods of the Hindu religion indicates that they usually wore clothing and ornaments. Some of them, however, were partly naked. Very few completely naked men and women appear in ancient Egyptian statues or wall paintings, although young boys and girls are sometimes so depicted. Representations of the philosophers Buddha and Confucius are sometimes worshipped in many Eastern countries as deities, but they are usually partly or wholly clothed, as indeed are most of their followers. In the Christian religion, Jehovah or God, when depicted at all, is usually shown in the form of a dignified bearded father-figure wearing long robes in which a mere mortal would probably have great difficulty in navigating. Michelangelo has painted some superb examples of such clothing in the Sistine chapel. He is also shown symbolically in the Masonic pictures as an All-Seeing Eye, certainly a more acceptable representation. Robes and loin cloths cover Jesus and the Apostles, as well as His disciples and enemies.

As to the gods of the Mayans, Aztecs and other Mexican Indians, these derived from the fact that over 4000 years ago these groups exploded into civilization after settling on the Mexican plateau. An examination I have made of a large number of statues, bas-reliefs and pictures left by those peoples indicates that in depictions of gods, rulers, priests and populace, these are almost always shown with their sexual parts covered by clothing. *From this we may deduce that clothing played the same role in advancing the civilizations of these agricultural peoples as with those already mentioned. We are therefore in a position to state that in all the ancient polytheistic religions, most of the gods wore clothes, and people clothed their gods as they clothed themselves (and often in their most dignified clothing), thus establishing a relationship which fortified their self-esteem and gave them faith and courage to rise above their origins and achieve as godlike humans.*

Most of the statues or wood carvings of the humanlike gods or spirits of primitive religions not only wear no clothes, but some have exaggerated male sexual organs to denote power or to stimulate fecundity. They usually arrive in this country and Europe either mutilated or covered by loin cloths which have been added by the Christian missionaries in much the same way as successive Popes

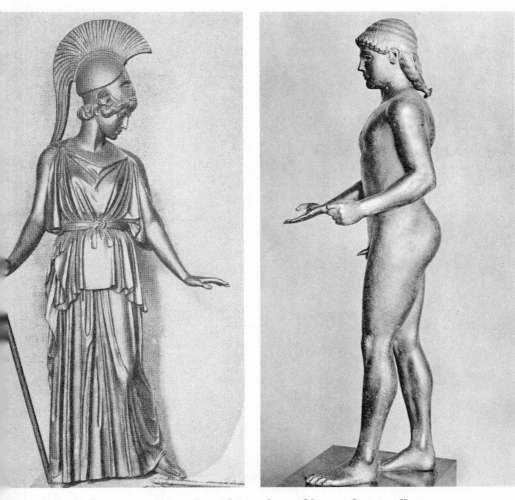

Pallas Athena was always draped from her ankles up, but Apollo was usually naked! (Louvre.)

Egyptian and Hindu gods and goddesses all wore clothes. Left, Egyptian goddess Neit, wearing crown of Lower Egypt, about 663-525 B.C. Right, Hindu goddess Parvati, about 900 A.D. (Metropolitan Museum of Art, New York.)

have insisted that all naked Greek and Roman male statues in the Vatican must be furnished with fig leaves.

The fact that the ancient Greeks were not divided as individuals, with their minds in rebellion against their bodies, and especially the sexual aspects of their bodies, may be one of the reasons why Greek civilization developed so extraordinarily not only in the field of creative art, but also in science and philosophy. When men feel free to inquire into the nature of their own bodily functions, and to satisfy their curiosity objectively, they tend to allow their imaginations to rove over the outside world and all it contains. Thus I believe their creative thinking was much freer than that of the Israelites, who were inhibited by their religion and clothing both artistically and physically in relation to their own bodies. The Jewish type of civilization thus tended to be subjective rather than objective during

Buddhist figures, often worshipped as gods or spirits, always wear clothes. Left, seated Buddha, China, dated 618-907 A.D. Right, Buddhist deity, Tibet, 17th century. (Metropolitan Museum of Art, New York.)

Mayan, Aztec, Zapotec, Tolupec and other Indian gods always wore clothes. Left, funerary urn representing god Xipe Totec, Zapotec. Right, rain-god Cocijo. (National Museum, Mexico City.)

the time when both races were making important strides in the progress of civilization. However, the clothing of the Jews during the periods of their greatest achievements in law and hygiene appears to have been resplendent in color and fabric, as evidenced by pictures of Hebrews shown on Egyptian and Assyrian wall paintings and descriptions in the Bible, while appreciation of feminine beauty found expression, not in statues, but in the erotic images of the Song of Songs. However, the Hebraic-Christian religion ultimately superceded the Hellenic or Graeco-Roman, since it provided in Jehovah or God a considerably higher and more satisfying deity to aspire to in place of the barbaric gods of Greece which, in their various metamorphoses, became the gods of cities and states.

Aristotle, in the "Poetics," as quoted by Edith Hamilton in *The Greek Way*, expressed the Greek philosophy as regards art and science in better terms than any modern reappraisal: "The glory, doubtless, of the heavenly bodies fills us with more delight than the contemplation of these lowly things, but the heavens are high and far

off, and the knowledge of celestial things that our senses give us is
scanty and dim. Living creatures, on the contrary, are at our door,
and if we so desire we may gain full and certain knowledge of each
and all. We take pleasure in a statue's beauty; should not then the
living fill us with delight? And all the more if in the spirit of the
love of knowledge we search for causes and bring to light evidences
of meaning. Then will nature's purpose and her deep-seated laws be
revealed in all things, all tending in her multitudinous work to one
form or another of the beautiful."

*Once men settled down in agricultural communities, wore a sub-
stantial amount of clothing, and believed that they were created in
the image of the gods or God, or partook of godlike qualities, then
progress in developing civilization under the influence of men's belief
in themselves as superior beings was immediate and continuous.
Indeed, it is suggested that no great civilizations have existed without
the goal of superiority imparted to mankind by religion and clothes
co-acting to sustain man's belief in his kinship with the gods.* Inasmuch

*Gods or spirits of primitive religions were usually naked. Left, Maori an-
cestor figure worshipped as a god, New Zealand. Right, ancestor figure,
Easter Island, Polynesia, kept in wrappings and unwrapped only for special occasions. (Brooklyn Museum.)*

as the monotheistic religions (the Hebrew and one branch of the Moslem) forbade the making of graven images or painting which reproduced human beings and their attire, these peoples created mainly in law, medicine, science, music, architecture and mathematics. The polytheistic religions such as those of ancient Egypt, Greece, Rome and India, gave the artists the opportunity to work creatively on images to be placed in temples; as did the Catholic Church later on in the statues and pictures of Jesus and the Saints exhibited in churches. *Creation along artistic lines seems to have carried along with it a desire to beautify human beings as well as their clothing. Suppression of such artistic activities seems to result in the creative faculties developing mainly along other lines of abstract thinking or science.*

The existence of our modern scientific culture may well be ascribed to the forces of reform in religion and to the individualistic philosophy which freed the will and which were let loose upon the world by Calvin and Martin Luther when the Old Testament, with its puritanical prohibitions, was reintroduced to the world of artistically ornate Catholicism. This reform movement and those which followed it were not only monotheistic and puritanical, but they also attacked the luxurious clothing of the clergy and the laymen, as well as the adornment of the elaborate Gothic churches with pictures and statues of the Trinity and the Saints which had absorbed most of the creative urge of the previous era. While modern science began in the Renaissance, the modern scientists prospered to the greatest extent in the northern countries under the influence of Protestantism and the diversion of the creative mind from artistic to scientific pursuits. Together with them came clothing which fitted the mood of the times. They were simple in design and drab in color. (I do not exclude the fact that many fine scientists came from France and Italy; these, as a rule, were not ardent believers in the Saints.)

Flügel in his *Psychology of Clothes* hints at the influence of clothes on science, stating: "It is perhaps no mere chance that a period of unexcelled scientific progress should have followed the abandonment of ornamental clothing at the beginning of the last century." It is true that very few modern scientists are dandies. But I suspect that lack of interest in his person and his clothing, in contrast with his interest in his work, is one of the main reasons that many scientists pay little attention to clothes. Charles F. Kettering, one of America's most prolific inventors, took so little interest in his clothing that his wife once told me she always bought them for him, "otherwise he'd wear the same things until they dropped off his back."

The interaction of clothing and religion during the Renaissance was undoubtedly a reason why the clothes of that great period were surprisingly beautiful compared to those of the puritans. The painters and architects responding to the artistic urge resulting from the rediscovery of Greek classical art, produced the great paintings, statues, both nude and otherwise, and other works of art uninhibited by puritanical considerations. This freedom in art was also reflected in the opulent, colorful clothes of the period, as was equally the case in ancient Greece and India. This is also why Leonardo da Vinci was more valued for his creative genius in painting than in scientific invention, in which he was also remarkable, for he belonged to a period in which artistic achievement was considered more important than science. Galileo was persecuted by the church, as was all science which ran counter to the Scriptures. Today, the situation is reversed, and our present clothes undoubtedly influence the culture of today, and in turn are influenced by it. *Plainness in clothing is the enemy of art. Were we to dress entirely in plain clothes, we would live in a drab world indeed, from which beauty in sculpture and painting would probably be abolished, as with the Mennonites and Amish of Pennsylvania, who put their creative urge into their craftsmanship and painted furniture.* What has been stated above applies also to some extent to literature and the theatre. Puritanism and drab clothing have usually been the enemy of the theatre, which until recently flourished mostly in periods of beautiful clothing, such as the Greek, Elizabethan and Restoration. Literature and poetry, however, belong to all periods, and seem to have escaped from the direct influence of clothing, if not of puritanism.

It is not possible in the present confines to do more than to point out above some of the broader aspects of the relationship between clothes, cultures and religions. This is a field for future study which may well be rewarding.

We shall turn now to the purposes of the clothing worn by the priests and ministers of religions. Once men recognized the existence of beneficent spirits or gods who were personally interested in them, clothes and decoration played a large part in ceremonies in which they tried to control or asked the help of these spirits or gods in their various pursuits, such as hunting, and later on agriculture. Our knowledge of the first medicine men or wizards and the costumes they wore came from the Ice Age cave paintings already referred to.

The purpose of these cave pictures and ceremonies is well explained by Loomis Havemeyer in *The Drama of Savage Peoples* in relation to the aborigine who, "when he wants the gods or spirits to do something in his behalf, proceeds to dramatize (act out) his request, that is, to give a rehearsal of a hoped-for performance. . . . When rain is wanted for the crops, a man will climb a tree, and out of a bucket pour a large amount of water on the ground, thus symbolizing the falling of rain. Before going out on a hunt, he will go through the motion of killing the animal with the hope that the gods will see his actions and grant him success. . . . This is known as imitative or empathic magic."

The ornaments and clothes of the medicine man, sorcerer or magician of present-day primitive religions are intended to indicate his special relationship to the spirits or gods and his control or power over them. Thus feathers, horns or antlers, amulets in the form of shells, claws and teeth of animals, and complex systems of painting or tattooing having special magical meanings, and symbols of the

Clothing to indicate religious authority: Bishops at enthronement of Patriarch of Rumania, Sofia, November 19, 1925. (Underwood & Underwood.)

Clothing to indicate religious authority: Zulu medicine men, their clothing and ornaments showing their tribal authority, attend Congress of Witch Doctors, Johannesburg, 1957. (Photo by Nickolas Muray, permission from Wenner-Gren Anthropological Foundation.)

totems, form part of the medicine man's or shaman's stock-in-trade which varies all over the world.

With the development of the higher forms of religions, priests of various kinds entered the picture on a high level of authority, and their highly colorful robes attested to their closeness to their deities and their power over their congregations in religious matters. *The reciprocal relationships between the king or tribal ruler and the priests or priesthoods was usually affirmed in ancient times by their ornate clothing and adornment which testified to the divinity of the king, and to his support of and by the priests and their separation from the rest of the people.* Priestly robes exist in all the great religions of today except those faiths in which there is no intervention of a special order of priests between man and his deity, or certain Protestant sects in which the preacher dresses in the same clothes as his congregation, such as the Plymouth brethren. (The priests of the Shinto religion of Japan wear priestly robes of green for temple services, but since they also follow other occupations, they wear the standard work-a-day clothes for these.)

Since most priesthoods involve a hierarchy with a head priest and subordinates, robes and vestments play an emphatic role in showing the superior rank of one priest over another and the priesthood over the secular world. A succession of magnificent Papal robes, of a richness which would have confounded Saint Peter, testifies to the Pope's authority to speak as head of the Roman Catholic Church. He is followed in authority by the Cardinals, Archbishops and Bishops, whose lesser positions are indicated by robes of lesser richness. Among the ancient Hebrews, the raiment worn by the silver-tongued Aaron, High Priest of Jehovah, as described in Exodus 28:5, must have made him the best-dressed individual in the desert, for he wore a "breast plate and an ephod and a robe and a coat of checkerwork and a mitre and a girdle. . . ." The ephod was a sacred vestment and was made "of gold, of blue, of purple, scarlet and fine twine linen." The robes of high priests of various religions have been thought to confer blessings on those who touch them—a function of clothing which goes back to the old days of magic.

The robes of Roman Catholic priests and nuns have their roots in the early Middle Ages and usually represent the type of ceremonial or upper-class clothes which were worn by people at the time of the founding of the order. In the case of monks and priests, however, it is noted that their costumes involve the wearing of long skirts which hamper free movement and have feminine rather than masculine characteristics, since similar skirts are used to handicap women in their movements. It is certain that these clerical robes were provided for entirely different reasons, yet the effect is the same. The priest is restricted in his movements as compared to men wearing trousers, and this restriction must affect his entire life, since he lives in his clothes. Veblen believed this placed the priest in the servant class, since he wore the clothes of a servant of God, and that "priestly vestments show, in accentuated form, all the features that have been shown to be evidence of a servile status and a vicarious life. . . . The priests at the same time, expected to refrain from useful effort and when before the public eye, to present an impassionately disconsolate countenance, very much after the manner of the well trained servant." This somewhat warped picture does not take into consideration the fact that the priestly robes are in general regarded as indicating the superiority of the wearer, rather than his servility.

Clothes have also been used as a badge to indicate special religions such as the plainly-dressed Quakers who disdain "finery."

Clothes also distinguish the priests and members of one branch of religion from another, such as the various orders of monks, and the superiors of the orders. To perform these functions, many special clothes were invented. Among these in the Western world are the clerical collar and round hats worn by Protestant clergymen, the simple robes of the various orders of Catholic priests and nuns, and the austere black or gray clothes of some American sects such as Shakers, Mennonites and Amish—the latter with their well-known aversion to using buttons on their garments, as "being too handy for the devil to hang something on."

The invention of special clothes to denote the superior position and denomination of the clergymen created a desired attitude of respect on the part of the public on meeting him in his clerical garb. Not long ago in France, the Roman Catholic Church decided to send a group of young "working priests" to the factories where the Communists were predominant, in order to convert them to Catholicism, and decided that these young men should not wear priests' clothes which might inhibit free discussion. So many of the young men had

Clothing to indicate religious authority: Tarascan Indian medicine men wearing hats with rabbitlike ears, Michocan, Mexico. (From MD *Magazine, photo by Bernard Cole; from the private collection of Dr. Abner Weisman.)*

their faith shaken by the Machiavellian arguments of the Communists that the Church hastily ordered the young men to resume their clerical robes. The priest's robe or the clergyman's cloth also generally protects him from injury in wars, and even in brawls.

Time Magazine recently stated that "The Roman Catholic priests of Spain had better climb off their motor scooters, put out their cigarettes, and stay away from soccer games and bullfights. So decreed Spain's primate, Enrico Cardinal Pla y Deniel, 80, in the bulletin of the Archbishopric of Toledo. Scooters and motorcycles may be used only with special permission and on church business—and never with a female passenger. Priests with permission to use motorcycles or scooters will be permitted, however, to substitute a beret or crash helmet for a clerical hat, and the cardinal's letter urges them to take out insurance with Mutual de Clero (Clergyman's Mutual)."

The same kind of respectful public attitude protects the nun, whose costume indicates the holiness of her calling, and counterbalances the fact that her clothes create the effect of mystery which so many roués are tempted to fathom, as was the case with Don Juan. The nun's clothing also has a quieting effect on the rowdy elements of the population, since she enjoys a respect which might not be accorded to another woman doing the same work but wearing ordinary clothes.

The wearing of special clothes for religious ceremonies in order to indicate the superiority of the priest and his closeness to God continues to the present day, and especially in the robes worn by Roman Catholic clergy for Communion. The vestments worn at services each have a meaning beyond the obvious functional one, and according to the Roman Missal, the sacred vestments worn by the priests such as the maniple, the cincture, the stole, and chasuble, each have a present use, an historical origin, and a special symbolism for each garment. For example, the maniple began historically as "a strip of linen worn over the arm. During the long services, and in the intense heat of the southern countries it was frequently used to wipe the perspiration from the face and the brow." From this humble origin the maniple has become a strip of silken cloth worn on the left arm of the priest. And according to the Roman Missal the maniple now represents a symbolic reference to "(a) the rope whereby our Lord was led, and the chains which bound His sacred hands, (b) an emblem of the tears of penance, the fatigue of the priestly office and its joyful reward in heaven." Thus is human imagination able to elevate the humble perspiration wiper to a prime symbol of Christianity.

It has been suggested earlier that no great civilizations have existed without the goal of superiority imparted to mankind by religion and clothes co-acting to influence man in his belief that he is akin to the gods. Communism is now attempting by government decree to impose a disbelief in religion, and seems to be succeeding to some extent. There are indications, however, that religion is by no means dead in Communist countries, and indeed may be on the upturn. *Life* Magazine reports the following information from China which reveals the true feeling of some of the Chinese masses: "A directive from the provincial authorities in Kwangtung in 1951 forbade communist party workers to use sacred images for target practice or to wreck temples. Such behavior, the directive explained, 'antagonized the masses' and played into the hands of the enemy." No matter what governments may decree, people have a way of creating their own gods. Eva Peron is already on the way to becoming a saint in Argentina. The Empress Candida introduced Christianity into a part of old China, built hospitals and did other charitable deeds, and on her death the Chinese worshipped her as a goddess. Confucius, a philosopher, was raised to the ranks of the gods, and was finally promoted in 1906 to the highest position, a place beside Heaven and Earth. Buddha, also a philosopher who made no claim to supernatural origin, was also ultimately made a god by his worshippers. If Communism should eventually succeed in China, we may expect that Karl Marx and Lenin, who denied God, will ultimately be worshipped as gods themselves. It is but a short step from Little Father to Big Father.

Biblical research and the recent findings of the Dead Sea manuscripts indicate that some of the gaps between Biblical truths and historical truths have been filled in, and that scientific truths are often hidden in the Bible in poetic symbolism. The Bible represents a story-telling technique which substitutes the simple legend of Adam and Eve and the invention of the first clothes, which can be understood even by children, for a complicated historical and evolutionary hypothesis which can be understood only by a considerably smaller number of people educated to some extent in modern science. Thus the poets who write our legends are usually more understandable than the scientists who attempt to explain them.

Has the combination of monotheistic religion and drab clothing in modern times contributed to our believing in science to the detriment of religion? This may be true in some areas and for some periods, but one of the most interesting phenomena of recent times is the flirtation which has been going on between science and religion and has now amounted to a reconciliation in many quarters. When all the laws of the universe have been explored, some of our leading scientists find that there is still room left for God. Shakespeare's saying from *Hamlet* that "There are more things in heaven and earth than are dreamed of in your philosophy" seems the truer the more we extend our knowledge. In an address to the Papal Academy of Sciences at Rome, the late Pope Pius XII gave his views reconciling modern atomic discoveries with the Creation as described in Genesis, and stated among other conclusions, "Modern science considers the idea of the Creation of the Universe wholly reconcilable with the scientific attitude and that on the ground of its own researches. Creation in time! That presupposes a Creator, presupposes God!"

Men of religion and men of science can therefore agree on the grandiose conception that man's future in the world depends upon the continuation of his belief in his own godlike qualities which in my opinion he has derived in the past largely from the combination of his religion and his clothing.

CHAPTER *9*

Clothes and Government

It is a startling thought that without the invention of clothing it would not be possible to develop the highly complex systems of governments with their armies, navies and police forces, which are now in existence all over the world. Yet this is obvious when we realize that all government is based on the domination of the population by an individual or small governing group which is, as we say, "clothed with authority." This authority is generally indicated by clothing.

Perhaps one of mankind's most ingenious uses of clothing is to employ it to demonstrate the authority of individuals or groups and to transform this authority into the power of government. This has been accomplished mainly by means of the uniform. The invention of the uniform has served many important social functions, including that of indicating police power as well as rank. The use of uniforms has often been supplemented or superseded by badges or insignia which may also serve the same purpose. The clothing which indicates the power of a ruling class usually undergoes a change if the power of this ruling class is taken over by another class. These various uses of clothing for purposes of government, as well as for some other purposes, will now be considered.

Since one of the primary purposes of clothes through the ages was to demonstrate the wearer's superiority, we may assume that one of man's first innovations was to use clothes to assist him in dominating others. The superior adornment and finery of the tribal chief which, added to his ability and prowess, enabled him to surpass in appearance the rest of the tribe, helped to produce the feelings of admiration, inferiority and submission among his followers which caused them to accept his leadership. The warrior, his body stained in unnatural hues, his face painted with frightening colors, his ornaments bristling with teeth or claws, his clothes of animal hides reminiscent of the strongest beasts of the forests, produced an effect which intimidated both friend and enemy. This form of terrorism found its counterpart in modern warfare in the clothing of the Prussian Death's Head Hussars and Hitler's terror-producing S.S. troopers. These inventions in clothing also enabled their users to disguise themselves as more powerful blood-thirsty creatures than their opponents or victims, and thus brought into play the power of fear to paralyze the defenses of their enemies.

Clothes were also of particular importance to indicate the stratification of society, and enabled the king with his crown jewels and magnificent robes, as well as the nobility, to show their superiority to the common man over whom they exercised authority. In their ceremonial robes, as members of the court, the nobility wore coronets or circlets on their brows, a minor or subordinate crown showing that the wearer was superior to "thee and me," but inferior to his leige lord, the king. In England the rank of the nobleman was further indicated by the number and size of the tines in his coronet, also an invention to distinguish one rank from another, while the robes and lengths of trains trimmed with one or more rows of ermine, according to the wearer's title, also served to indicate rank. The heads of the Fascist states, such as Hitler, Mussolini and Peron were also fond of dressing up to show their superiority, and adopted uniforms such as brown shirts, black shirts and many decorations to flaunt their brief authority to the world. Even in American political life, our Senators once had a habit of wearing large black hats and spreading coats. In giving expression to their position by their clothing, they were merely following the example of the Roman Senators, who wore a special kind of toga called a Laticlavan which lent dignity to their calling.

But government would never have been possible had it not been for the invention of the uniform, the apparel by which the government, whether it be that of a monarch, dictator or a democracy, indicates by its soldiers and police force its power over the masses. These uniforms distinguish the limbs of authority from the common herd and secure immediate obedience. Even in Communist countries where the use of distinguishing clothes for the governing hierarchy is absent, the uniformed police, and the soldiers and overdecorated

Rulers indicate their power to rule by their clothes. Some modern examples include: Left, *the late Kaiser Wilhelm von Hohenzollern, German Emperor.* Right, *Haile Selassie, Emperor of Ethiopia. (Underwood & Underwood.)*

officers of the Red Army who supply the force on which they must ultimately depend, are very much in evidence at all times, and there would be no government without them.

How governments depend on the use of uniforms in order to govern is shown by the following incident which I witnessed in the Unter der Linden in Berlin three days before World War I. The entire street was filled with a milling mob of Socialist workers demonstrating against Germany's going to war. A platoon of the Kaiser's Uhlans in full military regalia was thrown across the wide street. The sight of the soldiers in the uniforms which symbolized the power of the Kaiser was sufficient to cause the angry demonstrators to melt helplessly out of the street as the soldiers moved quietly forward sweeping them out of their way like a gigantic broom. The wearing of uniforms by large masses of the population was a particularly Germanic trait at the time, and was repeated in the events which led to World War II. It also made possible the famous hoax of *The Captain from Köpenick* which is described more fully in Chapter 12.

One of the two occasions when French soldiers landed on British soil since the Norman conquest occurred in Wales, at Goodwick near Fishguard Bay in the year 1797. The Welsh women, wearing their

national costumes with red skirts and shawls and shiny high hats and carrying broom-sticks for muskets, lifted their skirts over their shoulders, showing their white thighs, and paraded like a regiment of soldiers on the sea front. The French, mistaking them for British soldiers in red-coat uniforms with white trousers, beat a hasty retreat to their ships, leaving their muskets behind them. These are still to be seen in a Welsh castle piled up in silent testimony to the fact that by Welsh women's wits and French fear of the British uniform, England was saved from invasion by Napoleon.

Another use of uniforms is to build up the *esprit de corps* of the men wearing them. The desirable feeling of belonging to a group which cherishes courage, honor, patriotism and other virtues, is produced by wearing the uniform of a given regiment whose members are comrades in war and peace.

Not only would it be impossible for governments to govern, but it would also be impossible to conduct warfare (other than guerilla warfare) without using clothes in the form of uniforms in order to distinguish friend from enemy. From barbarous times until today the uniform of the fighting man is regarded as a necessity, and there could be few wars without its use. A disarmament conference which resulted in a general agreement among the nations to prohibit the use of soldiers' uniforms as contrary to international law might possibly bring the world closer to universal peace than any other measure!

As a substitute for uniforms under conditions where there were none obtainable or usable, revolutionaries sometimes use other distinguishing symbols, such as colored arm bands. Badges and ornaments to distinguish the wearer have also been used for warlike purposes from time immemorial. For example, in the civil wars of England, red roses were used to symbolize the House of Lancaster, and white roses the House of York.

The invention of the uniform had significance other than to indicate the armed power of a government. Basically, the uniform was invented as a means to indicate the relationship of an individual to a group, such as members of the same tribe. So many are the uses of uniforms today that we tend to forget the origin of the word

The uniforms which enable governments to govern: Upper left, the London "bobby." (British Travel Association.) Upper right, the American cop." (N. Y. Daily News.) Lower right, Italian policemen. (Hamilton Wright.) Lower left, Kenya (Africa) native police. (Wide World Photos.)

(uni-form: one form, all alike). *By wearing the uniform of a particular group, a man shows by his clothing that he has given up his right to act freely as an individual but must act in accordance with and under the limitations of the rules of his group.* From early times the livery of the servants or slaves, or the uniform of the soldier or policeman, have represented the submission of the individual to the rule of the chief, ruler, or commander. This use of the uniform has continued to modern times.

It is noted that in many forms of Socialism, either tried experimentally or in actuality, attempts to do away with class distinctions or inequalities of wealth are usually accompanied by the use of special clothing or uniforms to indicate the equality of the wearers. Thus, the participants in many of the communal experiments in the United States, described by Nordhoff and Webber, customarily wore special clothing, as in the Oneida Community and with the Shakers. The Salvation Army with its special mission of community service is another example of the use of the uniform to indicate a religious organization in which there is no class distinction among the rank and file.

Under Marxist-Lenin Communism, the tendency toward uniformity of clothes—as in modern China where a substantial part of the

Attractive Indian policewomen, armed with old-fashioned rifles to enforce law and order (and to protect themselves). (Information Service of India, New York.)

Communism and uniformity: A Chinese boy and girl, both wearing padded winter uniforms of the Red Army. Clothes for both sexes tend to be similar in most parts of Red China. (Wide World Photos.)

male and female civilian population has adopted a sober blue "boiler-suit" uniform, or in Russia where a few models of clothes with bell-bottom trousers for the men are turned out in huge quantities by government factories—indicates the subordination of the individual to the state. The clothes of the convict, demonstrating complete loss of freedom, is the ultimate use of the uniform. In the famous Czech play *R.U.R.* by Capek, the mechanical men to whom the name "Robot" was applied were all clothed exactly alike and given numbers instead of names, thus indicating their complete lack of individuality.

Quite recently (1958), in New York City, we have witnessed the use of the uniform to secure complete obedience to authority in connection with the Philharmonic Orchestra. Leonard Bernstein, its brilliant new conductor, wishing to weld the orchestra into a sensitive instrument completely responsive to his baton, decided that the musicians should discard their evening dress and white tie (itself the evening uniform of gentlemen) and wear instead blue trousers

and coats without collars which transformed the appearance of each
and every one of them into a musical cousin of the Robots of *R.U.R.*
Bernstein claims that the uniform is producing good results, but this
will obviously depend on whether the wearing of such a uniform by
the individual musicians will ultimately produce a feeling of inferiority or one of superiority.*

After the uniform was invented to indicate that the men wearing
it were all uniformly subject to the same rules of authority, humanity
found itself in a dilemma. The uniform denoted uniformity, but there
was also a need to distinguish the superiority of one or more persons
in uniform over the others. *Man's ingenuity came into play again,
and he invented the insignia, the stripe, the epaulette, or some other
variation in the uniform to indicate the difference in rank. How
simple it seems today—but what a great invention it was when it was
first made, since it has lasted through the ages and will continue
long into the future.* Thus we distinguish our "non-coms" from our
commissioned officers and our lieutenants from our generals by their
stripes and insignia. This invention became of much greater importance after the first Boer war when the British army discarded the
brightly-colored uniforms and crossed belts of white leather which
made excellent targets. The British Redcoats and their officers had
worn such uniforms for generations, and now replaced them with
the drab khaki uniforms of today. But for the insignia worn on their
clothes, our generals are not readily distinguishable from the rank
and file. Before this, the generals and admirals, their dress uniforms
trimmed with gold braid, epaulettes and brass buttons (familiarly
called "the brass" by the present generation), stood out so brilliantly
that it was necessary to furnish them with special field uniforms to
prevent them from being easy targets for their enemies.

The adoption of the drab khaki or field-gray uniform in place of
the dashing, handsome, romantic red, gold, blue and scarlet of
soldiers' uniforms took a great deal of the glamor out of war. Even
today it is counteracted by the desire of almost every soldier to cover
his breast with a patchwork of vividly colored ribbons and medals
indicating his campaigns and orders. And in the Soviet army the
amount of gold braid and size of epaulettes to show the officers'
superiority of rank over the common soldier provokes an ironic smile.

Somewhere along the road of history a series of inventions were

* Since the above was written, according to the *New York Times* "Leonard Bernstein's Thursday night uniforms for the New York Philharmonic have been dropped
by the conductor, who suggested that they 'pass into history as Bernstein's folly.'"

Taking the glory out of war: Left, *the colorful field uniform of the past, U.S. Army, 1700.* Right, *the drab uniform of the present, U.S. Army, 1957. (Wide World Photos.)*

made in the form of clothes to show the particular calling or occupation of the wearer. The American judge in his gown in this country and the judge in wig and gown in England still wear their traditional robes which denote their calling. The schoolmaster or professor in his mortarboard cap and gown has impressed generations of school children and college students with his superior knowledge merely by donning this peculiar attire from time to time. *The use of such uniforms to denote the wearer's profession was invented in order to provide a man, by his clothes, with credentials in regard to his superior professional ability or position.* We assume, when we are placed in the charge of a hospital nurse in uniform, that she has some sort of a diploma. The ship's captain in his braided uniform produces a

feeling of confidence among the passengers which might not otherwise exist. We do not ask the policeman in uniform to show his credentials, but the "plain-clothes" policeman is given no credence until he shows his badge.

The use of clothing to denote class distinction has continued from mankind's early history down to the present time. By style, color and materials it is usually possible to tell a man's class by the clothes he wears. Even the color of the servants' livery tells its particular story, red being the color still used by the British royal family. The entire art and usage of heraldry, with its symbolic emblems embodied in clothing with special quarterings, insignia and livery, is based fundamentally on pride of ancestry and superiority of the family to which it appertains over other families of lesser importance. The tartan performs a somewhat similar function for a Highland clan.

After the aristocracy was shorn of its power in the modern world, the flamboyant clothing which denoted its authority as the ruling class became an empty symbol. The classes which succeeded them to power repudiated this ornate clothing and substituted their own business uniform in its place. They continued, however, to show the authority of government by the uniforms of their soldiers and police. And so today, as in man's earliest days, the clothing which denotes superior authority continues to be an essential factor in the governments of the nations, whether these be democracies, dictatorships or otherwise.

ostumes which testify to the position, special knowledge or ability of the ?arer: Upper left, *academic cap and gown indicate that Virginia C. lldersleeve, Dean of Barnard College, is as learned as she is beautiful. hoto by Pach Bros.)* Upper right, *Betty Ford, woman bullfighter.* Below, *iglish judges in wigs and gowns at the opening of the Law Courts, Lon- n. Note trains are carried by attendants.*

PART

CLOTHES

AND

SOCIAL CONDUCT

Queens of the annual costume carnival, Port of Spain, Trinidad, 1957. Girls make and wear their own elaborate costumes for the annual carnival.

CHAPTER 10

Clothes and Behavior

How does our clothing affect our social behavior? Do we tend to put on good or bad behavior along with our clothes? And can we change from good to bad behavior by changing our clothes, or by taking them off altogether? There is no doubt about the answer. We can!

As part and parcel of our civilization, we have set up standards of good social behavior, and we achieve a certain measure of unconscious superiority when we conform to them. We also tend to look down on those who ignore these standards, or who set up patterns which we regard as poor or bad behavior. In all these activities, clothing plays an enormously important part.

We shall first discuss the subject of clothing as it affects the behavior of children and teen-agers—a subject which I fear will be topical for many years to come. Then we shall consider how clothing affects the behavior of grown-up members of society, including some of the less admirable sorts such as the Ku Klux Klan. We shall also observe how the wearing of masks and fancy-dress costumes affects the behavior of the wearers, with particular reference to costume carnivals, such as the Philadelphia Mummers Parade, and the New Orleans and Trinidad Mardi Gras costume carnivals and parades. We shall also consider how courage and self-confidence are imparted by certain kinds of costumes while the opposite effect results from the lack of proper clothing. We shall finally consider the behavior of nations and peoples as affected by their clothes.

Men have made the discovery that special kinds of behavior can be influenced by wearing special kinds of clothes. This behavior can be either good or bad, and begins with children. The young boy,

141

wearing trousers for the first time, attempts to live up to them, and experiences a thrill of maturity. This same boy, ten years later, may dress himself up in an exaggerated coat and baggy pants known as a "zoot suit" which gives him a feeling of superiority, and he may behave like a hoodlum or hooligan as a consequence. The phenomenon of present-day juvenile delinquency seems to be associated with clothes, not only in the case of gangs whose members wear emblems on their sweaters to distinguish between friend and foe in teen-age gang warfare, but also in youngsters who wear clothes which carry a challenge to authority, such as their parents, schools and the police. *When these youths put on these garments, they also put on a behavior pattern of which the clothes are symbolic.*

The effect of wearing completely informal clothing by school children was discussed in Washington at the convention of the National Association of Secondary-School Principals on February 24, 1957. At this convention, according to the *New York Times,* "several high-school principals put their backs up against blue jeans, the duck-tail haircut and Elvis Presley. Said R. B. Norman of Amarillo, Texas, High School, 'You can't put a kid into a monkey suit like one of these blue jean outfits and expect him to make any kind of good record for himself.' Howard F. Horner of David Douglas High School near Portland, Oregon, stated 'It's a rare, rare day that anybody comes into school in that kind of outfit and his record does not show a long list of difficulties in and out of school.' "

It is curious to note that an attempt to improve children's behavior by banning such clothes is now being tried in many cities under intelligent auspices. It seems that the youthful delinquent responds to soap and water and good clothes just as the rest of us do. The James N. Kieran Jr. High School in the Bronx recently enacted a code (Jan. 14, 1957) which placed a taboo on hair curlers, leather jackets and dungarees or blue jeans as a badge of superiority.

Dorothy Barclay who recently investigated the question of clothing in American schools collected reports from schools for more than a year on the subject of appropriate clothing for school children. She stated in the *New York Times* Magazine, January 27, 1957, "that scattered schools all over the country have been trying to get the girls into skirts rather than shorts or slacks, and the boys into clothing more 'appropriate' for the classroom than tight cowboy pants, engineers' boots, leather jackets and the like. School people are willing to admit that dress regulations may not 'cure' individuals

Dressed for trouble, U.S.A.: Left, *youngster in trouble, wearing sport shirt and leather windbreaker typical of delinquent youth gangs. (UPI Photo.) Dressed for revolt:* Right, *the typical dress of a "Teddy boy," Britain's brand of juvenile delinquent. The style is copied from the era of King Edward VII. (Wide World Photos.)*

but, said one, 'they limit the individual's effect on others.' The girl who must give up tight sweaters during school hours in favor of a cotton blouse is, this principal agreed, probably just as boy-conscious as ever but, he held, fewer of the boys will be conscious of her. Similarly, he said, boys who have derived from 'tough' clothes a kind of 'fool's courage' for belligerent behavior often 'shrink down to normal size,' during school hours at least, when deprived of the uniform and insignia of their cult."

This type of juvenile behavior accompanied by the wearing of special clothing is by no means limited to the United States. In far-off New Zealand there is also a juvenile problem accompanied by the wearing of special clothes by teen-agers. There are different categories of these called "bodgies" (male), "widgies" (female), and "milk bar cowboys" according to a report in the *New York Times* under a dateline from Auckland, March 22, 1958. Rape, relations with under-age girls, riots and vandalism are characteristic of the "bodgies." Even in Moscow the Soviet juvenile delinquents are causing troubles as evidenced by an Associated Press dispatch dated October 5, 1958: "Members of the Young Communist League were told today they should try to stamp out Western fads like zoot suits, but not resort to violence. Komsomolskaya Pravda, the league's newspaper, said league patrols had been nabbing youths in extreme attire, cutting off their long hair and ripping off their cowboy shirts. The paper suggested educational guidance rather than force. The newspaper warned that those who adopt Western fashion extremes might provide ready soil for capitalist ideology. It conceded that the style and color of some clothing produced in Russia was not good."

That vandalism is also an accompaniment of special clothes for teen-agers in the United States is indicated by a news item in the weekly periodical *Variety*, November 13, 1957, from Columbus, Ohio: "Hard-pressed by teen-age rowdies, Ohio motion picture exhibitors are studying new methods of foiling the teen-age rowdies bent on mischief and disorder. One of these was a 'vandal-proof' seat. The Secretary of the Independent Theatre Owners of Ohio noted that an angle worth exploring is insisting upon better dress for youthful patrons. 'Several exhibitors have told us,' he said, 'that the attire of the youngsters has a great deal to do with their behavior.'

"Alliance Theatre in Indianapolis has a 'code of dress' for juveniles, and boys are required to wear pants that fit them properly along with belts. 'Girls are to be dressed properly, too,' he stated, 'with a ban on short shorts, shirts hanging out and dirty jeans. This has been the practice in the Southern Theatre in Columbus for many years, and it caters to more well-behaved children and teen-agers than other theatres in town. When a youngster is dressed up, he or she invariably changes his behavior to conform with his attire."

The truth of the last line above will sound a familiar note to all of us who remember the feelings of restraint engendered by wearing our "Sunday best" clothes to church or Sunday school. The Boy Scout and Cub, and the Girl Scout and Brownie whose good behavior is well recognized, put on their resolve to do a good deed each day along with their Scout's uniform.

The general problem of children's clothes in the United States deserves more attention than it has received in the past. The clothing of teen-age girls and their behavior pattern can be best understood by comparing the behavior of these children in this country and some

School uniforms: Left, *to avoid too abrupt a change of habits, Australian aborigine children attend school in the nude. (Australian News and Information Bureau.)* Right, *Japanese children of both sexes in school uniforms.*

other countries. In the United States, young girls at a fairly early age use lipstick and rouge and ape the dresses of mature women. Compare this with the usual behavior of young girls of the same age in England, British colonies and other countries, where lipstick and rouge are taboo, and a plain school uniform is generally worn. Consequently, young girls tend to mature more slowly and grow to womanhood without a hot-house forcing of their emotions. In this country, the youngsters often attain superiority by copying the appearance and sexual behavior of girls considerably older, without having achieved the maturity which goes with such conduct. As a result, they are precocious in a harmful way, achieving too early in life experiences for which they are not ready. This of course is not true of the children of parents who are aware of and guard against this situation, or of children who attend convents or church schools where uniforms are worn. Of interest was the behavior of a young Catholic girl who confided to me "when I wore my white Communion dress I felt beautiful, spiritual and close to God. I almost wanted to be a nun!"

In Trinidad, British West Indies, the boys and girls who attend

Dressed for violence: Hiding behind their robes and masks, Ku Klux Klan members and masked initiates parade behind Klan officer carrying cross, near Stone Mountain, outside Atlanta, Ga. (Wide World Photos.)

the public schools all wear school uniforms, usually a white shirt or blouse and dark-colored shorts or skirts. An additional advantage arises because of the mixture of many races in Trinidad, these including white, mulatto, Negro, East Indian and Chinese. By wearing the same uniform, these children tend to de-emphasize racial differences in public life, no matter what takes place at home. No one is regarded as racially superior at school because of his or her clothes. A lesson in democracy can be learned by the use of such clothes in all countries where racial problems exist. On the other hand some British educators deplore the conformity imposed on school boys in England by wearing school uniforms. If the American and British methods of dressing children represent a choice of two evils, I prefer the British as the lesser of the two.

The behavior pattern and sexual characteristics of men and women can be affected for life by the improper use of clothes in early childhood. Thus the parents who always wanted a son, and compensated for their disappointment in a daughter by dressing her in boy's clothing, are responsible for giving her a tendency towards male behavior which in extreme cases may result in lesbianism. Similarly, the doting mother who always wanted a girl, and dresses her little son in girl's clothing, or keeps his hair in curls long after the usual time for clipping has passed, should not be surprised if he tends to become effeminate and develops homosexual tendencies. The average young boy and girl have a healthy distaste of being dressed differently from the rest of the "gang" at school, and parents will do well to let their children conform to the school fashions to avoid making them feel inferior and the butt of ridicule which may cause permanent harm.

Parents have also had an unfortunate habit of dressing their children in clothes which are miniature replicas of the fashions of the day. Thus, in the days of crinoline, the fashionable little girls wore little crinolines around their little hips, while in the days of the bustle, the little girls wore little bustles on their little behinds. Mother and daughter wearing the same clothes may land one or both of them on the analytical couch if it results in a rivalry between them for the affection of the father! The modern child's clothing allowing free movement and adapted to school, play and sports, represents a considerable improvement over the overdressed little moppets of the past. Polaire Weissman, Director of the Costume Institute of the Metropolitan Museum of Art in New York City, states, "The day of the 'miniature adult' is gone and not regretted. But too much empha-

Dressed for penitence: Holy Week, Seville, Spain. Confraternities parade to the cathedral wearing medieval penitents' masked costumes.

sis on the free and easy, reflected in children's dress, may at times be reflected also in children's behavior."

Coming to the world of "grownups," bad behavior often governs the choice of clothes without the wearer's being necessarily aware of the fact that these clothes build up his aggressive self-assurance or effrontery. Thus, the "spivs" of England, the black-market operators who came into being with shortage restrictions after World War II, attained superiority by wearing a distinctive type of loud, oversmart clothes which were too exaggerated for good taste. These are paralleled in the U.S.A. by the loud suits of the American gangster, whose tough face never quite matches the softness of his opulent silk shirts. In England the so-called "Teddy Boys" dress in Edwardian clothes and their behavior is such that many restaurants in London refuse to admit them when so attired. Latterly they have been indulging in behavior which is reminiscent of our own juvenile delinquents.

Another example of a behavior pattern put on with clothes is that of the hooded members of the Ku Klux Klan who, in their ordinary clothes, appear and act like normal well-behaved citizens. But when they don their sheets and hoods to mask their faces (but not their intentions), the masked hoods not only terrify their victims, but also by disguising their wearers and protecting them against identification, encourage them to excesses which they might not otherwise commit.

Masks produce very different effects when they are used at Mardi Gras or carnivals to symbolize the mysterious unknown who is released from the shackles of convention for the time being, and is willing to participate in a mild form of Saturnalia just so long as his or her real personality is not discovered. Thus the masked ball has been a favorite environment for romantic behavior throughout the ages, and will no doubt continue so long as some men and women need an outlet for sexual adventure from time to time to break the monotony of respectability.

Masks, usually worn with fancy dress and used for gala events, give their wearers pleasure by lifting them out of the commonplace of life into a realm of make-believe in which they achieve a superior and more glamorous existence. They serve to enhance the wearers, either by giving anonymity as in the case of the half-mask worn by men and women at carnivals or fiestas, or by giving the wearer a different identity, such as masks in the form of white faces, clown's

Dressed for Mardi Gras: Maskers on Canal Street, Carnival Day, New Orleans.

faces, animal or bird's heads, etc., worn at fiestas or celebrations such as Halloween. (To say nothing of the confidence imparted to a burglar when he wears a mask while holding up a bank!)

In general, fancy dress was invented to enable humanity to escape from its every-day existence, if only for a few brief and sometimes disillusioning hours. Indeed, fancy dress enables us to wear the costume of the superior being we aspire to be, for a fleeting evening of enjoyment. The selection of the fancy dress costume is never an accident when there is full freedom of choice, but is an expression of a conscious or unconscious desire of the wearer. So is the behavior which is often put on with the costume. The man who goes to a fancy dress ball attired as a sheik is more apt to believe himself to be irresistible and to make a fool of himself with the women he encounters than if he wore a sober black dinner jacket and tie. The young woman who makes a point of dressing as Cleopatra to emphasize her sexual attractions is more apt to misbehave than if she dressed more conservatively, since she invites the complementary misbehavior on the part of the men to whom she obviously conveys her feelings by her clothes.

A unique example of clothing and masks to give expression to mass feelings, and to influence gay behavior, is found in the Mummers Parade celebrated on New Year's Day in Philadelphia. This custom, brought over from England and Sweden, goes back to pagan days. Thousands of men and boys march through the streets each year dressed in every type of Commedia dell' Arte costume, but with the Pierrots and Clowns predominating. As they are dressed, so they tend to behave. Philadelphia would be a wild city of misrule on this day were it not for the fact that most of the Mummers, after their long march, are too tired to celebrate further. According to the *New York Times,* "at the Mummers Parade of 1957 about 12,000 followers of King Momus paraded four miles up Broad Street. The gaily costumed marchers, bands and clowns were seen by a crowd estimated by the police at nearly 1,000,000. Many more thousands saw the festivities on television. The Mummers are a Philadelphia specialty. For the last fifty-seven years members of a score of clubs, composed only of men and boys with women excluded for some long-forgotten reason, have strutted a welcome to the New Year. Even before, there were smaller neighbourhood parades that gave birth to the present city-wide celebration. Costumes are planned months in advance and their details are guarded secrets within club ranks. The city puts up $52,000 in prizes."

The same spirit of carnival exists with the famous Mardi Gras in New Orleans, the Carioca Carnival at Rio and the Junkanoo or John Canoe Festival at Nassau in the Bahamas. Carnivals have also

The prize-winning band of fifteen hundred Greek gods, celebrities and warriors march in the costume parade, Port of Spain, Trinidad, 1957.

Girls and men costumed as Egyptians march in the costume parade, Port of Spain, Trinidad, 1957.

achieved world fame at Nice, Venice and other cities in Europe. All these include fancy-dress parades, floats, masquerade balls and other picturesque costume events. Because of its special significance in illustrating the effect of fancy dress in creating a feeling of release for the slaves who first participated in it, I shall dwell in some detail on the Carnival at Port-of-Spain, Trinidad, which represents probably one of the greatest costume spectacles in the world. Many thousands of Trinidadians of all colors and creeds participate in the parades and competitions which take place for two days before Lent. Hundreds of thousands of dollars are spent on the costumes, and no sooner is one carnival over than the natives begin to work on their costumes for the following year.

In addition to an unusually large number of Carnival Queens, large groups of merrymakers are formed into "bands" all wearing related costumes. The prize band of the year 1956 was a group of Norse gods and vikings, while the 1957 prize was won by a band of over 1,600 Greek gods, celebrities and warriors.

The Trinidad costume carnival takes place under the surveillance of the town authorities. The following description is taken from the official announcement of the 1957 Carnival. "The panoramic splendour of Carnival, like a giant canvas on which a colour crazed artist has daubed his myriad hues with nightmarish frenzy, is here again. For two days, disregarding the two weeks spent in getting into stride,

Dressed for a Shriners' Parade: Middle-aged members of the Damascus Temple of Rochester, N. Y., march in close formation at the Shrine Convention in Atlantic City, N. J., June 29, 1954. (Wide World Photos.)

all inhibitions will go by the board, imagination will run riot, and the streets will be a gyrating, flowing stream of humanity. It has become a national institution as much as July 4 is to the American and Bastille Day to the French. And yet, Carnival as we know it today sprang from the pages of immoral serfdom, developed in spite of it, and matured because of it.

"The original Spanish settlers appear to have contributed little to the Trinidad carnival spirit, but the French brought with them the ancient Roman custom of celebrating two days before Lent, in preparation for the rigorous self-denials of the Lenten season. The practice spread to the slaves who must have felt 'released' in more senses than one by wearing Carnival clothes. They in turn colored it with their love for music, expression and imitation. The early rhythms and songs by the slaves, called the Bongoes and Calindos, were relegated to other functions, and in their place came Dame Lorraine, Pierrot, Columbine, Clowns, Diable Malaises and other costume characterizations."

The same official explanation adds: "It was in this manner that the Calypso, twin sister to the Mas' was born. The young bucks (white) who attended these shows enjoyed themselves and were treated with deference and respect. No one would dare inform their parents of their participation, or even presence at such goings on. From this state, it was but a short step to actual participation in the road celebrations. But in this the operative term was 'Mask.' That was the only way that the middle class could risk joining in the fete. Their faces had to be covered, along with other ruses calculated to defy identification. In time, the women too joined in the fun, safe behind their masks. Even now, tales are still repeated about the brothers and even husbands smiling tolerantly and even flirting with masked females on the streets without knowing who they were. This form of deception continued until the last war. With its end, came a revolution of outlook, a freer mixing of the formerly segregated groups and classes, a more developed manner of social intercourse."

There are voices to be heard in discreet criticism, however. The following is taken from an article by M. E. Farquhar in a local newspaper in the year 1957: "Overzealous officialism, and a resort to unbending discipline, have now yielded pride of place to friendly cooperation in the indulgence of—harmless fun! In the face of all this glowing advertisement of magnificent achievement, it may seem churlish or cussed to point out weaknesses and drawbacks to the festival, so often discounted or minimized as being purely superficial, evanescent and therefore inconsequential. In my view, this unhappy feature of Carnival is inclined to be glossed over as unnecessarily prudish and fussily grandmotherly. Even so, surely there is room for friendly concern over the prodigality in relative waste of time, money and valuable energy."

It is whispered in Trinidad, I do not know how reliably, that many marriages and "affairs" result from the Carnival, and that nine months after the event, the population of the colony is increased by a substantial crop of what are known as Carnival babies! Whether the exuberance due to wearing fancy dress should be criticized or praised for this, depends largely upon the point of view of the critic.

Apparel which imparts courage to its wearer is also part of the behavior pattern which we assume with our clothes. The soldier feels braver, the policeman more courageous, the boy scout more adventurous, when they sally forth dressed in their uniforms. The story of a long-suffering teller in a bank who one day chances to wear a "dog suit" to a masquerade party forms the subject of a recent novel, *Three Ways to Mecca.* The sense of freedom which the bank teller experiences when dressed in his masquerade costume, in which he impersonates a dog, eventually enables him to overcome his inferiority feeling and break the barriers of conventional living by setting forth in pursuit of his own ideals. Children are particularly responsive to the effect of clothing on their personal courage. The child in a soldier's, cowboy's or Superman's suit may even carry bravery to the point of personal danger, as evidenced by the child who, wearing a "space suit," jumped out of a second-story window in Los Angeles, fully convinced that he could actually fly.

A unique American fancy-dress phenomenon is the oriental "Zouave" costumes with baggy trousers and fez headdresses worn by otherwise normal businessmen who belong to the very worthy and respectable Order of Shriners. These men attend their annual Shriner conventions (usually in the large cities) and appear to enjoy hugely the wearing of these garish uniforms whose oriental origins are said to go back to the days of the Crusaders and Freemasonry, and came to America about 1850, after the French conquest of Algeria. A certain number of the less responsible Shriners appear to spend their time when not at meetings wandering around forlornly in the cities in an effort to enjoy themselves without their wives and families. After several days spent in listening to speeches, or attending unhappy parties, these worthies are poured back into the outgoing trains and aircraft, and depart to their small towns and villages where they end their butterflylike existence and return to the humdrum of normal life in their every-day clothes until another year comes by.

Hair shirts which cause skin irritation are sometimes worn by the religious to do penance for their sins. This is a form of self-inflicted suffering which also found expression in the Middle Ages when pilgrims placed pebbles in their shoes. In this way such clothes may be said to influence behavior by leading the wearer from a state of sin to a state of grace.

The clothes of the very poor, and the feeling of inadequacy or inferiority which is experienced by those wearing them, strongly affect their behavior pattern. The jobless man who knows that his clothes are worn out, or threadbare, or ill fitting, or dirty and dishevelled, or that he lacks underwear, stockings or adequate shoes, is handicapped from the outset in looking for work or bettering his mental outlook. The Salvation Army and other charitable organizations have long recognized that second only to proper food and shelter is the need for decent clothing to improve a man's ability to help himself. When it is generally recognized that this problem is deserving of special study, a solution should certainly be found in a country which does not lack the material means to solve it.

There is a valid lesson to be learned from our examination into the behavior of people as a result of their clothing. *If we want our nation to consist of self-reliant individuals interested in personal as well as national achievement, one of the ways to bring this about is by raising living standards so that all our people can afford to wear clothing which adds to their morale, dignity and self-respect. In the last analysis, a well-dressed population may not necessarily be a happy one, but it is likely to be far happier than an ill-dressed one.*

Dressed for gaiety: London's best-loved characters, the "Pearlies," cockney costermongers. (British Travel Association.)

CHAPTER 11

Clothes, Mass Emotion
and Communication

It is generally recognized that clothing, in addition to performing its usual function of covering the body, can also be used to indicate and communicate special emotions such as happiness and grief, and to carry special messages such as greetings or even insults.

For thousands of years primitive and civilized peoples have utilized special clothing to indicate mass happiness, grief or other emotions, so that the wearer can live up to accepted standards of superior social behavior suitable to funerals, weddings and other occasions of sorrow or rejoicing.

An early Israelite devised a method of advertising grief for his dead by publicly wrapping his body in sackcloth and strewing his hair with ashes. The rough cloth irritated his skin, the ashes made his hair and body dirty, and he felt thoroughly unhappy and in some cases he probably enjoyed it. In this way his emotion was communicated to the onlookers and an individual emotion of grief was successfully transformed into a mass emotion. This he could not have achieved had he stayed home in his ordinary clothes and left the ashes on the hearth. *Later on, he could behave in the same way even when he did not feel grief at all; but others watching him believed he did, because his clothes and behavior had become symbolic of grief.* In this way mourning clothes enable some of us less perfect mortals to pretend to a grief which we may not actually feel. Indeed, we often enjoy a measure of unconscious satisfaction in having outlived the corpse!

For countless generations special clothes have been worn by civilized or savage people all over the world as symbols of mourning. These special clothes are worn for longer or shorter periods according to the superior rank of the person being mourned. With state or court funerals, mourners are often hired to walk behind the coffin. And even the horses of the funeral cortege wear black plumes, as though to suggest that they too are feeling sad, though they have never been observed to shed tears. The invention of a special mourning color is widespread, purple being used in some parts of China and white in other parts of the East. When the American Chicle Company started selling chewing gum in China in purple wrappers instead of green, the sales suddenly stopped. The Chinese thought the gum was to be chewed only at funerals!

The special black garments, the crepe veils known as "widow's weeds," were invented to symbolize the wife's unhappiness, and she often wore these for years, long after her first grief had subsided. In some cases this garment also conveniently indicated that the lady was available for another husband once her grief had sufficiently abated.

The wearing of mourning clothes or mourning body decoration is generally practiced among primitive peoples. Sometimes this is because the dead are thought to be hostile. According to Radin in *Primitive Religion*, "In funeral rites, in which emotion became intense, the belief that death was caused by magic aroused anger and the feeling that the dead should be avenged." Undoubtedly some of the roots of our modern mourning clothes go back to earlier pagan ideas of driving the souls of the dead, or evil spirits, away from the living.

Wearing these mourning garments today is a rule of good social behavior in modern society rather than a religious or individual necessity. This is demonstrated by the fact that the very real grief sustained by the loss of the beloved has nothing whatsoever to do with wearing special mourning clothes, even though many people may feel a need for an outward expression of grief by wearing mourning. The fact that the greater the rank of the deceased, the greater the display of mourning also indicates that the wearing of such clothes is a symbol of social stratification as well as respect for the dead. However, some poorer people revel in a good funeral, sometimes followed by a lively wake, and pay far more attention to these outward manifestations of inner grief than do some of the wealthier classes.

The custom of using ashes to indicate mourning is still carried out in the churches by placing ashes on the forehead on Ash Wednes-

Dressed for mourning: Upper Congo wives mourn their husbands for about a year by smearing their bodies with white clay. They are then distributed among his brothers or other members of the family. (Photo by H. M. Whiteside.)

day, while "rending the clothes" as a sign of grief in the Old Testament (Job 1:20) is still observed symbolically by modern Orthodox Jews who tear the seam of a coat or cut up a necktie to mourn the death of a relative or friend.

The ability of clothes to create an emotional effect is nowhere better illustrated than at weddings in Western society, where the symbolism of pagan times continues to be observed in the wearing of the gayest party clothes by all the relatives and friends. If the bride is marrying for the first time, she wears a white wedding gown to symbolize her virginity. If, however, she is marrying for the second, third or fourth time, a condition none too rare in these United States, her lack of a white wedding gown tells her friends and the world at large what they already know—without putting it into embarrassing words. If she wears a veil, it is interesting to remember that these were first used to keep evil spirits away from the bride, while her orange blossoms symbolize the fertility which is hoped for.

The bridesmaids usually wear a uniform which not only adds to the beauty of the ceremony, but also informs the group present that they too are virgins available for marriage. The bridegroom also dons a special suit, which varies in different countries, but since his own virginity does not come into question, it is seldom white, but usually the same black suit which we associate with funerals. To show that this is apt to be a happier affair, he will wear a light tie and a light vest, and sport a light flower in his lapel. At Austrian peasant weddings, however, it was the fashion for the brides to wear black, thus taking nothing for granted.

Clothes also express feelings of individual happiness to be communicated to others, as indicated by the colloquial term "glad rags" consisting of a black coat and bow tie, and an amply exposed white shirt worn at parties. The wearing of these festive clothes, instead of working clothes, gives men the thrill of the unusual if they are of the class which does not habitually wear such clothes at night. The women, in turn, wear their richest, prettiest, most useless and sex-revealing apparel, and like the men, their evening or party clothes give them a "lift" which is contagious, and they too are ready to enjoy themselves more than they possibly could in their work-day clothes.

The cult of the "tuxedo" or dinner jacket with black tie to indicate the superiority of the wearer at parties or evening functions has reached extraordinary proportions in the U.S.A., as evidenced by the following from the *New York Times* of July 7, 1957, regarding a Philadelphia clothing business started by two farm boys named Rudofker. "The Rudofkers realized that a market must exist for tuxedos in the $16.50 range and decided to concentrate on the product. Thus two farm boys began to show the sophisticated city dweller how to dress for important evening functions. The volume of men's

Dressed for mourning: Funeral procession of Dom Carlos, Madrid, Spain, 1908. The hearse is followed by his horse, in full mourning.

'formal' wear last year was more than $66,500,000 and Rudofker claims a good deal more than half the production in the country. Last February the company sponsored a prizefight. Every one attending, from the spectators to the seconds and the contestants had to wear 'formal' attire to be admitted to the arena. Many celebrities are under contract with Rudofker to appear in After Six 'formal' wear. Movie stars, sports figures, singers and even young child stars that frequently appear before the public are induced to wear tuxedos as often as possible. The industry's volume now is four times that of the peak pre-World War II period and about ten times that of 1946." And you may be sure that when every Tom, Dick and Harry wears tuxedos or dinner jackets, all the snobs will start wearing something else!

We also wear clothing to reveal the emotions arising from ceremonies or dignified occasions, such as attending a public dinner or reception (black or white tie obligatory). A man will "dress up" most carefully to meet the President, or a Senator, or even a high superior in business. His clothes symbolize a feeling of respect towards his superior which society ordains, no matter how he may feel personally. Conversely, clothing which marks menial or humiliating service, such as the white uniforms of street cleaners or "white wings" who used to clean up after the horses, often have a humiliating effect on their wearers.

The use of clothing to convey mass emotion is also present in festivals of a different character from the costume carnivals referred to in the preceding chapter. From remote periods in agricultural societies, men have desired to convey the emotions of hope for a harvest, fecundity for their cattle, or prayers for success or gratitude to the gods. Such festivals have customarily taken place in the winter or the spring after the sowing of the crops or in the autumn after the crops have been gathered. The country fair which exists in one form or another all over Europe and America, with its competitions in fruits, vegetables, crops and animals, athletic prowess and skill in horsemanship (the ancestor of the Rodeo in the U.S.A.) and its spirit of revelry along the Midway in which clothing plays a part, is a lineal descendant of the ancient seasonal festivals. The heavy farm work being halted, the farm workers don their best clothes, and sometimes arrayed in masks and carrying colored balloons, toss conventionality to the winds and match their gay clothing with their behavior. Deep indeed are the roots of these seasonal festivals which found their counterpart in prehistoric sacrificial rituals, and which modern society seeks to imprison in air-conditioned auditoriums and aluminum tents.

In the days of the ancient Greeks (about 2,700 to 2,600 years ago) similar festivals were held, and for substantially the same reasons, with the added difference that religion and drama were also involved. One particular difference was the frank dedication of the people to the worship of Dionysus (Bacchus), god of wine and fertility, which took place in festivals known as the Dionysia held at various times throughout Attica. The desire of the people for increase in their crops, wine, herds and children was expressed in the great Dionysia of Athens which began by a parade of the god Dionysus, a representation of whom, seated on a wagon, or in a ship on wheels, passed through the streets while men dressed as horse-tailed satyrs accompanied it, some of whom carried a large phallus. They proceeded to the temple of Dionysus where the festival was held each year. A sacrificial bull led the procession, followed by wagons and maidens of noble birth. Mention is made in old documents of the scarlet gowns and the gorgeous robes of Chorigoi (chorus) carrying phalli. When the revellers arrived at the auditorium, comedies and later on tragedies were acted on the same days. It was these festivals which gave birth to the great Greek theatre of comedy and tragedy, and also to the popular theatre of mimes which finds its counterpart in the vaudeville and side shows of the modern country fair. (Such side shows were known as "show-booths" in the Russia of the Czars.)

The great Dionysia was usually held about the end of March and lasted three or four days, and the lesser festival, the Lenaea (festival of female Meneads), was held in January. The bearded head of the god Dionysus was carried through the streets mounted on a pole and the worship was performed by women in various stages of ecstasy and apparently all fully robed. Rural Dionysia were also held in the villages. As in our modern fairs, trading on the side in produce, cattle and horses took place during the festivals, despite their religious character.

Later on, in Rome, both spring and autumn festivals were held. The most famous of these was the Saturnalia in honor of Saturnus, one of the Roman gods patronizing the sowing of next year's winter wheat, and during it the god, whose legs were tied together to prevent him from running away, was released for the week of rejoicing which took place at about our Christmas season (December 19th).

In the Roman Saturnalia fanciful clothing again played its part in releasing the pent-up repressions of the revellers. Among the excesses permissible were drunkenness, uninhibited sexual freedom (within certain limits), and unrestrained feasting, drinking and dancing. Gladiatorial combats took place in the arenas, which were not only given over to the spectacles of animals devouring Christians, but also to single combat between men, and men and beasts. The magnificent clothing of the spectators played its part in these affairs, as indicated by many contemporary descriptions and pictures. The modern equivalent, the Spanish bullfight, is also a thrilling costume spectacle. The Spanish women attending the arena are attired in all their finery, and drape their vividly colored embroidered shawls (usually made in China) over the low walls of the boxes. The entrance of the toreadors, matadors and picadors to the strains of martial music is a dazzling costume display. The bullfighters dress in resplendent costumes as though to proclaim to the cheering spectators their superiority over the bulls. Then, getting down to business,

Dressed for marriage: Singapore youth poses with his two brides at their wedding ceremony. Brides wear similar dresses. (Wide World Photos.) Also dressed for marriage: An Indian child wedding. The Gadaba boy of eight wears a loin cloth but the bride of thirteen wears extensive ornaments and clothing. (From Primitive India *by Vitold de Golish.)*

Dressed for mourning: Widow's "weeds" are actually weeds in some parts of New Guinea. Contrast the widow, left, wearing a hempen halter, with the chic Parisienne widow, right, wearing black veils.

two animals, man and bull, face one another, and gorgeous clothing does not disguise the fact. Though the bull meets man on uneven terms, he sometimes wins, and then the blood-stained costume does not help the limp figure which is carried out of the arena. He fought like an animal and died like one, albeit a courageous one. But the bull is seldom or never permitted to leave the ring alive. If a bull-fighter is disabled, another takes his place, and then another, until the bull is killed. The spectators usually insist on seeing the final demonstration of man conquering animal. That the colorful costume of the bullfighter gives him courage for the combat no one can doubt, but that men and women can be enthusiastic spectators to such proceedings proves that under our clothes, the primitive animal is still not far below the surface.

A questionable use of clothing which may be regarded as an outgrowth of the carnival or parade, is the employment of clothes for advertising purposes. One particularly prevalent form in the United

States is to select beauty queens of certain industries, localities or resorts, and either robe them in absurd coronation ceremonies or disrobe them in bathing suits. Philip Wylie, reviewing Eric John Dingwall's *The American Woman* in the *Saturday Review of Literature*, remarks that American men "have not only abandoned woman for 'business' but now exploit female physical sexuality (within certain rabid limits retained from Cotton Mather) as a means to create marketable 'entertainment' in all media, and as a means to sell goods via all media. Americans are thus, Dingwall says, sexually the most self-titillated, self-stimulated, yet self-inhibited and antisexual people on earth. The liberated ladies are sore because—so to speak—the males are mere machine-age manikins, de-sexed sex salesmen—and, even more horrible, because American men are afraid of women as men have never been, anywhere, before."

I disagree that the use of woman in various states of undress for advertising purposes, which is now particularly prevalent in magazine and television advertising, is an indication that American businessmen are "de-sexed sex salesmen" or are "afraid of women." It is my opinion that by using women in this way, the American male boosts his own ego by emphasizing female vanity and love of adornment, while exploiting in the service of commerce the masculine interest in normal sex relations which still prevails in the United States to a greater extent than in many European countries.

With his astounding fertility of invention, man has also created methods to communicate messages of all kinds, including messages regarding his personal importance or the importance of others, by means of clothing. To challenge a rival, the knight in armor threw a glove in the rival's face or on the ground, while he showed his devotion to his mistress by wearing her glove or kerchief on his helmet. The cowboy threw his hat in the ring to denote his willingness to challenge or compete. Man also used his hat or head covering to indicate his feelings. He raised it to greet a friend on the street, or to show respect on passing a funeral, and he threw it in the air to denote joy. He also used it to show respect by removing it on entering a church or a home, or by wearing it on entering a synagogue. The sovereignty of a monarch is acclaimed by publicly placing a crown on his head. This process is also carried out in reverse by the public removal of the stripes or insignia denoting rank on a disgraced soldier, as for example in the famous anti-Semitic incident known as the Dreyfus Case.

Anti-Semitism has also written in the history of clothing a page of messages involving the Jewish race. Shylock mentioned his "Jewish gabardine" as the target for Bassanio's contemptuous spitting. A yellow armband was revived by the race-maniac Hitler to carry his message of hatred to the unfortunate Jews he was too busy to exterminate completely in the time allotted to him. Other apparel carrying messages include the "Sheitel," a wig worn by orthodox Jewish married women which said, "I'm married, so don't make love to me." Her husband's praying shawl communicated a message of religious orthodoxy which he displayed proudly within the synagogue, and wore in abbreviated form under his outer garments, and in which he was buried to insure his quick recognition in the afterlife.

The Bible contains many references to the use of clothing to convey emotional feelings or messages, in addition to the wearing of sackcloth to advertise grief, for the loose-flowing character of the

Dressed for marriage: At an old-fashioned Bavarian wedding procession, the bride leads the cow which is her dowry.

Hebrew robes admitted of a variety of symbolical actions; rending them was expressive of grief (Job 1:20), fear (I Kings 21:27), indignation (II Kings 5:7), or despair (Esther 4:1). Shaking the garments or shaking the dust off them was a sign of renunciation (Acts 18:6), spreading them before a person, of loyalty or joyous reception (II Kings 9:13), wrapping them around the head, of awe (I Kings 19:13), of grief (II Sam. 15:30), casting them off, of excitement (Acts 22:23), and laying hold of them, of supplication (I Sam. 15:27).

Women and girls sometimes use their clothing to express various feelings and intentions: to indicate coquetry by a slight lifting of their skirts and display of the stockings; to express indignation by flouncing their skirts; disdain by tossing their curls; and derision by lifting up the backs of their skirts and "bumping" with their posteriors.

While widows' weeds carry the message that their husbands are dead, modern women do not use clothes to indicate that their husbands are alive. On the contrary, a young married woman may often go to extreme lengths to display, by wearing décolleté evening gowns, as much of her charms as the law and her husband will allow. While such décolletage in a courtesan would indicate that her wares are for sale, in the respectable young married woman her low-cut dress usually carries the message, "Look how much my husband is to be envied, you husbands who are not married to me!" On the other hand, clothing or tattooing is sometimes used to indicate matrimony. Among some of the more primitive tribes, where the men and women are habitually naked, clothing or decoration for the wife or husband is sometimes put on for the first time during the wedding ceremony. In Tahiti the chief part of the wedding consisted in the groom throwing a piece of cloth over the naked bride. Women when married in Old Japan wore the same clothes as when single, and had their teeth blackened (but not their eyes). However, their eyebrows were shaved and their faces left unpainted, thus conveying in unmistakable terms their subservience to their husbands.

Other examples, too numerous to be mentioned, could be given showing the function of clothes in conveying emotions or messages. In most cases, the goal of superiority, conscious or unconscious, is responsible for the choice of such clothes, and also for the desire to publicize the emotions they represent.

A final example of the use of clothing to arouse or communicate mass emotions such as patriotism or nationalism is by parades or processions in which the costumes worn, and the flags carried, symbolize mass or national pride or other feelings of superiority. The May Day parades of union labor in many cities, the Communist May Day parade in Russia, the Columbus Day and St. Patrick's Day parades in New York, the Lord Mayor's procession in London, the Easter parades in Seville, and so forth, all employ colorful costumes to stir the emotions of the crowds.

Among these processions may be mentioned veteran's parades, parades for returning armies, and for national celebrities such as war heroes, Presidents, royalty and (on occasion) movie stars. Dictators are especially partial to such parades, as they give unequalled opportunity to hypnotize the masses into a state of adoring submission.

Thus, clothes are universally used to communicate constructive or destructive mass emotions and behavior, which is a far, far cry from the purposes for which clothing was originally invented and worn.

What New York City does not allow, 1959: Native dancers from Ghana in Les Ballets Africains were ordered by the License Commissioner to wear brassières. Taking the hint from New York, the Prime Minister of Ghana, Kwame Nkrumah, later ordered all Ghana girls to cover up. (Photo by Friedman-Abeles.)

CHAPTER 12

Clothes and the Law

Man is ever an ingenious creature. Although he first invented clothes
for his own good, it was not long before he discovered how to use
them for purposes of evil as well. He found in them a fruitful aid to
committing colorful and dangerous crimes, for some of which the
penalty is death or life imprisonment. Often the clothes enabled the
criminal wearers to gain advantages by simulating positions of social
superiority to which they were not entitled.

To protect society against false impersonation by means of clothes,
a number of laws were enacted and now form part of the penal codes
of many states in this country and abroad. Exceptions were made to
these laws to allow permissible impersonation by the use of clothing,
such as impersonation on the stage. Other laws have been passed
covering permissible removal of clothes in the theatre or on the
beaches. Laws also exist in most countries dealing with sex perversion and crimes related to the wearing of clothing, as well as crimes
in which clothing aids and abets the criminal. There are also a large
number of sumptuary laws, dating from ancient times, usually prohibiting the lower classes from aping their superiors by wearing luxurious clothes. Finally, repressive laws regarding the wearing of certain clothing have sometimes resulted in brutal treatment of the
wearers, leading in some cases to riots or insurrection.

Unauthorized wearing of a military or police uniform is a crime
punishable by imprisonment everywhere, the term of which usually
varies with the purpose of the impersonation. One of the most
famous stories of military impersonation is that of the adventurer of
Köpenick, a small town in Prussia, who, wearing the uniform of a

captain, took charge of the town and was feted for days before the hoax was discovered. Gogol's famous play, *The Inspector General,* is a satire on bureaucracy during the Czarist regime and was based on the hero's impersonation of an inspector general by wearing his uniform. A favorite form of impersonation during World War II was for a soldier to wear the insignia of a superior officer while off duty in order to "show-off."

The Sunday Advocate, a Georgetown, Barbados, newspaper, recently described the amusing case of a Negro who was arrested under the Barbados Uniforms Act for wearing a naval uniform in a bank holiday parade under circumstances "likely to bring contempt upon that uniform." The defendant argued that he was innocent since he was wearing a mixture of an admiral's coat and a surgeon's trousers. The judge offered to let him off with a nominal fine if he would pledge himself not to wear the uniform again. The defendant "boldly stated he intended wearing another uniform no matter what happened." On account of his behavior he was made to pay a fine of forty shillings! Rule Britannia!

The impersonation of a warrior or soldier by wearing the uniform of the enemy in order to penetrate the enemy's lines is a trick which is almost as old as war itself. The penalty for the impersonation, if caught, is death. Similarly, when enemy soldiers wear civilian clothes to secure information or to deceive for any purpose, this carries the penalty of being shot as a spy.

Reference has already been made earlier to laws prohibiting the impersonation of one sex by the other in public; this may or may not be deceptive or for immoral purposes, but such laws exist in most countries. Under the so-called "Masquerade" Section of the Penal Law of New York State, Section 888 (7) of the Code of Criminal Procedure, the impersonation in public of the opposite sex by male or female is regarded as "vagrancy." Therefore, persons "disguised" in clothing of the opposite sex are liable to prosecution as vagrants who are subject to imprisonment up to six months at hard labor under sentence of a magistrate. An interesting case occurred in New York City in the year 1912 when a man dressed as a woman was arrested in the lobby of a theatre advertising a play called "The White Slave." He was held not to be a vagrant, apparently because he was wearing female clothing only as an advertising trick or stunt.

It may be news to some of our girls who innocently wear men's clothes on the streets that the police sometimes pick up women "dis-

What the law tolerates: Early American feminists who dressed as men. Left, Dr. Mary Walker in the clothing she wore at a reception at the White House given by President Arthur; right, wearing reform clothes of earlier date. Center, Private Deborah Sampson, who dressed and fought as a soldier in the American Revolution.

guised" as men. But they have nothing to fear so long as they are clearly identifiable as women. The law is difficult to enforce when the individual partakes of sexual characteristics of both man and woman. It is not an uncommon occurrence for a masculine-looking woman to dress as a man, and to live for years following men's pursuits until death or some accident reveals the impersonation. For a woman to wear a uniform in order to impersonate a soldier, and to join the army during a war, is also a well-known occurrence. One of the most famous of these was Deborah Sampson who impersonated an American soldier in the Revolutionary War.

Dr. George W. Henry cites the case of Dr. Mary Walker, a surgeon in the Union Army, "who wore men's clothes and high boots much like Lincoln's. She had been awarded a medal for her services in the Civil War, and it was assumed that she had permission from Congress to wear masculine attire. On one occasion she was arrested for appearing in public dressed as a man, but as soon as she reached the police station she was recognized and released."

The prohibition against men wearing women's clothes in public is far more strictly applied and is based on the belief that this would, if permitted, increase male homosexuality. Since many women are

What the law does not allow: Above, *Lord Cornbury, Colonial governor of New York and New Jersey from 1702 to 1708, often dressed publicly as a woman. (By W. H. Lippincott, from H. S. Ellis'* History of Our Country.) Below, *the Chevalier d'Eon, 1728-1761, dressed as a woman to aid his diplomatic career when he felt this would be useful.*

now habitually dressing in men's clothes, it is interesting to speculate whether or not this will also increase female homosexuality.

There is an additional New York statute which is applicable to prevent "drags" or males dancing together dressed as women. It is Section 710 of the Penal Law, and states: "An assemblage in public houses or other places of three or more persons disguised by having their faces painted, discolored, colored, or concealed, is unlawful, and every individual so disguised, present thereat, is guilty of a misdemeanor; but nothing contained in this section shall be construed as prohibiting any peaceful assemblage for a masquerade or fancy dress ball or entertainment. . . ."

The desire on the part of men to dress as women is exemplified in some celebrated characters. One of these was Edward Hyde, Lord Cornbury (1661-1723), who was colonial governor of New York and New Jersey from 1702 to 1708. He bore a resemblance to his cousin, Queen Anne, and was fond of appearing in public in her clothing. He was finally requested to return to England for "cause." Another well-known character was the Chevalier d'Eon (1728-1761), who although a famous duelist in his early days, later dressed as a woman and was so convincing that people believed he actually was one; bets were made on his sex, even songs written about him. Philippe, known as "Monsieur," Duc d'Orléans (1640-1701), brother to Louis XIV, although married on two occasions, was also a transvestite. According to St. Simon's description, "He was a little pot-bellied man, mounted on such high heels that they were more like stilts, always dressed like a woman, covered with rings, bracelets, and precious stones everywhere. He wore a long wig, rouge, and had all the manners, mannerisms and interests of a woman." Though, like the Chevalier d'Eon, he also fought admirably.

Female impersonation on the stage, where the fact that the performer is a male is so advertised to the public, is not in itself a misdemeanor. Although this kind of impersonation is no longer fashionable in New York City, it is nevertheless extremely popular in San Francisco where a revue of some of these entertainers was recently assembled. A theatre still exists on 42nd Street, New York City, named for Julian Eltinge, one of the most celebrated female impersonators during the early part of this century. It is, of course, well known that in the Chinese theatre of today, as well as in the theatre of Shakespeare and the Elizabethan period, the roles of women were always played by men and boys.

What the law allows. Female impersonation on the stage. The laws of U. S. A. and Great Britain forbid such impersonation on the streets.

The question of permissible nudity in public has attracted the attention of legislators from Moses to present-day Solons. Appearing or dancing in the nude by women is regarded as indecent exposure and subjects the female who publicly appears without clothes to the penalty of the law. This is covered by Section 1140 (a) of the Penal Law of New York State which makes it a misdemeanor to perform or procure or permit indecent shows, exhibitions, tableaux and entertainment.

American ingenuity invented the strip-tease in which a girl removes her dress and most of her underclothes, one by one, on the stage before an audience largely composed of men. The strip-tease still exists as a waning form of entertainment in some of the burlesque theatres of America. This strange outgrowth of American culture has been transported across the Atlantic and is now the rage of every other *boîte* in Paris. The question of whether a misdemeanor is committed by the strip-teaser in this country depends on the amount of clothes the performer takes off. The Superior Court of the State of New Jersey recently decided that even "if the illusion of nakedness" exists, the young woman is guilty. After the arrest of twenty-seven performers during January, 1957, the burlesque houses of Newark, New Jersey, called it a day and closed up for good. The learned New Jersey judges seemed not to appreciate, however, that the real excitement is not due to the "illusion of nudity" of the performer, but to the curiosity of the male whose erotic desire to see the girl naked is stimulated by the step by step removal of her underwear. In most parts of the country, the "stripper" is usually adjudged innocent if she retains a G-string and a flower on each breast!

Whether it is legally permissible to appear on the stage without sufficient clothes has been the subject of controversy for years in many countries. Total nudity on the stage is not permitted in America or England, except in the case of the so-called living statues where the naked girl stands motionless as though life had departed from her. This form of aesthetic titillation was introduced by the late

What the law approves: Mr. T. C. Jones is not only a highly popular American female impersonator, but brilliantly satirizes the actresses he impersonates, such as Tallulah Bankhead and Bette Davis.

What the law allows: Left, "strip-tease," French Casino, New York. Now popular in Europe, this form of entertainment constitutes one of America's lesser contributions to world culture. (Camera study by Ormond Gigli.) Right, *stripper in action.*

Power dressing: Native North American elders and tribal chiefs proudly displayed their symbols of spiritual and political power for all to see.

I

Western symbols of power: The use of clothing as exclusive symbols of status and authority was an important factor in the evolution of Western dress. Laws were enacted forbidding the wearing of such garments by those without rank or status.

II

Top Left: *The Prussian Guard, 1871*. Bottom Left: *Court Ladies, Henry IV, 1590 and Louis XIII, 1614*. Top right: *Medieval women wore high conical hats to denote their position in society*. Bottom right: *Special vestments separate the sacred from the secular*.

An ostentatious display of wealth: In periods of great prosperity, it was considered the duty of all members of the elite to display their wealth in a mode of dress which visibly and immediately separated them from the lower social strata—the poor and working classes.

*The professional beauty: During the late 19th century, it was the
demi-mondaine—professional beauties of somewhat questionable virtue—who,
together with actresses and dancers, created most of the luxury fashions of
the period and introduced lingerie as an item of fashionable apparel.*

*Extremes of fashion: Men and women have often gone to extremes, wearing
styles that would openly display their natural physical attributes one year,
or wearing tight lacing another. Corsetting is thought to have originated in
the Middle East during times of famine to stave off the sensation of hunger.*

VI

Country weddings: Traditionally, the mode of dress worn by both bride and groom at a Hungarian country wedding was used as a symbol of fertility. It is only in more recent times that the wearing of a white wedding dress, a Christian symbol of purity and virginity, has become commonplace.

VII

Wealth: Ready-to-wear, changeable fashions are a very recent innovation. Most pre-1914 fashionable styles were reserved for the wealthy elite who wore specific modes of dress to convey specific functions—such as a long gown for an evening at the opera, or more tailored styles for an afternoon out shopping.

Authority: The traditional gathered skirts of the Greek Euzones soldier and the mantle of courage of the African tribal chief specifically denote virile strength and vested authority within their respective cultures. How particularly symbolic forms of dress are perceived from outside the culture is an issue usually not taken into consideration.

Greta GARBO
John BARRYMORE
Joan CRAWFORD
Wallace BEERY
LioneL BARRYMORE

LEWIS STONE   JEAN HERSHOLT

GRAND HOTEL

A METRO-GOLDWYN-MAYER PICTURE

Greta Garbo, James Dean and Marilyn Monroe: The immensely powerful influence of Hollywood film fashion, most notably from the 1920s through the '60s, remains with us even today and will continue to impact upon clothing design and taste for decades to come as each new generation views these cinematic classics for the first time.

The influence of Pop and Rock music culture has exceeded that of the film industry since the early 1960s. In matters of dress and body styles, the younger generation of the '80s and '90s have a much broader spectrum of visual imagery from which to select. (Photographs on this page courtesy of Mary Quant, and KISS, Great Britain. Lower opposite page: Jeff Harris, U.S.A.)

The ancient traditions of Mardi Gras and other similar ethnic festivals continue to inspire highly diverse and exciting sartorial experimentation.

Florenz Ziegfeld in the famous "Follies" revues, in which exotic "living pictures" of nudes were posed by such well-known American artists as the late Ben Ali Haggin. Similar regulations as regards total nudity without movement exist in the French theatre. Exposure of the breasts is permitted both in French and English theatres, and has constituted for years one of the routine attractions of the Folies Bergère in Paris and the Windmill Theatre in London. Similar exposure in American theatres would usually result in the police moving in. However, in the case of Les Ballets Africains, in the spring of 1959, some of the Negro girls danced with their breasts exposed, which did not disturb Philadelphia or Boston, but resulted in the New York License Commissioner ordering them to wear brassières under threat of closing the theatre. Ghana, in Africa, from which these girls originate, has since followed the ideas of our License Commissioner and passed a law that all women in Ghana must now cover their breasts. Thus civilization follows the brassière.

Havelock Ellis, who opened so many windows to let in the fresh air of truth about sex and morality, has the following to say about nudity in the theatre: "Some day, perhaps, a new moral reformer, a great apostle of purity, will appear among us, having his scourge in his hand, and enter our theatres and music halls to purge them. It is not nakedness he will close out, it will more likely be clothes."

The Prophet Moses would not have agreed with Havelock Ellis. He was aware that problems arising out of nakedness in family life lead to trouble, so in Leviticus 18:6 the Israelites were enjoined that "none of you shall approach to any that are near of kin to him to uncover their nakedness." This prohibition went so far as to include not only fathers, mothers, sisters, brothers, aunts, uncles and cousins, but also the mothers-in-law, daughters-in-law and so forth. Furthermore, if any man pawned his garment during the day, the lender had to return it by sundown so that the borrower could sleep in it during the cool night, an accommodation which no longer exists today (Exodus 22:25).

Both men and women are usually permitted under law a degree of nudity on the beaches which would be regarded as indecent exposure in the city streets and dealt with accordingly by the police. In the city of New York, women are not permitted to wear shorts which expose too much of the legs, presumably under Section 1140 of the Penal Law already referred to in connection with "indecent exposure." In Chicago, where women and children pass through streets to the bathing beaches which line Michigan Boulevard, the police seem less interested than in New York. In Nassau, the English colonial resort in the Bahamas, women are prohibited from walking on the streets in "shorts which are too short." In Majorca, Spain, until recently the police did not permit men and women to bathe together in the Mediterranean in public, even if clothed from head to toe; nor is this permitted on the orthodox Israeli beaches. And indeed, not so long ago women were not permitted by the police to bathe in many American resorts without covering their entire bodies; later on this strict ruling was modified provided the women covered their legs with stockings.

Little by little the police attitudes changed as more and more of the female leg was revealed by the short skirts of the twenties. As a result, many of the men and women of today spend their summer leisure almost naked on the warm beaches of the U.S.A. without police interference, and with somewhat the same results that occur with seminude primitive peoples—that curiosity is blunted, and boys and girls remain more attractive to one another with their clothes on. When the moralists finally realize this, they may follow Havelock Ellis' advice and have us all arrested for wearing clothes rather than for discarding them!

Laws prohibiting indecent exposure are also intended to prohibit sexual crimes based on the disrobing of the body by men. The compulsion which causes the unfortunate victim of this mental illness to adjust his clothes to expose his sexual parts to women or children should be properly treated as a disease calling for the psychiatrist rather than a term of imprisonment. Revolting crimes in which clothes play a part are those where sexual perversion produces violence due to clothes fetishism. A perverted interest in women's underwear recently resulted in the murders of several women by a mentally afflicted sex criminal who was run to earth by the Federal Bureau of Investigation and finally paid the death penalty. This was reported in the *Reader's Digest,* May, 1957.

Clothes serve to conceal weapons and other aids to crimes of violence, as well as to aid and abet the kleptomaniac who haunts the department stores and steals objects by dropping them into pockets in voluminous clothing. The crime of smuggling is also materially aided and abetted by the use of clothes. Other crimes which are aided by clothes are those of the pickpocket, the robber who places his hand in his coat pocket to simulate a gun or to conceal it and

What the law allows: Completely nude girls as "living statues" stand stock-still in the revue "Time Will Tell," at the Windmill Theatre, London, 1934.

threatens to shoot his victim, and the judo or jujitsu expert who, taking hold of the lapels of his victim's coat, pulls it over the shoulders to imprison his victim's arms.

In the past there have been numerous sumptuary laws regarding clothing which would make half of us criminals were they in force today. The purpose of most of these was to prevent the lower classes from trying to ape the clothes of their so-called betters. Among these, Greek women were not permitted under the laws of Solon to wear more than three garments at a time. In Rome, where color and material denoted rank, at one time the law restricted peasants to one color, officers to two, commanders to three, and members of the royal household were permitted to wear ermine. In the reign of Charles IX of France, the amount and quality of ornamentation of clothing was regulated according to the rank of the wearer, and most of these laws remained in force until the French Revolution. In England Henry VIII insisted that a countess must wear a train both before and behind, while those below her in rank might not have this distinction. History is silent as to whether his eight wives dressed in eight different styles, but at least several of them probably wore a "going away" dress of the period. Good Queen Bess, who possessed an enormous wardrobe, was autocratic regarding the dress of her subjects, and among other things restricted the use of great ruffs or any white color in doublet or hose, or any facing of velvet in gowns. Her successor, James I, swept these restrictions away on the ground that extravagance in clothes was of advantage to business.

Massachusetts restricted extravagance in clothes on the ground that "excess of apparel among us is unbecoming to a wilderness condition and the professions of the gospel." New Jersey when still a British Colony passed a law with the same penalty as for witchcraft or like misdemeanors for any women "whether virgins, maids or widows, who shall after this Act impose upon, seduce, or betray into matrimony any of His Majesty's subjects by virtue of scents, cosmetics, washes, paints, artificial teeth or high heeled shoes."

Insurrections and rebellions have been caused as a result of a too stringent application of laws against clothes or hair ornaments which caused the wearers to feel inferior. Professor Hurlock states: "The Chinese people were aroused to great fury and open rebellion when ordered by their Tartar conquerors to cut off their hair as a sign of servitude. In many cases they preferred to lose their heads rather than lose their hair. When the Spanish prime minister, in the eighteenth century, attempted to abolish the sombrero, which had become a part of the national costume, a rebellion arose which resulted in the banishment of the prime minister. Queen Elizabeth's stern enforcement of her clothing edicts brought about a great deal of ill-feeling against the crown, and during the next reign all such laws were abolished to avoid open rebellion."

Whether the clergy of England should wear the vestments, or a square or round cap or hat, together with changes in the form of worship, was a question which arose and was responsible for many secular demonstrations in the reigns of Elizabeth and James I. Demonstrations have also been started by the appearance of strange new garments. When Directoire skirts and hobble skirts were first worn, police escorts had to be called out. The same thing happened when girls first wore knickerbockers for cycling, as well as the first time women wore one-piece bathing suits, when the demonstrations were so numerous on the New Jersey coast that special police had to be stationed on the beaches.

Since it is but a step from insurrection to wars, it is not out of

What the law quibbles over: Above, *the clothing of the Solomon Islands holiday dancers would not be permissible in New York City, 1959. (American Museum of Natural History.) However, the dubious posturing in a satire of Minsky's burlesque,* below, *is entirely permissible. (M.G.M.)*

place to mention here that the desire for luxurious clothes on the part of the upper classes has been responsible for certain wars in the past. R. Turner Wilcox states: "The causes of many wars can be laid to the quest of valuable furs, trade routes being seized by one nation from another. The conquest of Siberia in the sixteenth century was prompted by the wealth of furs to be had there. France invaded Canada for the same reason."

Clothes also motivated the Russian settlement in California at Fort Ross, Russian River, above San Francisco, from the year 1812 to 1841. The Russians settled there in order to extend their seal and sea-otter fisheries into continental American territory (then Mexican), and often hunted for furs in San Francisco Bay. The promulgation of the famous Monroe Doctrine on December 2, 1823, in part grew out of the question of Russian claims on the coast of North America. The Russian Emperor had issued an ukase in 1821 prohibiting citizens of other nations from navigating and fishing within one hundred miles of the northwest coast of North America from the Bering Strait to the 51st parallel of north latitude. In July, 1823, Secretary John Quincy Adams informed the Russian minister that the United States would contest the right of Russia to any territorial establishment on this continent. It was in this connection that President Monroe declared in his famous message that "the American continents are henceforth not to be considered as subjects for future colonization by any European powers." *Consequently the desire for seal pelts for clothing was largely responsible for the Monroe Doctrine, which itself was one of the contributing causes for the departure of the Russians from California after about thirty years!* Imagine what might have happened had they stayed on!

It will be noted from the above that disputes and crimes of all kinds, including murder, have resulted from the wearing of clothes, to say nothing of a few rebellions and minor wars. Most of these would not have taken place had we lived in a state of nakedness. But we may be sure that man, with his never-failing ingenuity, is capable of inventing other crimes which would be equally obnoxious to society should nudism ever become the order of the day.

What the law allows: The degree of permissible nudity on the stage in the United States is carefully regulated. Thus, the dancing costumes of the Iban women, above, whose husbands were formerly head-hunters, would be banned by the New York authorities, while the considerably more naked chorus of the motion picture, "Dames," with Joan Blondell, is permissible.

"What was good enough for my great-grandfather is good enough for me."
Conservative clothing for the dandy of about 1830 and the dandy of 1959.
(Photo, Abbey Imports, Inc., Byford Socks.)

CHAPTER 13

Clothes and Conformity

Why does modern man wear such drab uncomfortable clothes for business and formal wear? And when did he start wearing the sober two- and three-piece suits which change only slightly year after year and give him the appearance of an animated stove, with stovepipe legs, stovepipe sleeves and a stovepipe hat, cap or lid?

Since the dawn of history, as appears from ancient pictures and sculptures, men have taken the lead in adorning themselves in beautiful clothes when their positions and wealth have enabled them to do so. Costume books are replete with illustrations showing the gorgeous robes of Eastern potentates and Western monarchs, their courtiers, retinues and priests. Superior men showed their superior position by wearing elaborate and colorful clothing. When Shakespeare speaks of the divinity which attends a king, the clothes worn by him contribute a great deal of majesty to his appearance before his admiring subjects. Men followed nature's example which usually gave the gaudiest plumage to the male, and during many periods of history women's clothes were far inferior in point of adornment, beauty and expense to those of the men. And in those periods where it was the European fashion for men's clothing to be dark in hue, as in the Spain of Philip II (1556-98), the richness of materials, embroideries and laces made up for the lack of color. Shakespeare, writing of such clothing, had Polonius give his son the advice, "costly thy habit as thy purse can buy, but not exprest in fancy; rich but not gaudy."

During the times of the Tudors and the Stuarts in England, the clothes of royalty and the nobility were extraordinarily sumptuous and immediately proclaimed the position of importance of the wearer as a member of the ruling class. When Sir Walter Raleigh laid down his cloak in the mud for Queen Elizabeth to walk upon, it created such gossip that we are still talking about it. George Villiers, first Duke of Buckingham, one of the two richest men in England in the reigns of James I and Charles I, is said to have worn a suit of white velvet trimmed with precious stones valued at over seventy thousand pounds. The extravagance, corruption and licentiousness of the nobility were part of the contributing causes of the conflicts between the Cavaliers, who were men of fashion and wore their hair in long ringlets, and the Roundheads, who were Puritans and dressed in drab clothes and wore their hair closely cropped around their ears.

After the end of Cromwell's Commonwealth, which lasted from 1649 to 1653, the monarchy was restored with the return of Charles II from France, and he brought his elaborate French clothes with him. Great was the glee when "Merrie England" threw off its black, grey or brown Puritan attire, but the populace was not so happy with the fancy, femininelike costumes which Charles brought back with him from Paris. During the Restoration (1660 to about 1688), the nobility and their imitators were slaves to fashion and far surpassed the women in the elegance of their laces, the daintiness of their linens, and the "chic" of their broad-brimmed hats plumed with ostrich feathers. Courtiers emulated the peacock and matched the sharpness of their wit with the flamboyancy of their apparel. The repartee between the wits and the women, which has been recorded by Wycherley, Congreve and others in the plays of the Restoration, shows that the "men of fashion," as they were called, not only copied the women's long hair in their wigs or ringlets of curls, but also appropriated their feminine chatter along with their feminine frills. Many of the favorite characters of the stage of those days were frankly effeminate and given such names as Mr. Vainlove, Lord Froth, Tattle, Petulant and so forth. England was deluged with a tidal wave of male finery and worked its way out only after a considerable period, with the advent of the frumpish House of Orange and the stolid House of Hanover.

Clothes in America were balanced between the drab costumes of New England and the gayer attire of the Southern gentry. After the American Revolution, the gentry no longer aped the unpopular English. During the Revolutionary War, the perfumed dandies who belonged to a club known as the Macaronis in London were the

The Look of Leadership changes in three hundred years: Left, *the Duke of Bavaria, about 1658.* Right, *clothes described as having "The Look of Leadership" in an advertisement in* The New Yorker, *by Wm. H. Goldman, Bros., 1958.*

laughingstock of the lower classes in both countries. Hence the origin of the American Revolutionary song:

> Yankee doodle came to town
> Upon a little pony
> He stuck a feather in his hat,
> And called it Macaroni.

Later on, the French people's hatred for the nobility was so great during and after the French Revolution that upper-class men and women for their own safety discarded the elaborate clothing of the aristocracy and adopted the clothes of the common people. The highly decorative, beautiful costumes for men no longer symbolized the opulence and power of the governing classes, and as their power waned or was broken, their clothes no longer represented superior authority.

Beginning about three hundred years ago, a startling revolution took place in Western men's clothing, and its aftermath is still with us. After the doctrine of the divine right of kings was replaced by that of the divine rights of the people, the men of the middle classes gradually took over the authority of the aristocracy and made their own drab Puritan clothes the badge of male superiority, and this has continued right down to today. It will be interesting to trace how and why this happened in England, France and the United States.

The changes in men's clothes from the flamboyant to the drab first arose from the acceptance of the teachings of Calvin and Martin Luther, and from the Protestantism which was responsible for the general adoption of Puritan clothes during the Commonwealth under Oliver Cromwell. The Puritan settlement of New England was also accompanied by the wearing of drab clothes in these colonies. In this connection, it must be remembered that the middle and lower classes have always worn work clothing, usually of a drab hue so as not to show stains in use. However, the farmers and peasants were usually possessed of at least two sets of clothing, one of which was used for work, while the other (often known as "Sunday best") was used for ceremonies, parties and church.

Many writers on the subject ascribe to the French Revolution the change of male clothing from the ornamental costumes of Louis XVI and his court, to the sober, male business suit which, with changes in colors and small details, has been with us for the past hundred and fifty years. This is only partially true. The change to the drab male clothes of today was gradual and took place in successive steps as the feudal aristocratic system was replaced by the rise of Parliaments and the Puritanical middle classes, and still later by the working classes. Revolutions whether violent or gradual usually affect costumes, as one class supersedes the power of another. Communism, one of the latest revolutions, has produced the drabbest clothing. Fidel Castro's revolution in Cuba has produced the "Barbudos," the bearded, long-haired, green-clad revolutionaries who have pledged themselves to retain their beards until Cuba's wrongs have been righted.

During the First Empire, Napoleon attempted to revive the custom of wearing colorful clothes for men, and even commissioned the design of a special costume which turned out to be a dire failure. According to Laver, the French court adopted a modification of the English country squire's costume, but the tight male trousers of the Napoleonic era were almost as erotic as the hose and codpieces of Elizabethan times. These clothes for the men vied with those of the seminaked, high-waisted robes of the Classical Revival for women. In an era when the victorious French armies were continuously going to and from the Napoleonic battle fields, members of the fair sex dampened their transparent bodices to reveal to the homecoming soldiers the beauty of their breasts. The Classical Revival returns as a fashion every few years, but the ladies of today who wear Empire gowns are not apt so frankly to display their charms.

Classical clothes began to pass out of fashion about 1806. As the commoners rose to power, they rose with their common clothes on. These in turn became a badge of superiority, and the male commoner who flaunted ornamental clothes with lace and embroidery incurred the contempt of his fellow commoners who were held together by a determination to be loyal to their own class down to the last button. This had nothing to do with the rise of democracy, as suggested by some writers, for clothes still differentiated between rich and poor, leisured and working classes, religious fanatics and gay dogs. They had but one thing in common, an aversion to ornamental display in masculine attire such as had been worn previously by the nobility.

The businessmen and "the landed gentry" in England, as well as the monied classes in America ceased to wear embroidery (except on their waistcoats) just before 1800 and their clothes changed from colored to dark as well as plain about 1850. Since then they have usually worn sober, dark-colored, uniformlike coats and trousers which have varied but slightly during the last hundred years, and are descended in part from the costumes of the Regency which reached their apogee in the sartorial perfection of the famous dandy Beau Brummel and in the romantic appearance of Lord Byron.

The dandyism of this period represented the rise of a new factor of social superiority, the "gentry" in opposition to "aristocracy." Laver writes that "Brummel himself was a parvenu yet he made himself the acknowledged arbiter elegantiarum, the veritable tyrant of the mode. The Prince Regent himself is said to have burst into tears when Brummel told him his breeches did not fit." Professor Nystrom states that "In a sense, the development of this movement

What the well-dressed man was wearing in 1820. There has been but little change in his clothing since, except for the collar and coat length. The "Bond Street Loungers" above are, from left to right, the Earl of Sefton, the Duke of Devonshire, "Poodle" Byng, Lord Manners, and the Duke of Beaufort.

of dandyism, if it may be so termed, rose during the eighteenth and nineteenth centuries as a protest against the rule of kings in the field of fashion, as democracy rose as a protest against the rule of kings in politics."

Baudelaire, an admirer of the English dandies, summed up the situation by writing that dandyism is not, as many unthinking people seem to feel, an immoderate interest in personal appearance and material elegance. "For the true dandy the perfection of personal appearance consists in complete simplicity—this being in fact the best means of achieving distinction."

During the Romantic period when Lord Byron led the world of fashion, the unruly hair parting, the flowing cravat and the tight-fitting tail coat and breeches all did their part in creating a romantic style for the upper classes which for a few brief years triumphed over the prosaic attire of the majority of Englishmen. But it did not last long. Victoria herself, as well as her consort Prince Albert, exerted a sobering influence on fashion during her long reign. The Prince Consort was one of the innovators of a particularly funereal black frock coat named after him in the United States. Throughout this period, middle-class men were not desirous of becoming conspicuous by their rich and elegantly tailored attire, but wished to shine by their own gentility, personal abilities and fortune, no matter what clothes they wore. This era of middle-class supremacy has continued substantially unchanged among British and American society and businessmen to the present day.

Since the middle classes set an example for sobriety and conformity by their dark clothes, these were followed by the clerical office workers or "white-collar" workers who imitated their superiors to overcome their own feelings of inferiority, and became even more inconspicuous and drab. During the Wall Street regime of the late J. P. Morgan, Sr., so many bankers dressed exactly like him that cartoonists used his style of dress to symbolize the entire capitalist fraternity. The conservative investment banker continues to set an example of conservative dressing for businessmen. Their clothes, like their bank buildings, say to the public, "You may safely leave your money in my care. I haven't a vestige of recklessness in my body or soul." And thus their sober clothes are appropriately fitted to the responsibilities of their calling, as well as to their bodies, and to the impression of security they wish to create.

Man's tendency to fit the appropriate clothing to the responsibilities of his profession is a deep-rooted one. If you wish to test it, try going to business in your pajamas. And if you feel this is a far-fetched example, and you are what is termed a "white collar" worker, try going to the office without wearing a necktie, as suggested earlier. You will suffer all the embarrassment of a nightmare in which you dream you are walking on the street in your underwear!

Why is it that businessmen, so proud of their common sense, continue to wear the present stuffy uncomfortable business clothes so inappropriate to much of every-day living? *The answer is that conformity is a mark of superiority in the business community and gives a feeling of security to the wearer and his business associates.* Nobody wishes to be an innovator by wearing comfortable clothes which would tend to brand him as a radical or an irregular or an irresponsible businessman, or "screwball." In England in the seventies and eighties there was a movement to apply common sense to men's clothing. It resulted in the cranklike clothes known as "Jaegers" which were worn only by a few faddists, such as Bernard Shaw. During World War II, Sir Winston Churchill, who was im-

Evening dress and Court dress, left, *for gentlemen at the time of Queen Victoria's Golden Jubilee. (From* The West End Gazette, *London, 1897.)* Right, *gentlemen's cutaway coats, London, 1909. Quite similar clothing is still fashionable for formal occasions fifty years later.*

portant and popular enough to be above ridicule, designed for himself a special utility suit in which he looked like a cherubic sausage, but his suit is never likely to become fashionable, for all its utility.

Fifty years ago Thorstein Veblen pioneered in explaining dress and fashion as an expression of the "pecuniary" cultures and asserted that labor is regarded as a mark of inferiority, and therefore clothes which were unsuited for labor were the mark of the leisured class. He stated that "much of the charm that invests the patent-leather shoe, the stainless linen, the lustrous cylindrical hat and the walking stick, which so greatly enhance the natural dignity of a gentleman, comes of their pointedly suggesting that the wearer cannot when so attired bear a hand in any employment that is directly or immediately of any human use." Since practically all the articles mentioned above, except the stainless linen, have been discarded in the United States, and we no longer tend to regard work as a mark of inferiority, Veblen's theory hardly applies to the clothing of today. And with the levelling of society due to taxes and other economic causes, the "Theory of the Leisure Class" may ultimately become as obsolete as the clothing and society on which it was based.

The clumsy, uncomfortable and ugly businessman's uniform of black, grey, brown, or blue, and stiff white shirt and collar, of the last hundred years is now being somewhat modified for business. After losing the frock and coat tails in the early part of the century, the next object of male apparel to be modified was the stiff starched collar and cuffs. These were replaced by a soft collar and cuffs, and by the invention of a collar which looked stiff but was actually soft, *i.e.* the Van Heusen collar. The New York judge who decided that the patent on this collar was valid was a famous liberal, Judge Learned Hand, who liked to observe the decorum of his position but disliked all forms of stiffness in society.

Business suits are of course subject to changes in fashion, but these are so slight and subtle as to be almost imperceptible except to the wearers and their tailors, who often become eloquent on the subject of whether coats should have three buttons or two, or are to be an inch longer or shorter. One American clothing house makes its proud boast that its clothing for men has not altered in fifty years. During that period we have moved from the horse and buggy to the Sputnik, but men's business clothing has remained by and large as solidly unchanging as the Rock of Gibraltar—so great is modern man's need to feel secure in his environment.

Matters are not improving in this respect. The businessmen of today have become more conservative than ever in the use of the business uniform as a symbol of business superiority. Russell Lynes seeks to explain this when he terms "the most recent paradox in male attire, the popularity of the charcoal-gray suit, the drabbest garment to appear as a man's costume since the early days of the industrial revolution when men, though they dressed their wives magnificently in tremendous crinolines, affected the solemn black of factory chimneys for themselves. The charcoal-gray suit is the costume of the successful and would-be successful businessman. . . . It is a uniform that covers a multitude of uncertainties and a multitude of platitudes." The "man in the grey flannel suit" has become the national symbol of conformity and middle-class security.

John G. Fuller, a New York writer and editor who is in revolt against the drab business uniform, has given me the following account of his one-man crusade in New York for more comfortable clothes in business: "I began wearing Bermuda shorts to work as a form of protest against the idiocy of the tailors' inhumanity to man. My main motive was *function:* why shouldn't man be comfortable instead of harassed? But in addition, I'm sure there was a hidden vein of the feeling of superiority: I would be above the slavish worship of convention. I would refuse to be a member of the herd. I would be an Individual.

"The last four years have been a futile battle against convention which has left me bloody and scarred. For four summers I have mounted the 8:17 train from Norwalk to Manhattan, immaculately dressed in Bermuda shorts and knee socks. From the other spineless Exurbanites, I have received nothing but disdainful glares or hooting derision. In Manhattan, it's usually a less gracious form of whistles and catcalls. But I continue to march to my own drum beat in spite of this. As Heifetz said when he picked up his violin, it takes guts. But it has gotten me nowhere. The herd clings to its hoary traditions, and I suffer the slings and arrows of outrageous insults. Instead of being the Messiah of the Liberated, I have become only the Buster Brown of Fairfield County."

Since World War II, American businessmen have begun to wear gaudy sports shirts in the suburbs and in the country during weekends and over the summer. We are now witnessing a return to finery for men during their leisure hours. They are presently wearing brilliantly colored beach robes, Hawaiian shirts and colored Bermuda trunks, while the stiff, starched evening shirt is being replaced in some quarters by a soft, billowing frilled affair which our fathers would have regarded as offensively effeminate.

The laxity which is creeping into the male attire in the U.S.A. is also partly due to the greatly increased wages paid to factory workers, enabling this large group to purchase clothes at all prices and qualities without the restraining influence of the conventional standards of middle-class taste. Indeed, it may well be that the rise of the working classes will result in modifying the standard businessman's garb, since these classes are under no social pressures to imitate the "gentry." Indeed, the opposite is often true. Thus we are entering a new phase when blue jeans and windbreakers, and all kinds of fantastic and colorful country clothes, are worn by businessmen in their leisure or on weekends, although these have not yet begun showing up to any substantial extent at city offices.

The wearing of sober business clothes to create a feeling of belonging to a superior class also finds its counterpart in specially designed work clothes, clothes for outdoor occupations and sporting clothes which make the wearers feel they are better workers or sportsmen. Among these are clothes for mechanics, house painters, carpenters, chauffeurs, engineers, lumberjacks, and others to express their callings in which they often take a conscious pride.

The invention of the jockey's ingenious costume, in which the color and quartering of the shirt (itself a hangover from feudal times) indicates the owner's name, while the number on his back identifies the horse and his description in the racing program, represents an achievement in beauty and utility. It also gives the jockey a feeling of pride in the stable he represents and a desire to win races for it. The pink jacket and white breeches worn for fox hunting and imported from England with a host of traditional emblems, including the insignia of the hunt club on the lapels, the "pink" (really red) tail coats for the hunt balls and the black riding costumes of the women, all contribute to a sense of class distinction. The golfing tweeds, loud shirts and stockings (usually products of Scotland along with the game of golf itself) not only help the golfer's game, but may sometimes proclaim his unconscious feeling of superiority over his non-golfing friends.

The superiority conferred by traditional clothing for men is so inbred that it is almost impossible to imagine prizefighters without their traditional shorts; a rodeo without the cowboys in tight pants; a circus arena without the clowns and trapeze artists or acrobats whose traditional costumes give them confidence in their performances; a cricketer or tennis player without his "whites," or a baseball player without his baggy knickers and cap. And who can doubt the feeling of solid strength imparted to our American football players when they don their padded jackets and helmets which remind us vividly of the armor of the Middle Ages?

Contrariwise, the painters and bohemians have a contempt for conformity and have invented special clothes for their own class to indicate this contempt. For generations they wore velvet coats, large bow ties and unconventional berets, which advertised to the world their superior attitude towards the bourgeoisie and its traditions. This type of costume, worn by Oscar Wilde, was satirized by Gilbert and Sullivan in *Patience* in the character of Bunthorne, who "walked down Piccadilly with a poppy or a lily in his medieval hand."

Other classes of creative artists, writers, composers and actors show their feeling of superiority over their bourgeois contemporaries today by wearing tweed or corduroy coats and slacks. Special clothes have been designed for the clothes-conscious bohemians who originated in Hollywood, where the creative artists are a race apart from the bourgeois middle-west settlers in that very new land. The artists' reaction to their neighbors is to dress as unlike them as possible. One has usually only to glance at a man to tell by his clothes that he belongs to the "movie" industry. His wardrobe usually includes lounge shoes or moccasins, colored socks, baggy slacks, a blazing shirt open at the neck, and a brightly colored coat, the elbows of which bear leather patches. Young Hollywood actors thus attired travel back and forth to New York, where they encounter another group, the young New York actors, this time a more "socially-conscious" variety, who dress in blue jeans and windbreakers of plastic or leather such as are commonly worn by mechanics, laborers or motorcyclists. The two groups of actors meet in sartorial battles which take place in Hollywood, on Broadway and in the airways between. The New York contingent, being better trained for argument and more conspicuously and blatantly dishevelled, has so far won hands down.

A few years ago I interviewed a young actor for the part of a banker's son in William Inge's play *Picnic*. He was so unkempt and unshaven that only the gleam in his eyes made me aware that the youth might possibly play a young man of education and refinement. After he left me I drew a sketch of him under which I wrote "American Actor, 1956." He was Jimmy Dean, who later became the posthumous idol of the teen-agers.

Clothes which are a symbol of non-conformity have become so commonplace that they are, in essence, the conformist uniform of the non-conformist. The careless undisciplined uniform of the "coterie" actor often connotes a careless undisciplined behavior in relation to life generally. No one introduces fashion faster than the popular motion-picture actor whose clothes are seen all over the world. As a result, the "slob," a new creature to appear on the American horizon, wearing sweaters, blue jeans and plastic windbreakers, is being copied throughout the world with unfortunate social consequences. His undisciplined conduct is another example of the part played by clothes in creating society. We should not condemn this entirely, for the "slob" psychology and attitude may be essential in breaking down obsolete conventions of clothing and conformity. But unless this is replaced after it has done its work by some attire which spells out cleanliness, discipline, and order, its effect will be cathartic only, and will not supply the sustenance needed for a well-ordered

Oscar Wilde, who lectured on art and manners on a tour of the United States, was widely ridiculed for wearing a velvet jacket, vest and knee breeches. He is shown here in a cartoon in Harpers Magazine, 1882, lecturing to the miners of Leadville, Colorado, his pockets stuffed with American dollars.

society which, strangely enough, seems to begin being "orderly" by its use of clothes.

Let us look into this matter of the clothing for "a well-ordered society" more deeply. The world's drudgery is not done by actors, writers, artists and college boys who wear tweed coats and slacks or baggy trousers as a symbol of defiance, but by the millions of working men and farmers in their workaday clothes, and by businessmen and office workers in their sober uniforms. These clothes bespeak their responsibility to their families, their businesses and their country. Should these men lose their social discipline, the world's work would rapidly deteriorate. Each man who wears his working clothes or business suit which conforms in a general way with those worn by his fellow man derives an unconscious satisfaction from the fact that he is making a disciplined and orderly contribution to the gigantic machine of production, distribution and consumption without which the economy of the entire world would fall. This uniformity of man's clothes therefore bespeaks our interdependence on one another in a world made possible only by individual cooperation. The business and work suits are the uniforms of the people. They symbolize their responsibility to maintain law and order and to keep this world running smoothly in its orbit. Changes will take place in this male uniform, but they will probably be slow, as heretofore.

I hasten to add that there are many reforms desirable in our attitude towards "conformity," and in men's business suits or work uniforms to indicate this, which could be made without introducing anarchy into the business structure. I leave it to the women clothing reformers, such as Elizabeth Hawes, to decide what reforms are desirable, but I warn them that if they try to introduce anything too drastic or too relaxing or comfortable, I, for one, along with millions of others, will refuse to wear it. For when we buckle on our male armor for the jobs of the day, we do not expect to relax at the same time, any more than our primitive ancestors expected to relax when they seized their bows and arrows and set off for a day's food hunt.

Englishmen have been laughed at by others not qualified to know because of their habit of continuing to wear formal evening dress in the tropics, thousands of miles away from Piccadilly Circus and The Mall. They have seen too many Americans and others relax, "go native," succumb to alcohol and the torpor of the climate when the discipline of civilized life is not insisted on. Experience has shown that this can best be accomplished by wearing certain formal clothes for the social intercourse which sustains the Western pattern of living. Schools and colleges are faced with a similar problem in this country today, and in some it is almost a major issue between the teaching staff and the student body.

English insistence upon the discipline exercised by clothes has been a beneficial influence in another direction. The English monarchy continues to hold court with traditional court costumes, complete with feathers and trains for the women and knee breeches for the men. British royalty also provides a hard core for the performing arts which no longer exists anywhere else in the world, except in Germany, Scandinavia and Russia. The effect of this on the British classical theatre and ballet is to give them a superior stature which is the envy of artists the world over. The Sadlers Wells Ballet was

The "slob" costume: Actors wearing plastic windbreakers, T-shirts and slacks satirized by Judy Holliday in Comden, Green and Styne's musical play, Bells Are Ringing, *New York, 1957. (Photo by W. J. Kuhn.)*

recently taken under the royal wing, and made the "Royal Ballet." We Americans who work in the world of art, and receive nothing from our government but the obligation to pay more unfair extra taxes than any other segment of the community, might well benefit from an American Queen or King in this respect!

Finally, it is not intended to suggest that clothing which denotes "conformity" is a desideratum of mankind, but rather to explain its value and purpose in modern civilization. *Conformity is the enemy of individualism, and the great achievements of man have usually been created by individuals who have refused to conform to a fixed pattern and have followed their own bent.* Perhaps when the creative artists of the world have grown tired of rebelling against conformity by wearing so-called "slob" clothing, they may lead us back to beauty in men's attire by adapting our present flamboyant, decorative leisure clothing to our every-day life.

But sober reflection argues against relying on the creative artists for anything of the sort. Remembering the futility of Oscar Wilde with his velvet coat and knee breeches which he discarded in his later life, we turn to the real arbiters of male fashion, the businessmen. *If, as may be expected, mass leisure will be expanded in the machine age to the point where men will spend only a portion of their time in productive employment, they may spend the first half of the week wearing their drab business suits, and for the balance they will be arrayed as the lilies of the field in their colorful leisure clothes. Let us look to them to take the leadership and to transport us back to bravura living in a world of bravura clothing—on a half-time basis!*

PART V

CLOTHES

AND

FUNCTIONAL IMPROVEMENTS

Improving on nature: Left, Turkish armor of steel plates and chain mail, 15th century. Right, Chinese medieval armor of steel plates covered with embroidered satin. (Metropolitan Museum of Art.)

CHAPTER 14

Clothes to Improve
Upon Nature

Shakespeare wrote in a frenzy of creation "What a piece of work is man! How noble in reason! How infinite in faculty! In form and moving how express and admirable! In action how like an angel! In apprehension how like a god!" And he might truthfully have added "And in dissatisfaction with his own body, how like a human!"

Man differs from the animal world not only in his goal of superiority but also because of his persistent desire to improve on nature. Nowhere does he demonstrate this desire more stubbornly than by his clothing. Man was not happy with nature's handiwork so far as his body was concerned. He set out to improve it from his early beginnings by inventing clothing not only to improve his appearance, but also to supply what he felt to be missing in order to overcome his physical deficiencies. Most parts of his body came in for attention, but especially his feet, his skin, and his physique; and in the case of his woman, her bust, her neck and her waistline all seemed susceptible of improvement from time to time.

One of man's first needs was to protect his handlike feet as he walked on the hard ground or in the swamps or forests. The soles were relatively soft, compared with the hornlike hoofs of the sheep, goats and other animals which he domesticated. He solved this problem by interposing a layer of animal hide or bark between the soles of his feet and the ground. To secure this bark or other material to his feet required a fastening cord or thong passed around the instep and ankle to hold the layer in position, and thus was born the sandal, the progenitor of all the inventions in footwear, from moccasins and clogs to shoes, slippers and boots. Hundreds of patents are still taken out annually to cover improvements in footwear, and with the advent of every new material, such as rubber or plastics, a host of new inventions appear. Skins or leather fastened around the shins or ankles also fathered a host of inventions later on in the field of shin guards, leggings and spats.

Consider the enormous industries created by the development of the invention made by that primitive ancestor of ours who first tied a piece of bark or leather to the soles of his feet! Reportedly, American men buy over 100,000,000 pairs of shoes each year, while American women buy over 220,000,000, or more than three pairs each year (1957). Huge manufacturing concerns such as the United Shoe Machinery Company have factories in the United States and abroad for the manufacture of machinery for making footwear automatically, thus bringing down the price to within the means of the poorest parts of the population. Hundreds of research engineers are engaged in improving this machinery and countless millions of hides pass through tanning processes to supply the assembly lines from which a seemingly endless flow of boots and shoes flood the markets of the world.

Let us remember, in passing, that none of this would have been necessary had we been provided by nature with natural hoofs like our horses! But of course, in that case we would have "looked like the devil" in more ways than one!

It is interesting to note that men, with their persistent ingenuity, were not long in inventing footwear which also improved on nature by indicating rank and social position. The shoe, sandal and boot of leather with soles, worn by all except the slaves, derive from the earliest civilizations of Egypt and Mesopotamia. A wall painting of about 3500 B.C. shows an Egyptian king being followed by his servant who carries the royal sandals. A magnificent sandal, the wide straps of which were decorated with pictures of the Nile, was found in the tomb of Tutankhamen who died about 1350 B.C. The Egyptians had the quaint practice of painting pictures of their enemies on the inside of the soles, so as to tread on them. A picture in the British Museum shows a Jewish captive identified by his hair and beard painted inside the sole of a sandal, thus indicating that not much change has taken place in racial feelings during the past 5000 years. Footwear was the sign of a free man in Greece. R. Turner Wilcox notes: "In the Hellenistic period of 525 to 31 B.C. bare feet when out of doors became the insignia of slavery. Peak toe boots were said to have been introduced into Egypt and Greece from the

Assyrians. It is said that the courtesans delighted in wearing red shoes, and that the poet Sappho writing in the 6th century B.C. tells us that the soles of sandals were often dyed red; the purple straps made by the Syrians were coveted luxury accessories."

In the Middle Ages, the pontaine or long-toed shoe or boot was fashionable. It had a snouted toe which sometimes reached twelve inches or more beyond the foot. Havelock Ellis notes that in the fourteenth century the pointed toe cap of male and female pontaines was elongated into strange shapes such as a lion's claw, an eagle's beak, and even the shape of a phallus. Pope Urban V (1362-1370) and Charles V of France issued condemnations against the lascivious practice of wearing them, which, however, appear to have been ineffective.

Nor was man content, in improving on nature by means of footwear, to leave sexual attraction out of the picture. Among his efforts in this direction is the high-heeled shoe which enabled a woman to increase her height and make her feel more attractive and sexually more interesting. The dainty evening slipper with French heels also causes the wearer to walk with the helpless little steps which bring out the protective feeling which supposedly beats in every male heart. Consequently, it has been a symbol of femininity for generations. Inebriated gentlemen of the gay nineties distinguished themselves in public places by drinking champagne out of them, an unsanitary custom which has fortunately disappeared along with Dundreary sideburns and high silk hats. French high heels reached their greatest height in the reign of Louis XVI and the ladies of the court carried long staffs to keep them from tottering off their balance. Many of today's models are almost equally silly. In Old China the small size of the shoe not only hampered the woman's movements for the purposes already explained, but established her value as a wife. In medieval Spain, the shoe was an erotic symbol *par excellence*.

Primitive man also made inventions to improve on nature in respect to his skin. To retain the advantages of sensitivity and cleanliness which he derived from his naked skin, and also to gain the advantages of the protection which the animal world derived from their tougher hides or fur, man first invented the shield. This he made of hide or matting, and later on of bronze and wrought iron, to protect himself against the onslaught of animals or his enemies. But the shield was an inadequate answer to the problem. He regarded the turtle or tortoise encased in a hard shell of armor, and found

Leather armor was invented to provide the wearer with a protective skin which was later superseded by steel armor. Left, primitive warrior wearing padded leather breastplate, Boube Island, Africa. (American Museum of Natural History.) Right, medieval steel armor, Spain, 1498. (Hauser y Menet, Madrid.)

the solution he was looking for. Attaching the shield to his body, he first invented the breastplate of leather or metal, which he fastened in place by thongs or cords. From these inventions he developed the suits of mail or armor of the Middle Ages, which, because of their durability are among the few articles of clothing which have been preserved in quantity down through the centuries to today. We marvel at the skill and ingenuity of the armorer of those days who was the first smith to work in articulated wrought iron and steel. He was responsible for the most exquisite workmanship in making armor which was fitted to the body like the work of a tailor in metal. And this indeed he was, a tailor in tough metals which protected the life of the wearer. The armorer, ever anxious to lighten the weight of the armor without reducing its effectiveness, successively invented the coat of mail, the coat of chain mail, and the articulated metal plates which, like fish scales, covered the more vulnerable parts of the body. The "superiority" of the wearer determined the quality of the armor, the leaders wearing the most and the best, and the valiant men-at-arms, being more expendable, wearing the least, and certainly less than the horses of their liege lords.

As usual, sex came into the picture. In the so-called Age of Chivalry (a misnomer if there ever was one), the same armorer who sheathed his feudal lord in garments of steel in order that he might sally forth to the Crusades, his lady's kerchief in his helmet, also fashioned the peculiar garment known as the "girdle of chastity" which enveloped this lady's lower portions in a band of wrought iron which ensured her faithfulness to her marriage vows during his absence. Her outer clothes no doubt hid these barricades from would-be lovers who, if too aggressively ardent, found no comfort in the old adage, "Love laughs at locksmiths." While this article of apparel is a source of amusement today, this could hardly have been the case for its unfortunate wearer who found it an instrument of both physical and mental torture. For apart from the actual bodily and sanitary discomfort such a device entailed, its wearing carried with it a badge of distrust which was hardly flattering to the wife, nor to the husband who depended upon it for his peace of mind while abroad. So far as we know, no record has been kept of the kind of conversation which passed between husband and wife on the occasion when he locked her up and left her with the key in his pocket. It does not take much imagination to picture her feelings on his departure. "Come back soon," she must have murmured savagely between her clenched teeth, "I shall keep remembering you every moment you are away."

That there was probably a good reason for the popularity of the "girdle of chastity" is shown by the fact that during the Age of Chivalry many young men of family were brought up in the castles of the feudal lords, and gave their fealty and loyal love not only to their liege lords, but also to their liege ladies. Hauser remarks that the "patent idealism of courtly-chivalric love should not blind us to its latent sensualism. Nor can we fail to recognize that it grew out of a revolt against the Church's requirement of chastity. The success of the Church in repressing sexual love had at all times fallen far short of her ideals, but now repressed sensuality broke out with redoubled force and overwhelmed the manners not only of court circles, but to some extent of the clergy too. There is hardly an epoch of Western history whose literature so revels in descriptions of the beauty of the naked body, of dressing and undressing, bathing and washing of the heroes by girls and women, of wedding nights and copulations, of visits to and invitations into bed, as does the chivalric poetry of the rigidly moral Middle Ages. Even such a serious work, and one written with such a high purpose, as Wolfram's 'Parzival' is full of descriptions that border upon the obscene. The whole age lives in a state of constant erotic tension; one need only mention the strange custom—well-known to us from accounts of tourneys—by which the hero wore the veil or the chemise of the beloved lady next to his skin, with the magical effects ascribed to this fetish, to get a picture of this eroticism."

Armor eventually fell of its own weight and the invention of firearms. But men continued to feel the need to protect their bodies against the newer weapons. Body armor in various new forms has been invented continuously down to the present times, when the bullet-proof vest has served to protect our gangsters against the attention of their friends and the police. Modern armor in the form of vests made of many layers of nylon, and of the lighter metals, also appeared in the armies of World War II and Korea. Among the

Improving on nature, for under-sea and over-sky travel: Left, *diver's equipment for swimming under pack ice.* Right, *full-pressure, high-altitude flight suit. (Official U.S. Navy photos.)*

Improving on nature: Left, *modern armored jacket of laminated nylon.* (U.S. Army photo.) Right, *armor and helmet for A-bomb warfare, with radio receiver and transmitter, and eye protector in helmet and gas mask,* U.S. Army, 1959. (Wide World Photos.)

Paris fashion models displayed in the store windows of Algiers in the year 1957 were bullet-proof jackets to protect the French wearers from assassination by their Algerian neighbors. Scientists in the Army Quartermaster's Research Laboratory at Natick, Massachusetts, are now working to develop a new uniform which will not only completely protect the soldier against fragmentation missiles, but also against flame and the heat blasts and radiation of nuclear weapons. They hope to make it a standard uniform which GI's can wear comfortably in the Arctic, in jungles, mountains or deserts. "If it does work out, think what it will mean logistically," says Dr. Stephen Kennedy, chief of the Textiles and Footwear Division at Natick. "A single uniform will replace the 160 items of clothing that must now be issued for duty in all climates." No doubt, as we continue to progress in the Atomic Age, we shall all be wearing one-piece ray-proof armor covering our asbestos underwear.

Improving on nature: The "wasp-waist" corset of whalebone. Left, "Royal Worcester" kid-fitting corset, 1907. Right, "Clarisse" straight-fronted corset, 1902.

Man also found that he could improve upon nature by inventing clothes to hide those of his physical deficiencies which made him feel inferior. The man who is too short makes himself taller by adding lifts in his shoes, or if his shoulders are narrow, by placing padding in his coat, he can give the impression of a massive frame. Like James I of England, he may make padding fashionable so as to protect himself from stabbing, or from the winter cold as in China and Russia. If his arms or legs are spindly or otherwise ungainly, coat sleeves and trousers can hide the fact from the world. False calves are by no means rare. "Why doesn't the Bishop pad his gaiters?" asked a woman friend of the Anglican bishop's wife as they regarded his thin legs. "My dear," replied the bishop's wife, "they're padded already!"

Hurlock describes some amusing instances of clothes hiding some physical defect of an exalted personage being made fashionable. "Shoes with long points came into favor during the reign of William Rufus because one of his court favorites, Count Fulk of Anjou, had feet misshapen with bunions which he was very anxious to cover up. The king was so pleased with this novel method of concealment that he eagerly accepted the style and a fashion was thus established which lasted for nearly three centuries. Long skirts were brought

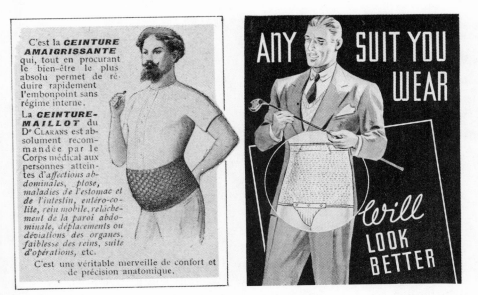

Improving on nature: Male corsets, except when worn for medical purposes, have generally passed out of use. Left, Paris advertisement, 1910. Right, London advertisement for rubber male girdle, 1937.

into favor because the daughters of Louis XI of France had misshapen legs and feet. Charles VII adopted long coats to cover ill-shaped legs, and Louis XIII, who was prematurely bald, used a peruke made in imitation of long curls. Hoop skirts were said to have originated with Madame de Montespan to conceal defects produced as a result of an accident.

"The high neck ruff which is so characteristic of Elizabeth's period, was adopted by the Queen to cover up a long, thin and unshapely neck. The late Queen Alexandra adopted a jeweled collar to hide a disfiguring birthmark on her neck."

Man also felt a need to improve on nature in respect to the shape of his body and its support, and to this end he invented the girdle or corset which at first was worn both by men and women. Pictures and statuettes appertaining to the Minoan civilization of about 5000 years ago show that it was not uncommon for the males and females of Crete to wear wide metal girdles or bands encircling their waist, thus providing them with the ancient equivalent of the late-Victorian "wasp waist."

Men wore corsets for generations. This went out in the Edwardian era, when aged dandies or military men no longer maintained an elegance of carriage by the use of a male variety of this garment. The corset itself is far better known as a female garment, and it has served many purposes throughout history as such. Today it has a bad name because of its dangerous uses in the past. The corset served a useful purpose when it supported the oncoming child, or the over-large abdomen, or fallen muscles due to age. It was only when the corset was used for deforming the human figure under the influence of fashion that its use became detrimental to health.

Why did man regard it an improvement on nature for so many years to constrict the feminine waist, thrusting the body organs both up above the waistline and below to exaggerate the hips and buttocks? First of all it contributed to the uselessness of women of society, for wearing such stiffening devices made it almost impossible for them to indulge in manual work or sports which required bodily agility. Second, it exaggerated the breasts and the hips, both zones capable of arousing erotic excitement. Thirdly, it provided a distinction between the "superior" woman of society or the middle class and the working-class woman who did not use exaggeratedly tight lacing. Finally, it also provided a pleasurable feeling in embracing and supporting the torso. Veblen described the popularity

Improving on nature: Left, the one-piece corset formerly worn by women is replaced by the girdle and brassière, right, 1929.

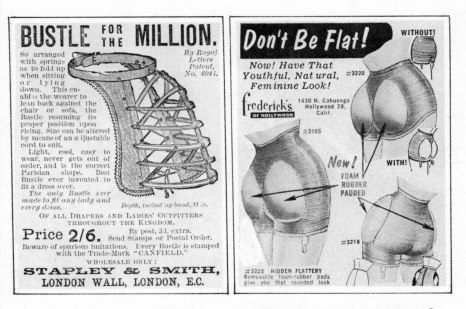

Improving on nature: The bustle exaggerated the female posterior in the 1880's. The modern foam rubber pads which "give you that rounded look" behind are advertised as "hip enhancers" and are obtainable at Frederick's of Hollywood, 1959.

of corsets among the upper classes of the nineties as "Substantially a mutilation, undergone for the purpose of lowering the subject's vitality and rendering her permanently and obviously unfit for work. . . . The women of the poorer classes, especially of the rural population, do not habitually use it, except as a holiday luxury." But Veblen goes on to note that "an increasing large and wealthy leisure class is discarding the corset," indicating that some objective, other than that of merely rendering wealthy women physically helpless and thus inferior to and dependent on the male, lies behind the use of this garment. When women began to vie for superiority with men, healthy muscles began to replace the unhealthy corset, and continue to do so to a substantial extent. We may well question whether the corset was an improvement over nature. Nevertheless it has, in one form or another, held sway for hundreds of years, and there are numerous garments being sold to women today under different trade names which are merely corsets in disguise.

The popularity of corsets for so many years led to countless inventions in this field. These range from the whalebone and metal atrocities by which the Elizabethans, as well as our Victorian grandmothers,

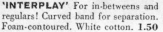

'INTERPLAY' For in-betweens and regulars! Curved band for separation. Foam-contoured. White cotton. **1.50**

'LASTIC LOVE' CONVERTIBLE Precious *and* practical! Nylon ruffle top, all-Lastex V-back. Foam-contoured. White cotton. **2.50**

'ACTION' The bra that moves v breathes with you, frees you! Ler sides, back and waist. White cott

Improving on nature: The cult of the brassière, here described as "foam contoured," New York, 1959. The pages of magazines and newspapers to-day are filled with similar revealing advertisements.

suppressed their natural girth in an effort to emulate the hour-glass, to the modern girdle which enables the girls of today to hide their muscular deficiencies beneath an elastic sheath of latex or rubberized fabric which tucks in their "tummies."

One of the most successful of the modern supporting girdles is that called "Playtex," made of latex devised by an ingenious inventor named A. N. Spanel, who conceived it as an improvement on the human skin and provided the thin layer of latex of which it is composed not only with pores for the passage of perspiration, but also with a permanent floral perfume, which is claimed to be better than that furnished by nature!

American inventors have performed a stupendous task during the past thirty years in improving on nature so far as the female bosom is concerned! Varying from time to time as something to be revealed or something to be suppressed, our native talent for invention applied to this part of the female body has soared to creative if misguided heights. For the lady whose breasts were too large, or had fallen, or had never risen, we invented the brassière, a garment which in its myriad forms is emblazoned over the advertising pages of every newspaper and magazine in the country. Visitors to the U.S.A. from all over the world are given the impression that the cult of the brassière is one of the obsessions of modern America—which is so close to the truth as to be uncomfortable.

American inventive ingenuity—that same ingenuity which has fashioned monster electric generators, huge airplanes, the Univac and the atom bomb—has produced in the American brassière a versatile object of attire which can be used not only to flatten the breasts of women when they are too large, but also during periods when "flat" breasts are fashionable. The same garment can also be provided with rubber pads to create the illusion of full breasts for those insufficiently endowed by nature, an illusion which will deceive all but the husband or lover who is privileged to caress these areas, and who may find himself affectionately massaging a bar of steel or plastic when the brassière serves the purpose of lifting the breasts from a fallen position to one of challenge.

The triple function of the brassière is amusingly illustrated by the story of the manufacturer who sold three types of this garment, one called "The Dictator" because it suppressed the masses, another called "The Salvation Army" because it uplifted the masses and the third called "The Yellow Press" because it made mountains out of molehills. The foam-rubber "falsie" is a relatively new invention, and before its introduction the upper part of the corset sometimes served the same purpose, with the assistance of a pair of pads shaped like round pincushions which were dropped into the top of the corset for creating the desired illusion.

Such "falsies," while seemingly a modern invention, are almost as old as the hills. The "plumer" was an article used for rounding out the female bust in the United States in the 1880's. James Laver

Improving on nature: The inflatable brassière invented by Forrest Daven-port, Perfect Contour Co., Stratford, Conn., has individual containers of Vinylite, puncture-proof plastic. Left, inflating the brassière. Right, the brassière in use.

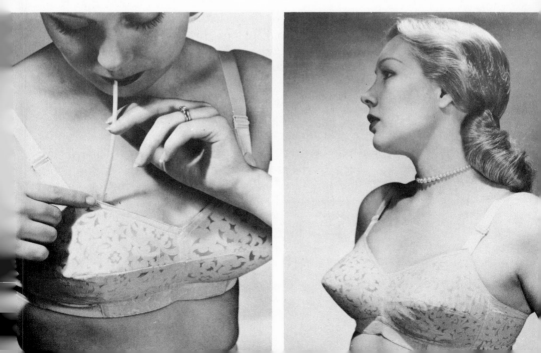

quotes the following, written by an anonymous monk of the fourteenth century on a similar subject: "And that wymenne were more nicely arrayed and passed the menne in alle manner of arraies and curious clothing, for their werede such strete clothes that they had long foxtailes sewed witthynne their garments to holde them forthe! The which disguisingges and pride afterwards brought forth and caused many mischiefs and myshappes that hapned in the rerme of England."

The amount of human effort and ingenuity which has gone into the invention and manufacture of corsets, girdles and brassières is staggering. In earlier days, fleets of sailing vessels set out on hazardous voyages yearly to hunt the whale which provided the whalebone stiffeners. Dozens of patents are taken out annually on the newest of these devices. Upon the advent of sponge rubber, a particularly large number of inventions appeared in the field of brassières. Not the least among these are the false breasts made of sponge rubber, or even the inflatable rubber bags like a pair of small balloons. "What size breasts should I wear for the Theatre Guild?" asked an actress when she was told at a dress rehearsal that her breasts were attracting too much attention under her sweater. "I have three sizes—my own, medium, and large." The Theatre Guild, noted for its moderation, chose the medium!

Perhaps the latest garment to appear in women's continuous attempt to improve on nature is the so-called "hip extender," used by thin women and those who have dieted to such an extent that their hips have become "boyish." These consist of foam rubber protuberances to restore a feminine look to our girls around their middles. These new hip extenders can also support the new crinolines. Thus, foam rubber is a commodity which promises to furnish many new variations of artificial body building, from brassières to bustles.

To those of my readers who may feel that I have approached the subject of these particular improvements upon nature's handiwork with too much levity, I offer my apologies. *Speaking seriously, anything which helps the wearer to overcome a feeling of inferiority and to build up self-confidence is deserving of approbation, and this applies not only to the brassière but to all the other garments which create an impression of beauty which nature herself has been too niggardly to supply.*

CHAPTER 15

Our Versatile Head Coverings

Among his many sources of dissatisfaction with himself, man has never been entirely pleased with his hair, originally provided by nature to protect his head. When it was long, it tangled in the bushes, and as woman's crowning glory it was decidedly dirty and dishevelled. Prehistoric man therefore dressed it in many ways to improve on nature's untidy handiwork, and also to indicate superior rank and beauty. Hair dressing and hairpins go back to remote periods in time, as evidenced by statuettes showing curls dressed in regular rows, and bone hairpins which have been found in ancient graves dating back to many thousands of years ago.

Since men and women have suffered from baldness from time immemorial, man invented the wig as an improvement on nature, and continued to use it for other reasons as well. Wigs display a surprising versatility, since they have been worn by men and women for thousands of years for three separate and different purposes: (a) to hide baldness, (b) to enhance the appearance by framing the head with blonde, white or dark hair, and (c) to indicate the superior social position of the wearer. Wigs in the form of toupees are still used for the first purpose, although American men fight shy of wearing these, a shyness which is not shared by their British and French contemporaries. Wigs for women move in and out of fashion, as does the chignon and other hair-pieces of the 1870's and today. To make life more complex, women in the winter of 1958 began wearings wigs as hats over their natural hair. These, like some of the Egyptian wigs of 5,000 years ago, were made of wool, fur, horsehair, human hair and even straw for summer wear.

The habit of wearing wigs to indicate social superiority comes to us from great antiquity. The ancient Egyptians were particularly fond of wearing them, and at one time the upper classes wore extremely ornate wigs, some of them of huge size and decorated with jewels or garlands. Many examples of actual wigs have been preserved on Egyptian mummies. The fashion of wearing wigs existed in other ancient civilizations, including the Persian, Minoan and Greek. In the Greek theatre, the actors who portrayed traditional figures wore traditionally colored wigs, such as a black wig for the tyrant, blonde curls for the hero, and a red wig for the comic servant; these traditions, even as to color, still exist in the theatre today. Wigs were equally popular in ancient Rome. Judging from the statues of Julius Caesar and other balding Roman politicians, the wearing of wigs was largely confined to the women. Indeed, Faustina, wife of Marcus Aurelius, was said to have had over two hundred wigs. There is a portrait statue of Plautilla in the Louvre so designed that the hair is made removable so that by changing the wig from time to time it is never out of fashion.

The most primitive type of wig was made of horsehair, goat's hair, sheep's fleece or even vegetable strands; human hair of slaves came later, the blonde hair of the Germanic tribes being favored by the darker Roman matrons.

But wigs to indicate social superiority did not really come into their own in the Western world until the seventeenth century. Louis XIII, who was almost bald, set the fashion about the year 1624, and his wigs were copied by the French court and spread all over Europe. Men and women cut off their own hair and replaced them with wigs of horsehair, or the hair of other humans. Pepys in his diary refers to having cut off his hair and "paid £3.0.0 for a periwig." *Wigs by their size and expense denoted the social position of their wearers, the aristocracy being able to afford the larger wigs which grew higher and higher in size and cost as the wearing of wigs spread to the middle and lower classes.* And since the wearing of such wigs lasted for over a hundred and fifty years, they fluctuated in size and appearance in accordance with the vagaries of the fashion of the day.

Wigs had their "ups and downs" and were reduced in size or omitted altogether during the "pompadour" period, when that brilliant woman, Madame de Pompadour, introduced the fashion of wearing the hair brushed back from the forehead and over a pad, giving a halolike effect. Wigs and hair, first powdered grey and later

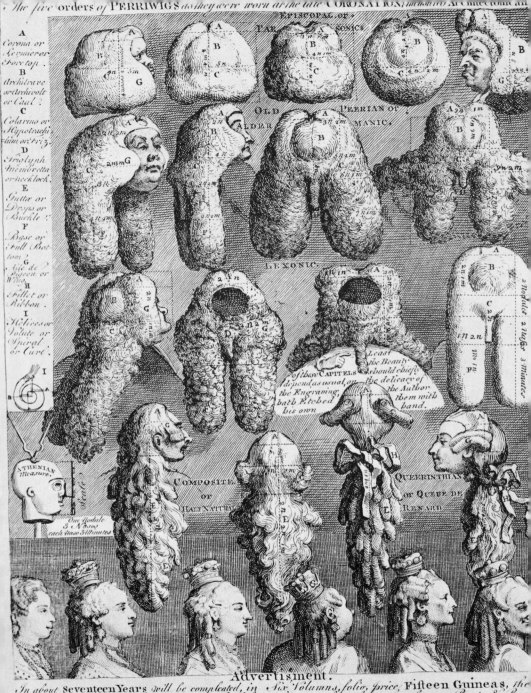

Superior wigs for superior people: Hogarth's famous satirical engraving of wigs denoting rank, social position and other implications "as worn at the Coronation," 1761.

on white, were favored by all classes, but in order to confer social distinction during the eighteenth century, they began to assume larger proportions again. In some cases the wearer's hair was spread over a frame carried by the head so that it resembled an enormous top growth. This was usually powdered or entwined with garlands and ribbons. In the period of Marie Antoinette and about ten years before the French Revolution, headdresses reached the absurd height of three feet or more. Marie of Oberkirch in her memoirs describes the wearing of little curved bottles in her hair, filled with water in which were inserted the stems of garlands of flowers to make a floral wreath which encircled her "snowy pyramid of powdered hair." According to A. M. Earle, the tops of sedan chairs had to be removed in order to enable a lady of fashion to sit in them without knocking down her high hairdress.

Men's wigs achieved their greatest development in England in the reign of Queen Anne, flowing like a waterfall over the head, shoulders and chest of the wearer; and women took an extramarital risk in accepting a man of this period for a husband, since on removal of his huge wig on the wedding night, what remained of the bridegroom might be far less than the bride had bargained for. The

The male wig in its most feminine embodiment, about 1680. Left, Charles Napier, Esq., right, Spencer Compton, Earl of Wilmington.

Superior wigs for superior people: Ancient Egyptian women show their social position by wearing wigs. Left, Egyptian lady of the court of Thutmose III, 1501-1447 B.C. (Metropolitan Museum of Art.) Right, modern American girl wearing colored wig over her own hair, 1959. Note revival of headband. (From Coiffures Americana Salons.)

bridegroom took an equal risk, however, for the bride's wig and ample skirts could be equally deceptive. "I expected far more of you" was apt to be remarked by either party on retiring.

Since such wigs required special servants to take care of them, as they called for frequent dressing and cleaning to remove the insects which took refuge in them, it is not surprising that after the French Revolution these monstrosities of aristocratic fashion disappeared in France. They continued on in England, however, until they no longer imparted any social distinction. Their departure was hastened by a tax on powder to help pay for the cost of the French wars. From the latter part of the reign of George III, their use was gradually limited to certain ceremonial purposes, such as to distinguish barristers and judges, the Speaker of the House of Commons, and so forth, and this has continued right down to the present day.

Having improved on nature by inventing wigs, man also invented hats to cover his head. The need for the hat is not so obvious as might seem to be the case, since nature provided man with a goodly

The "high hat" at its highest: French hairdressing and hats, Paris, about 1770-1776. Left, "Bonnet à la Victoire," right, "La Candeur."

thatch of hair which shielded his head from the sun. Indeed, prehistoric man's problem was to keep his mane of long hair from getting in his way before the invention of a cutting edge to rid him of the superfluity of hair on his head. Therefore, before the hat came useful or ornamental arrangements of hair which we are still continuing to invent for women with each change of fashion. *The hat came into existence as a decoration when the first human wove flowers, matted grass, feathers or leaves into his hair and felt superior to his fellow men as a result. We still refer to a "feather in his cap" which formerly denoted the use of a decorated hat to show achievement or rank.*

The hat began to blossom under man's inventive ingenuity. He not only developed hats and helmets to shield the head from the sun, rains and inclement weather, but also to protect the head from blows and bullets, and to indicate superior rank, as by a crown or coronet. Indeed, he found in the hat or turban a ready means of identifying the position, calling, race, religion and practically every other attribute it is important to know about a man before one meets him. Among such hats may be mentioned the ten-gallon hat of the Westerner, the opera hat of the *bon vivant,* and the silk hat formerly worn at selected functions to indicate rank or respectability, which itself replaced the high beaver hat when silk began to be imported into the West in quantities from China. And since man has seldom overlooked the opportunity of bringing sex into his apparel, he also in-

The "high hat" at its highest: Hats worn by ladies of quality, Paris, about 1770. Right, bonnet for night wear. Left, afternoon hat and chignon.

vented hats to make men and women more sexually attractive and to differentiate between the sexes.

Taking the first category, can there be any doubt that the chic little confections perched so precariously on top of milady's hair is there for any other purpose than to make her look prettier and more desirable? Or is there any doubt that the difference between her hats, whether they resemble cartwheels or bouquets of flowers, and those of the fatuous sex that wears the bowler hat, the felt hat and other male monstrosities, indicates the differences between the sexes? It did not take the inventive talents of women long, after men had discarded the feathered hats of the Restoration and the tricorne of the Georgian period, to seize on these articles of adornment and use them to top off her own perfection and to fascinate the opposite sex. The brazen nature of this theft is best illustrated by comparing the hat worn in the famous picture of the Duchess of Devonshire painted by Gainsborough with the hats worn by the Cavaliers a hundred and fifty years or so earlier. It is almost the same model. Women now having firmly entrenched themselves under the ornamental hat, there is nothing left for modern men but to make the best of the sorry Homburgs, Stetsons, bowlers, boaters, caps and the like, and to wear them jauntily or tilted to one side in a pathetic effort to use them to enhance their sex appeal.

But there is one position to which men can reluctantly retreat,

Caricatures of the exaggerated fashionable hairdressing, wigs and hats, about 1770: Left, shooting pigeons nesting in the hat, Paris. Right, curling Milady's hair with the aid of a stepladder and surveyor, London.

which is to refuse to wear a hat at all. This habit is now being re-garded as a sign of virility among the youth of the United States and will no doubt continue for some time, to the consternation of the hatters and the confusion of the bald-heads. But men did not hold this hatless distinction for long. Now many women wear no hats either, or wear them only to indicate superior rank, such as the women executives in department stores, or presidents of Women's Clubs!

The woman's new hat for Easter has become traditional in the United States, as is the change which takes place in the wearing of men's hats from felt to straws with a regularity which begins on the fifteenth of May each year. Not to conform with these traditions in-volves both loss of face and loss of that feeling of gaiety, once called vanity but now known as self-expression, which attends the wearing of a new hat. And nowhere is the adventurous attitude of women towards clothing more apparent than in the choice of a new bonnet. A mistake may be a disaster, yet most women are usually brave enough to take this risk and completely change their style of headdress as often as their purses permit. Contrast this with the frightened male who wears the same model of hat for years, and is often too lazy to change his battered headgear for a new one until his wife or daughter shames him into doing so.

The use of a headdress to avoid racial prejudice is amusingly illustrated in the story of a New Haven Negro clergyman who was angered by the segregation he encountered when visiting relatives in Alabama. He decided to purchase an East Indian turban and to wear it on his next visit. As an East Indian, all doors were magically opened to him despite his dark skin; he lived in white hotels, ate in white restaurants and rode in the white sections of buses and railroads. The climax came when he was invited to speak before a local Chamber of Commerce on the progress of Christianity in India!

Before leaving the subject, it may be interesting to note that all of the thousands of different hats and head coverings invented throughout the ancient and modern worlds are variations of seven basic shapes, which are (1) the flat hat, like the mandarin's, held onto the head by cords attached under the chin or back of the head (2) the bonnet, a variation of the above, with the brim flattened against the ears (3) the crown or bell which is held on the head by encompassing the cranium (4) the crown with a rim of many sizes and functions (5) the turban consisting of layers of fabric wound on the head (6) the beret or cap (7) and finally the cloth or scarf tied around the head.

And of course not forgetting the little feminine hat which breaks all the rules including the law of gravity, and stays on the head by animal magnetism, or by the piercing of the hair with vicious-looking hat pins which on occasion can serve as concealed weapons.

Finally, we must recognize that the hat is the most versatile of man's inventions in clothing, for not only does it indicate the superior or inferior rank or social position of the wearer, but it can also differentiate between the sexes, add sexual attraction to the wearer, indicate the season of the year, and keep the head warm or protect it against the sun or physical injuries. It can also denote the profession and often the age of the wearer as well as his religion or nationality. In the case of women particularly, the hat also often indicates the mood of the wearer. And all these functional variations, and even more, can be obtained with an object of apparel which seldom weighs more than a pound or two! And are we men and women now to discard the hat which serves all these useful purposes? Never!

Advertised as "Superior Ladies' Underwear," this kind of versatile under-clothing which combined utility and sex appeal was fashionable at the beginning of the century. (From J. & J. Cash Ltd. catalogue, Coventry, England.)

CHAPTER 16

Our Versatile Underwear and Bedwear

Why do we wear underwear, and how long have we been wearing it? It is usually thought that we wear it for reasons of personal cleanliness. However, until about two centuries ago, personal cleanliness was not considered important in America or England, and even less in France, either by the upper classes or, still less, by the commoners.

According to C. & P. Willett-Cunnington, writing about the English Restoration period, "Men and women, even of high rank, were generally dirty and often verminous. Exquisite lace ruffles did not entirely conceal grimy hands and black finger-nails, and the fashion for heavily perfumed undergarments imperfectly distracted attention from less agreeable odours. It was their experience that silk and linen garments next to the skin were less liable to harbour lice than the wearing of woolens, which did not become usual for undergarments until the era of physical cleanliness opened a century later." *It was only when men and women finally decided that cleanliness was a superior attribute and that it was disgusting to be dirty, that the wearing of underwear became general among the upper classes.*

After the notorious English dandies, known as the Macaronis at the time of the American Revolution, had introduced the conception of personal cleanliness, underwear began to be important and was washed weekly. Beau Brummel is said to be responsible, later on, for the startling innovation of wearing a clean shirt each day!

Underwear in sufficient quantities to keep their wearers sweet-smelling was a symbol of social superiority and reached its highest

point in the United States and England during the nineteenth cen-
tury. The possession of many changes of linen underwear, with the
servants to wash them, was distinctive of the upper classes who
bathed and showered daily. Respectable members of the poorer
classes in both countries took a weekly bath, usually on Saturday
night, in order that they might appear clean and shining in church
in their best clothes on Sunday.

We are so used to our underwear that we are unaware that the
first conception of such garments was a meritorious invention. Man,
having clothed himself in skins or fabric adapted to present a "front"
to the outside world, or to provide warmth or protection, found himself faced with a need to adapt this outer covering to the comfort
and functions of his skin and body. This included some way of pre-
venting the rough inside surfaces of the outer covering from contact
with the body; some way of absorbing perspiration; and some way
of providing "slippage" so that the heavy outer clothing would not
rub each time it moved against the body. All these desiderata and
many others were obtained by placing one or more independent
garments between the outer garment and the skin of the wearer.
The second garment was made of soft *washable* material which protected the skin, absorbed the perspiration which could damage the
outer garment, and could be readily cleansed by washing. *Man was*
thus arrayed in two sets of separate garments; an outer covering with
which he faced the outer world, and an inner covering with which he
faced his own skin and body. With the use of washable underwear,
man ultimately introduced sanitation into his wardrobe.

When and where was underwear first invented? In the warm
climates where man originated, underwear was neither a luxury nor
a necessity. In the temperate climates, a lighter garment was needed
for the summer than for the winter, and for the hot days and cool
nights. Place the winter garment over the summer garment and you
have, in effect, underwear. But this is not the correct answer, for
unless the summer garment was made of a soft washable material, it
would not serve the purpose of underwear as we define it today. So
we realize that, like most inventions, underwear was the product of
man in temperate climates, and it originated at a much later date than
the outside clothes.

There are in existence descriptions and pictures of early Egyptian, Greek and Roman underclothing which differs from our own
in that considerable portions were exposed and formed part of the

outer garments. Over the long periods of Egyptian history, the principal garment next to the skin was the short tunic or kilt usually made of linen or cotton, with an ornamental girdle placed over it. The women's tunic reached to the ground and was sometimes worn under a kilt. In ancient Greece, as evidenced by the Elgin marbles and vase paintings, the principal garment, the tunic, also called the Chiton, was worn next to the skin and draped around the body; the outer clothes were worn over it. Only in this sense was it underwear. The Doric Chiton was short and of wool; the Ionic Chiton was full and long. The Romans and Etruscans also wore a somewhat similar garment, the Toga, the length of which was a matter of choice with the men, but according to Cicero, was considered effeminate when it reached the feet.

In more modern times, Queen Elizabeth I of England left behind her a list of her clothes and underclothes, so we have a clear idea of what the best-dressed spinster of her day regarded as a good and sufficient wardrobe. She owned over three thousand dresses, and her laundry list included 126 kirtells, 135 foreparts, 126 petticoats, 13 saufeguardes (we might guess what these were, but would guess wrong) 43 saufeguardes and juppes, and 9 pantobles. Besides, she possessed hundreds of robes and gowns, as listed by M. Stone in her *Chronicles of Fashion* published in 1845. The modern counterpart of the kirtell is a petticoat; the foreparts are girdles or "stomachers"; the saufeguardes are an outer petticoat which keeps the other petticoats clean; the juppes are shirts or jupons; and the pantobles are embroidered slippers. All these made for warmth and comfort in English stone castles without central heating, where even the ghosts have colds in the head and rheumatism lurks in every corner.

With the general adoption of underwear in modern times, a host of additional inventions came into being, such as shirts, undershirts, vests, chemises and camisoles for the upper and middle parts of the body, and underpants, drawers, knickers, panty-girdles and petticoats to cover the middle and lower parts. And in order to keep these clean, laundries were established with equipment for washing them on a wholesale scale in place of the old-fashioned home tubs and river banks where the women used to gather for washing and gossip; soap manufacturers produced soap and detergents by the ton; and, finally, the inventors stepped in with automatic washing machines known as "laundromats" and home automatic washing, ironing and drying machines operated by electricity and sold by the millions.

Left, *French lady of fashion removes her peignoir, Paris, about 1760. (From engraving by N. De Launay.)* Right, *a young Abor lady removes her striped loin cloth and reveals that her underwear consists of ornamental discs.*

Thus the forgotten inventor of the first underwear set in motion industries employing hundreds of thousands of men and women in the manufacturing and cleansing of these garments all over the world.

The familiar sight of the family laundry hanging out to dry in public view, with the male and female undergarments shamelessly hobnobbing with one another on the clothesline, is a matter of indifference to the passerby, but invokes a feeling of social embarrassment on the part of the owner of the underwear who, when possible, will try to hide it from the inspection of his friends.

Man, having invented undergarments for good and sufficient purposes, also developed a sense of shame in appearing in them in public.

The man or woman is not born who will parade the streets in his or her underdrawers or undershirt—even though the body is completely covered. Yet the same man or woman will appear publicly in abbreviated bathing suits or trunks which are far more revealing without the slightest hesitation or embarrassment. This sense of shame is not strictly due to the fear of attracting attention on the part of the curious onlookers. It is because we have endowed our underclothes with the quality of intimacy and regard our wearing them in public as an act of social inferiority. They are private garments, and even those that cover the back and chest, such as the undershirt, are not displayed in public by what were once called "the better classes."

After the idea of the intermediate washable layer was established, a host of new apparel sprang into being. Most ingenious of these was the shirt, a two-faced fellow, the upper part of which was perfectly respectable and could even be used as an outer garment (as in the south and west of the United States), while the lower part with its embarrassing shirt tail was tucked into the trouser top and kept out of view, since it was associated with and covered man's everlasting source of shame. Another inventor took the collar or ruff, which once had an independent life of its own, and attached it to the shirt top, while sleeves and cuffs which also led a separate existence, were robbed of their freedom and anchored to the shirt. The collar and cuffs, by their stiffness, called for the use of starch to stretch the necks of the limp and impart a feeling of pride and social distinction to their middle- and upper-class wearers. The immodest drawers or underpants with their ability to slide up and down the body, met severe competition for a time from the invention of the combination or union suit in which the drawers and undershirt were formed in one piece, and gained in simplicity what they lacked in maneuverability.

Women followed the men in the use of most of these underclothes, including the wearing of drawers. These began as a strictly male garment and were introduced into the female world at the turn of the last century. Men regarded the feminine variety as a shockingly immodest garment and a threat to their male superiority. However, women finally overcame their objections and persisted in wearing them. This continued until it became the fashion in the nineteen-twenties to wear the fewest possible layers of undergarments around the middle in order to appear as slim as possible. Many women then discarded their drawers (once referred to as "unmentionables" and an almost nonexpendable garment) and replaced them by a rather ridiculous flap passing beneath the body and connected to the chemise, which provided insufficient protection either from the cold or sight. But enough of this destructive criticism. Fortunately, drawers and knickers will always be upheld by sensible women both for warmth and modesty, and as their clothes tend more and more to resemble men's, this garment is obviously destined to continue in its original position of importance.

Petticoats, an invention once associated with the utmost in femininity, keep coming and going and changing their function. Today, as was the case over a hundred years ago, they are often used to support a flare in the outer skirt. In Victorian days, their function was to create the impression that women's legs terminated just above the ankles.

Having invented underclothing for utility purposes, man was not long in employing his inventive ingenuity in using them to stimulate sexual interest. *Nothing appears to be more exciting to the average male than to witness a thoroughly respectable woman (usually though not necessarily his wife) in her underclothes, and although this thrill may be lost by constant repetition, it can be recovered almost immediately by substituting a different woman.* These garments, originally designed to give body protection for the female, and especially warmth, were perverted into instruments of temptation for the male at those periods in history when women were most particular in keeping their bodies completely swathed in clothes. For generations the layer upon layer of billowing lace petticoats, the drawers trimmed with flounces of lace, and the chemise with its openwork top which partly concealed and partly revealed the breasts, all played an important role in the game of sex. The petticoat peeped discreetly with its lace edges from under the skirt, while the drawers, during certain periods of fashion, were indiscreet enough to appear far below the skirt in the form of frilly pantalettes.

Man's ingenuity also modified his night clothes so that these took on sexual characteristics. Before the invention of beds, man slept on pallets of hay or straw which, later on, were covered with fabric. He covered his body with a blanket for warmth and, still later, the hay or straw was left in the barn and the pallets became transformed into mattresses. In the privacy of their own homes, men and women for generations wore the same kind of nightshirt or nightgown, a bulky shapeless shirt hanging from the neck like a deflated balloon, which looked absurd on men and adorable on women.

"Alas, my poor sister!"

Left, *the lady in the long, flowing nightgown is commiserating with her "poor sister" whose similar garment, not being of "Viyella" material, has shrunk and shows her feet and ankles. How much more distressed she would be, could she see her granddaughter wearing the "baby doll" nightie,* right, *made by Barbizon, New York, 1958.*

In the late gay nineties some unknown inventor of clothing must have looked at himself in a mirror dressed in his nightshirt and found he looked ridiculous and undignified. By a stroke of masculine genius he invented the pajama, a garment which preserved his male dignity by giving him trousers, yet was soft enough for sleeping in and was readily removable and washable. It also enabled him to continue throughout his sleeping hours the sex differentiation in clothing so important to him during his waking hours. Not for long was he permitted to enjoy this new-found feeling of superiority. Soon women began wearing pajamas, not only in bed, but in the home as well. As a result, they have destroyed any vestige of masculine dignity in the garment. Indeed, the more brazen of the sex have taken to sleeping in pajama tops only, thereby converting the pajama itself into an abbreviated feminine nightgown with all the seductive attributes of that garment.

Woman, whether she slept in the hay or on a mattress, rapidly converted her nightgown from a utility garment into a source of seduction. The fabric shoulders and upper portion, which should have kept her warm around her chest, were discarded in favor of open-work lace and, in case this did not reveal her charms sufficiently, she entwined a ribbon under her breasts so as to leave no doubt as to their existence. The ordinary fabrics, such as white silk, linen, or cotton, were not sufficiently revealing, so she invented the black-silk "nightie," which permitted the glow of her white skin to shine mysteriously through the transparent fabric. In the conflict between warmth and bodily comfort on the one hand, and sex on the other, warmth and comfort fought a losing engagement in the battle of the bed, and will undoubtedly continue to do so. Fortunately, there are still enough women left in the world who use the nightgown for its original purpose of utility to keep the garment from being discarded altogether.

Having invented underwear to be worn under the outer clothing, man's ingenuity led him to invent a special garment to be worn over the underwear when the outer clothing is removed in order to preserve the privacy of the former. This was the dressing gown or negligee, worn in the house or on the beach in the form of a bath robe. Man again displayed his inventive ingenuity in making the latter of toweling (terry cloth), so that it would dry his body after bathing or swimming. Since the dressing gown was usually worn indoors, it also gave the cowardly males a chance to bedeck themselves in colors and silks in which they would never dare to appear in public.

When we come to examine such humble garments as stockings, hose, socks, and tights, we are amazed at the inventive ingenuity which man has poured into these relatively unimportant coverings for our legs and feet. First, these extremities were encased in wrapings of wool, for it was only after the invention of knitting that men were able to provide elastic tubular hose which adjusted to the shape of the legs and did not hang in baggy folds. Then, with that interest in enhancing sex with which man ultimately embroidered almost all his inventions in clothing, stockings were designed and redesigned to show the beauty of line of the feminine limbs themselves, by using sheer silk which embraced the legs like a second skin, and shone with a sheen which invited the interest of the opposite sex.

Women emasculate men's nightwear: Left, *ladies' pajamas, "an exact copy of a Paris model,"* 1928. Center, *ladies' pajamas,* 1919. Right, *men's pajamas,* 1902.

For generations the colors black or white were used for stockings, and no respectable woman would wear any other colors. With the advent of short skirts in the nineteen-twenties, however, black stockings began to produce a somewhat startling effect. They pointed like two black sign posts to the lingerie above, and transformed what had been a mere suggestion to masculine interest into a positive invitation to set forth on a voyage of discovery. In vain the girls rolled the tops of their stockings and wore sheaths to encase their bodies. Their efforts to appear modest were unavailing until fashion discarded the black stockings for hose of light tans or various shades of skin color, or even transparencies, so that the paths leading to the borders of their abbreviated skirts lost their conspicuous quality. Appearing in public with what seemed to be naked legs naturally caused protest from the bewildered moralists of that day, but they were so busily engaged in storming against the abbreviated skirts that they ended by swallowing the transparent stockings whole. The result is that when the skirts came down again, the skinlike stockings remained, and they are with us to this day in silks, rayons and particularly nylons—an invention of the devil himself aided by the Dupont Company in whose laboratories the product was invented. For who but the devil would think of transforming the coal with which he feeds the everlasting fires of hell into the filament used in the nylon stockings which lure so many sinners into his clutches?

Nightgowns and pneumonia: Fashionable night wear in the year 1916.

Luckily for the historians of fashion, a handful of women of Montmartre preserved the tradition of wearing black stockings nestling in layers of ruffled petticoats, as shown in the Toulouse-Lautrec posters. Thus, there has been handed on to the present and future generations, in the performance of that boisterous dance, the Can-Can, the almost forgotten pleasure experienced by our grandfathers—the contrast of respectable black stockings against the billowing white background of seductive petticoats.

Whether the necktie should be included as underwear is a moot question. Unlike underwear, it is worn to be seen, especially in the loud colors which men now often display in the United States. Since at least part of the necktie is covered (and often more ought to be), it is given the benefit of the doubt and considered here. The necktie is unlike any other garment worn by man. He can encase his body in drabness, wear the most melancholy of hats and coats, yet suddenly blaze forth in a minor burst of colorful glory in the region just under his chin. The necktie once had a function as its name implies—to tie the collar around the neck. What impelled modern man to seize on this inoffensive little ribbon and emblazon it with all the flamboyancy he is too cowardly to show in the rest of his attire? The answer is that the necktie is a symbol of man's superiority, for be sure that in selecting and wearing a tie, he reveals his conservatism or bohemianism, or some other attitude towards life, and even in his day-by-day selection of the tie to wear, he fits the apparel to his mood. (I know of one individual who took at least twenty minutes each morning to decide which of his hundred neckties he would wear.) The man who wishes to attract attention, or to pretend to greater youth than he possesses, or to indicate that he belongs to a particular club, regiment or school (the old school tie), can do so at will by means of this extended piece of ribbon. And finally he can indicate his interest in horse racing (ascot tie); his loss of a friend or relative at a funeral (black tie); and even his membership in the Socialist Party in England (red tie). Or he can show his disdain for his class by refusing to wear one at all. Or he can refer to his necktie as a phallic symbol to confuse his lady friends. But why go on—this versatile little article has been invented to perform a dozen functions for you, including the possibility of strangling someone, if you happen to be in the mood.

Finally we shall refer briefly to that melancholy garment in which we robe ourselves for the last time—the shroud. Considering that we will wear it longer than any other article of apparel, very little attention has been paid either to its style or durability. It remains an inexpensive replica of that absurd creation, the male nightgown, and should give modern man a sense of shame when he compares it with the expensive and durable raiment of the ancient Egyptian mummy. But even in this field, progress is being made. More and more men in America tend to be buried in their evening clothes (black tie obligatory), thus gallantly putting their best foot forward at a time when they can walk no more.

Clothes, those mute survivors that outlive us, so much a part of ourselves, are difficult to give away after death, since, when we part with them, we part with the outer semblance of our beloved dead. Perhaps they should be burned in a funeral pyre along with the wife, as was once the custom in India; a good old custom which, like many other old customs invented by men, the wives are no longer interested in perpetuating!

CLOTHES

AND

THE ARTS

Shakespeare in modern clothes has been a successful feature of the American Shakespeare Festival at Stratford, Conn. Above, Kent Smith and Nina Foch in Measure for Measure *wearing Viennese costumes of the 90's.* Below, *Katharine Hepburn and Alfred Drake in* Much Ado About Nothing *wearing "Mexican" Texas costumes.*

CHAPTER 17

Clothes and the Performing Arts

With television bringing people dressed in all kinds of clothes into the homes of millions all over the Western world, the importance of wearing clothes and what they signify is multiplying a millionfold. And since plays and motion pictures are televised which range through every era of human history, all walks of society are now becoming acquainted as never before with what people wore through the ages.

The use of clothes to provide information about rank, feelings of inferiority and superiority and other attributes of their wearers, is nowhere more apparent than in the performing arts, such as the theatre, motion pictures and television. Costumes are employed in these arts to convey to the audience the psychological essentials of the characters. There is no time to beat about the bush. The actor, producer and director must use clothes to telegraph to you, almost in shorthand, all that can be learned of a person by his immediate appearance and his clothes. *Because of this, almost every aspect of clothing as explained with reference to such subjects as fashion, religion, government and behavior, come into play in the performing arts, and are often heightened on the stage to make a theatrical point.*

Dramatists have long known that clothes reveal the man, and that just as an actor's bearing or carriage betrays his inner feelings (slumped when dejected, rigid when proud, etc.), so his clothes betray a dozen or more facets of his character, such as his social position, his occupation, or his belief or lack of belief in himself. Great care is taken by some dramatists to indicate to the actors how they must dress. Among the most clothes-conscious modern dramatists may

241

be mentioned Bernard Shaw, Eugene O'Neill and Granville Barker, while Oscar Wilde, Pinero, Galsworthy, Ibsen and others were almost indifferent in describing their characters' clothes.

Costume and make-up also help to bolster the actor's self-confidence in the terrifying ordeal, to some actors, of appearing before an audience. Some managements obligingly place mirrors just before the entrances to the sets, so that as the actors pass they can see themselves and, if courage is needed, imbibe it by looking at themselves with deserved satisfaction.

Stanislavsky in *An Actor Prepares* describes the feelings of a young actor on putting on his costume: "When my make-up was finished and my costume put on I looked into the mirror and was delighted with the art of my make-up man, as well as with the whole impression. The angles of my arms and body disappeared in the flowing robes, and the gestures I had worked up went well with the costume. Paul and some others came into my dressing room, and they congratulated me on my appearance. Their generous praise brought back my old confidence." Such examples could be multiplied by the hundreds, all of which testify to the feelings of assurance imparted to the performer by his costume and make-up.

Because of the close relationship between good acting and appropriate costuming, great care is exercised by theatrical producers to see that actors and actresses are properly dressed. For this reason, specially trained costume designers are employed who have made a life-long study of what comes over the footlights to the audience in both modern and costume plays. If, for example, a woman from a small town is wearing an evening dress, your experienced costume designer will see to it that "small town" is written all over the dress, if that be desired. It may well be necessary to have such a dress specially designed to exaggerate somewhat the points which give the dress its special character, since it will be observed by an audience seated anywhere from ten to seventy feet away from the stage so that fine details will not be seen.

Actors and actresses (and especially actresses) feel uncomfortable and unable to perform properly if they are antagonistic to the clothes they are wearing. This antagonism may be due to a number of reasons, but primarily it springs from the fact that the costume does not produce the picture which the actress sees of herself in her mind's eye as the character she will be portraying. Secondary reasons spring from vanity; perhaps the costume emphasizes an overlarge bosom or hips. Whatever the cause may be, the actress refuses to wear the dress on the ground that she doesn't feel comfortable in it. Some of the most temperamental scenes in the theatre arise from disputes over costumes. I have seen a well-known American actress, not especially noted for her politeness, throw some dresses she disliked for a new play on the floor of her dressing room and trample on them to the accompaniment of a volley of oaths which would do credit to a longshoreman, while screaming "I don't care if they cost $3,000! I hate them!" The experienced manager usually allows his star to select her own clothes with the aid of the costume designer and the approval of the director. She will then have only herself to blame if she is "uncomfortable" in them. This is not always a safe rule, however. A temperamental star we once engaged to play the role of a storekeeper in a small Tennessee town insisted on having all her dresses made by the most fashionable New York couturier! Her mind was not entirely divorced from the next motion picture she was going to make, in which she was to play the part of a society lady.

Great must be the tact and versatility of the costume designer and costumier for the theatre, motion pictures and television. There is not only the actor or actress to be pleased. The author, the director and the manager must also be satisfied, and the livelihood of all of them is more or less involved. In the old days the managers came first, today they come last. I remember when the Theatre Guild was producing *Twelfth Night,* Madam Karenska, the famous costumier, who had recently arrived in New York from Paris, was engaged to make the costumes designed by Stuart Cheney. In typical European fashion, she invited me to her studio to see them being displayed by the actors and actresses. Helen Hayes, dressed as a page boy in striped pantaloons, came and stood on a model stand; Karenska asked me, "Do you think her pantaloons are too long or too short?" I begged to be excused.

I finally gave up making decisions on clothes for actresses and ballerinas in the theatre after I became involved in a violent dispute between a ballerina and a costume designer as to whether the former should wear frilly period pantalettes or modern silk ones under her ballet skirt in a Southern ballet in Walter Kerr's *Sing Out, Sweet Land.* "The friction from the frills prevents my skirts from billowing out," screamed the ballerina. "And the silk pantalettes are not in period," shouted the costume designer, firmly and with finality. My patent training led me to remark, "Can't you design her something

Many actresses yearn to play Hamlet attired in doublet and hose, but are seldom successful. Sarah Bernhardt, shown above, was no exception.

to overcome the friction, such as a roller or ball-bearing?" A compromise was finally effected. The designer gave the ballerina cotton pantalettes with frictionless frills.

In the costuming of musical plays, such as *Oklahoma!, Carousel, Porgy and Bess, Bells Are Ringing,* and others with which I have been connected, *it is interesting to note that "reality" is not a desideratum in the costuming.* On the contrary, the costumes are heightened in color, materials and design to provide glamorized pictures of the cowboys, fishermen, and subway passengers of these respective musicals. I remember in connection with the original production of *Oklahoma!,* the cowboys were glamorized to such an extent by wearing shirts of varying shades of lavender, pink and other pastel colors that all believability was destroyed. In the New Haven tryout we changed their shirts to primary colors which made them look less girlish. It is interesting to speculate on the effect these plays would have had on audiences had they been costumed completely realistically. The onlookers would have been in an entirely different frame of mind and would have been highly critical of many incidents which they passed over in the mood created by the fantasy or fairy-tale quality of a musical production.

In costume plays, clothes often act as a barrier between the char-

acters depicted by the actors and the audience. *This happens when the costumes worn do not telegraph to us the immediate significance of the character.* A perfect example of this is found in the character of Malvolio in Shakespeare's *Twelfth Night.* If this role were played by an actor attired in the clothing of today, he would wear a butler's or major-domo's uniform. This would indicate clearly his semi-inferior position, as a result of which his being in love with Olivia is a comedic impertinence. In Elizabethan costume, the fact that Malvolio is a superior servant is not at all clear, and the main situation is often misunderstood by modern audiences. Costume plays are often unpopular because our audiences have difficulty in identifying themselves with the strangely-clothed characters who appear in them. Because of this, as well as the expense involved, there is generally a reluctance to produce costume plays even though some have achieved great success.

Those who attend the final rehearsals of plays, before the actors wear their costumes, often remark that the play was never again so understandable or moving later on when the actors performed in costume. I remember on one particular occasion, the final run-through rehearsals of Werfel's *Juarez and Maximilian* which was set in the Mexico of 1867. Prior to the dress rehearsal there was a tenderness and moving quality in the play which was lost as soon as the actors appeared in the costumes of the period at the dress rehearsal. We were never able to recapture this quality in the actual performance of the play, and it was a failure with audiences, notwithstanding that the excellent cast included three of America's best actors at the time, Alfred Lunt, Edward G. Robinson and Claire Ames.

The reason for this failure is not hard to find. *When the actors appeared in their everyday clothes, they seemed to be close to us and our times. When they put on the trappings of another period and another country (Mexico), their costumes became a barrier between us and the people they were portraying, and their contact with us was lost.*

Because of these facts, it is often the custom to produce the plays of Shakespeare in so-called "modern dress," in which a period is chosen where the clothes and their social significance are more familiar to us than the Elizabethan. As a result the plays come more vividly to life. Among the best examples of these in the modern theatre are the *Hamlet* in modern clothes of Basil Sidney and Mary Ellis, and the G.I. *Hamlet* of Maurice Evans. By costuming *Julius Caesar* in black shirts reminiscent of Mussolini, this play was given a modern significance by its director, Orson Welles, which was missing in versions costumed in the period of the play. But perhaps the best examples were the productions of the American Shakespeare Festival Theatre and Academy, in the summer of 1956, of *Measure for Measure* directed by John Houseman, in costumes of Vienna of the nineties, and *Much Ado About Nothing* in the summer of 1957, directed by Jack Landau, in Texas costumes of Spanish origin suggested by Katharine Hepburn. *These plays succeeded for the first time in this country because the characters were made understandable for American spectators, since the actors wore clothes which indicated to a modern audience their social position and pursuits and were easily recognized for what they were.*

While we regard the costuming of Shakespeare's plays in this way as a modern innovation, this is not actually the case. In the days of the Elizabethans the plays were always given in contemporary costumes. For this reason, it was not necessary for the Bard to write lines to explain the rank or position of his characters. The actors' clothes did this for the audience without words; this is just the opposite of what takes place when we witness these plays in the theatre today, with the actors wearing Elizabethan costumes.

The custom of using the costumes of the day for Shakespeare's plays continued up to the beginning of the nineteenth century, and the real innovation was to go back to presenting these plays in Elizabethan or other period costumes. Nor was this a welcome departure. So expensive were the Elizabethan costumes when Charles Kemble introduced them at the Drury Lane Theatre, that he had to raise the prices of admission in order to pay for them. This in turn so provoked the members of the audience that they rioted in front of the theatre for several evenings. Similar riots would seem to be in order today, with the rising expense in the cost of costumes.

It is interesting to note to what extent the fashions of the day modify in costume plays the costumes worn by actors and actresses of this and other periods. This tendency exists at the present time and probably always will. The actress who can somehow modify her old-fashioned costume so that it will reflect the fashion of the day, achieves a measure of happiness out of all proportion to the effort it takes. Sometimes a manager tries to take advantage of the fact that an actor or actress would like to appear in his or her favorite clothing on stage. I attempted this with Katharine Hepburn in trying to persuade her to appear as Rosalind in *As You Like It*. Remarking her predilection for wearing slacks and low-heeled shoes in real life, I asked our scenic artist, Stuart Cheney, to sketch up several drawings of her in "modern-dress" boys' suits. She made me happy by agreeing to play the part, but only if she dressed in Elizabethan page-boy costumes with tights—in which she was actually bewitching.

The wearing by actors of clothing of the opposite sex was a favorite stage device in Elizabethan days. Boys were used to play girls' parts because the women of the lower classes available for the theatre were not usually sufficiently educated. Since boy actors could play the roles of boys better than they could play girls, a number of Shakespeare's plays were based on the impersonation of men by women, such as *The Merchant of Venice* where Portia impersonates a young male lawyer and *Twelfth Night* where Viola impersonates an ardent young lover. In the Elizabethan theatre, the impersonation of

Left, *Ellen Terry wearing a lawyer's robe as Portia in* "The Merchant of Venice," 1902. Right, *Katharine Hepburn in similar robes, American Shakespeare Festival Theatre, Stratford, Connecticut, 1957.*

females by boys wearing women's clothes was usually taken seriously by the audience. In modern times the wearing of women's clothing by grown men is usually treated as hilarious comedy, as in the old Victorian play, *Charley's Aunt,* in which the male clumsiness in wearing feminine apparel has been a source of mirth for generations.

Comedians who have provoked laughter throughout the ages have often achieved this with the help of clothing which caricatures or pokes fun at more dignified clothing denoting authority or just plain pomposity. Thus, the small bowler hat worn on the top of his head by Charlie Chaplin mocks the "conformity" of the normal wearer of this badge of respectability; the baggy trousers are an undignified guffaw at the well-creased pants of the well-dressed man, while the cane or walking stick and the tiny mustache complete the caricature of a man who wears his clothes to indicate the dignity of his position in life.

Costumes are sometimes used in the theatre to convey a stylized characterization to the audience. An example of this is found in the costumes of the Commedia dell' Arte which began in Italy in the sixteenth century and has spread to other countries. In these plays the actors originally portrayed the characters of Pierrot, Columbine, Harlequin, Punchinello, Pantaloon, the Captain and other traditional figures, and improvised their lines. Each character wore his or her own stylized costume, which immediately told the audience the kind of person being portrayed, thus relieving the improvisers of the necessity of writing characterizations. Thus the sad lover or deceived husband was portrayed by Pierrot dressed in baggy white trousers and blouse with a white conical hat; the not-to-be-trusted sweetheart or wife by Columbine in a short white skirt and similar blouse and hat; Harlequin, the gay deceiver or artful villain in his costume of skin-fitting tights with diamond-shaped patches; and so on. These costumes have lasted down the centuries as symbols of the eternal triangle and other follies of mankind, alike in the theatre, opera and ballet, and still live on the stages of the United States, England, France, Italy and elsewhere.

The costume of Pierrot fathered that of the circus clown whose painted white face caught the flickering light in the circus tent and symbolized man's ability to laugh at himself and his misfortunes. Children seeing his grotesque clothes and expressions, his falling down and being beaten by a slapstick, were told by his costume to find his troubles highly amusing and to laugh wholeheartedly at him

The desire to wear male costumes has led many actresses to play roles written for or dressed as men. Here are some outstanding examples taken from a London Sketch *of 1894:* Upper left, *Mrs. Lewis as Richard in* Richard III; upper right, *Mrs. Jordan as Hypolita in* She Would and She Would Not. Lower left, *Miss Wyndham as Count Pontigny in* Scaramuccia; lower right, *Mrs. Mountain as Matilda in* Richard Coeur de Lion.

without realizing that they are unconsciously laughing at all humanity, including themselves. The acrobats' and equestrians' tight-fitting costumes go back to Roman days and spell out athletic prowess, adventure, sex and utility at the same time.

The character of Punchinello with his curved cap and his hump continues to appear in the ancient Punch and Judy show which still delights some of the children of today. These youngsters escape the movies and television to witness the hilariously sadistic spectacle of Punch beating his wife Judy and *vice versa*—a sport which for some quaint reason is considered more appropriate for children than television plays about cowboys or gunmen.

The lighting employed in the theatre throughout the ages has had a considerable influence on stage costuming. With modern electric lighting there are no problems in illuminating the actors, except those which sometimes exist in the minds of the scenic artists, some of whom prefer to illuminate the scenery. It was not always thus. In the flickering gaslight of the Victorian era, the costume designer had to help the visibility of the actors by dressing them in ornate fabrics and using such light-reflecting materials as cloth of gold, satins and so forth wherever possible. And in the candle-lit evenings of the theatres of the Restoration and Molière, the actors had to stand over the candle footlights to put their witty lines across to the audience.

In Shakespeare's day the plays were usually performed in the daytime and the problems of illumination were lessened. Since the clothes were contemporary, no special lighting problems would seem to have arisen. Going back to the earlier days of the Roman and Greek theatres, problems arose which affected the appearance of the actors as a result of the enormous auditoriums in which these plays were given. For example, the theatre of Dionysus in Athens seated 14,000 spectators. According to T. B. L. Webster in *Greek Theater Production*, the distance from the front of the "stage" across the orchestra to the front row of spectators was 60 feet in the fifth century and over 70 feet in the fourth century. "The back rows of the theatre of Dionysus were about 300 feet from the stage. This means that an actor six feet in height would look about three and a half inches high to the spectators in front and three-quarters of an inch high to the spectators at the back. On this scale, without footlights, facial expression would mean little to the front rows, and the advantage of a mask, necessarily larger than the human face and the features firmly painted, is obvious." The shoes were also provided with raised heels and soles and together with the voluminous costumes contributed to increasing the size of the actor.

According to W. Beare in *The Roman Stage*, Donatus, an early writer on the subject of the Greek and Roman theatres (interrelated, since most Roman plays were adapted from translations of Greek plays), states the following as regards the costumes used: " 'Old men in comedy are dressed in white, as that is said to be the oldest style; young men wear garments which contrast with each other in colour. Slaves in comedy wear a short garb, either because of the poverty of early times or to allow of free movement. Parasites wear their mantles wrapped (presumably in some special way). White is the colour for a cheerful character; a man in trouble wears shabby clothes. Purple (purpureus) is the color for the rich, red (peniceus) for the poor. A pimp wears a costume of variegated hue; a harlot is given a yellow mantle to indicate her avarice. Trailing robes (syrmata) are worn by characters in grief to show their neglect of personal appearance.' "

Webster indicates that in the earliest type of Greek comedy, the actors did not show their own skin but wore tights which probably picked up the light. "The actor of Old Comedy, when he is to per-

Masks for comedy and tragedy were used in the huge Greek and Roman theatres. Note the upper right mask, the mouth of which forms a megaphone.

Shantiniketan acting company's modern presentation of Tagore's comedy, Tasher Desh, *New Delhi, 1954. (Information Service of India.)*

form a small part, wears a mask, tights with a phallos sewn to them which supports his padding, and over the tights any other clothing that suits his part: If he is stripped naked the audience sees him in mask, tights and phallos; his tights are his dramatic skin."

In the comedies of the sixth and fifth centuries in Athens, the clothing was often obscene in the modern sense. When presenting such characters as satyrs in the Dionysian festivals, they wore phalli as part of their costumes. Webster writes: "If the actor is playing a male part, he has a phallus stuck on his tights; it may be tied up, or it may dangle if obscene jokes are to be made; the two positions can be seen clearly on the Leningrad Ocnochee, and Aristophanes refers to them in 'The Clouds.'"

Masks which were used extensively by the actors in the Greek theatre were first invented by prehistoric man in his desire to propitiate supernatural beings or spirits, or to impersonate animal spirits or totems. The first plays were probably hunting plays given in the caves of southern France and Spain, in the last phase of the Ice Age of about twenty thousand years ago, in which the hunters served as

A Siamese play with incidental dancing, showing the elaborate costumes employed in plays in Bangkok, Thailand.

the actors in a mock dance hunt, while the wizards or witch doctors, dressed in ceremonial robes and masks, played the parts of the animals. *These were the first actors and dancers, and in this way they demonstrated to the gods the success they wished for in the hunt.* Masks, therefore, form a bond between religion, theatre and dance, and rank among the earliest devices created by man. We have learned about their prehistoric use, not by finding actual masks, but by pictures of them as worn by wizards or medicine men in the cave paintings mentioned earlier. The number of these indicates that masks were habitually worn in the animal food ceremonies. Kuhn in *The Rock Pictures of Europe* shows eleven such wizards wearing animal masks of various kinds. Animal masks are also shown in the Spanish Levant rock paintings which are dated at a somewhat later period.

Today masks of all kinds are found among primitive and civilized peoples alike. In general they enable the wearer to impress the public with their superior position, or to impersonate a superior being or spirit, as with the witch doctor or medicine man. Professor Havemeyer points out that masks "are to be found among practically all

Old-age insurance: The Duk-duks of the Bismarck Archipelago are old men disguised as masked figures who appear at an annual festival and intimidate the younger men into taking care of their aged.

Masks used in primitive African ceremonies have had an important influence on modern art. Left, mask from Belgian Congo. Right, mask from Balumba tribe, Gabun region, Africa. (Brooklyn Museum.)

peoples in the lower stages of civilization and even in so advanced a civilization as that of Greece. Grief was expressed by one actor's mask and joy by another. Not only each person, but also each emotion was expressed by the set face of wood and linen rather than by the actual countenances of the actors." Another use of masks in the Greek and the No theatres of Japan was to enable a small number of actors to play a large number of characters. In many of the masks of the Roman theatre, a megaphone was invented which formed part of the mouth and enabled the actor's voice to be heard in the enormous amphitheatres.

An additional reason for wearing masks is found in the Japanese No plays. M. S. Stopes in *The No Plays of Old Japan* states, "Only men can act, and for the women's parts they wear the conventional masks with the white narrow face and the eyebrows painted high up on the middle of the forehead, which is the classical standard of female beauty." According to Stopes, in these Japanese No plays the men were formerly not only given the outward semblance of women by every contrivance which the costumer and coiffeur could supply, but they were required to spend their lives from childhood in feminine costume and society so that their masculine proclivities might be as far as possible obliterated. This does not mean, however, that women did not act in some plays, for they did, but never with members of the opposite sex. The actors never appeared without masks, which were very elaborate.

The Asian theatre began with the dramatization of the Hindu religious legends of the Ramayana and the Mahabharata some fifteen hundred years ago, and spread throughout countries such as Indonesia, Thailand, Indochina, and Bali, which were influenced by Indian art and literature. The costumes of this theatre reached a high elaboration due to two factors: (a) the actors were mainly playing the roles of gods or devils who wore superb clothing, and (b) scenery, when it existed at all, was of minor importance, so that the entire spectacle was usually carried by the costumes and props. The special studies of the modern Asian theatre made by Faubion Bowers in *Theatre of the East* indicate that the Asian theatre, including the Chinese, retains certain similarities to the theatre of ancient Greece in its use of voluminous costumes and elaborate masks to portray supernatural beings, while all the women's parts are usually played by men. This type of female impersonation reached a high point in Old China in the work of Mei Lan Fang who toured the United States and Europe in a series of elaborately costumed classical plays and operas about thirty years ago, and who is responsible for continuing to give dignity and stature to the classical theatre during the present Communist regime.

Throughout India, China and most of the countries of the East, as well as in Oceania, Australia, Africa and Brazil, masks are also used to enable the wearer to simulate supernatural beings in religious ceremonies or processions. One of the most interesting of these uses is that of the Duk-Duk of the Bismarck Archipelago. The Duk-Duk is a spirit which comes to life periodically and frightens the boys and younger men of the tribe into providing food for the old men who are too feeble to fend for themselves. According to Havemeyer, the mask or head of the Duk-Duk is "a conical-shaped erection

Above, *Robert Keith looking at mask of his cynical self in* The Great God Brown *by Eugene O'Neill, Greenwich Village Theatre, 1926. Below, masks used in motion picture based on Sophocles'* Oedipus Rex, *directed by Tyrone Guthrie for Stratford Shakespeare Festival, Ontario. (Masks and costumes by Tanya Moiseiwitsch; photo courtesy of Leonid Kipnis, producer.)*

about five feet high, made of very fine basket work and gummed all over to give a surface on which the diabolical countenance is depicted. No arms or hands are visible and the dress extends down to the knees. The old men, doubtless, are in the secret, but by the frightened look on the faces of the others, it is easy to see that they imagine that there is nothing human about these alarming visitors."

One of the most interesting use of masks in the modern theatre was provided by Eugene O'Neill in at least two of his plays, *The Great God Brown* and *Lazarus Laughed*. O'Neill told me he was always disturbed by what he felt was the inability of many actors to portray the inner feeling of the character as well as the outer façade which he presented to the world. In *The Great God Brown* he attempted to solve this by the use of masks. Thus the young man Dion wears a mask which is a "fixed forcing of his own face into the expression of a mocking, reckless, defiant, gaily scoffing and sensual young Pan." When he removes the mask and we see his own face underneath, it is "dark, spiritual, poetic, passionately supersensitive, helplessly unprotected in its childlike religious faith in life." The device of alternately putting on the mask and removing it to show the real picture underneath was dramatically effective but did not entirely satisfy O'Neill, so that in *Strange Interlude* he substituted for the mask the asides to the audience which revealed the true personality and inner feelings of the character.

In *Lazarus Laughed* O'Neill also used masks for an entirely different purpose, to give a fixed characterization to a chorus. In a production of *Oedipus Rex* in Stratford, Canada, in the year 1955, masks designed by Tanya Moiseiwitsch were worn by all the characters, and transformed the faces of the actors and extras into magnificently sculptured legendary Greek figures. The illusion, while striking in the beginning, was soon lost. The masks appeared to become stiff and lifeless, for no mask is as interesting as the human face.

It is heartening to be able to end this chapter on a note of optimism as to the future of costume in the American theatre. After a drought lasting nearly fifty years, the plays of Shakespeare with their magic complement of costume, poetry, philosophy, color and music are returning to the stage, largely as a result of the success of the Shakespeare Festivals in Stratford, Ontario, Canada, and Stratford, Connecticut. Supported by all classes from workers to the wealthy, the audiences flocking to these two festivals have broken all records for summer engagements. There is therefore some hope that the drabness in costume and scenery of the socially-conscious play, which has to some extent characterized the American theatre since the thirties, may be in turn replaced by a more colorful *mise en scène*. As I write, audiences are flocking to half a dozen plays which bring back to our theatre some of the splendors of the Orient in costumes and scenery. The authors of the current musical play *My Fair Lady* ascribe some of its success to the beautiful costumes worn throughout the play, particularly in the Ascot number. Perhaps the success of Shakespearean plays and American musical plays represents a rebellion on the part of audiences against plays of futility and horror by angry young men and blasé older men. So does the nation-wide popularity of the ballet. I believe all this presages a return to the heroic in the theatre again—a theatre which holds up the mirror to nature instead of the microscope, and will bring back to the stage the glory of man's achievements as well as the ignominy of his failures.

Dancing costumes are universally worn. Above, *New York City Ballet in Gounod's "Symphony," by Balanchine*. Below, *dance of boys at Initiation Camp, Guekedou, Upper Guinea, West Africa. (From* Les Hommes de la Danse, *Edition Clairefontaine.)*

CHAPTER 18

Clothes in Dance, Fantasy and the Fine Arts

In the dance, fantasy and the fine arts we have found it necessary to devise special clothes to dress the creatures of our imagination or those who portray them in ballet or dance. How did the tutu, the ballet skirt which resembles a large powder puff, come into existence? How do we distinguish by clothing between our friends or foes in the fantasy world of fairies, elves, imps, angels and devils? How do we show our superiority to some of these and our inferiority to others? And how, in the arts, do our painters and illustrators use clothing to indicate their feelings about their subjects? These questions are all interrelated and we shall try to answer them in turn.

Dancing is almost as old as humanity and the part played by clothes in compensating for feelings of inferiority in the dancers is equally ancient. Many animals and birds dance and prance, and Kohler, in *The Mentality of Apes*, refers to the pleasure enjoyed by apes as they prance around with "pieces of rags generally hanging in long strings over their shoulders to the ground. The trotting about of apes with objects hanging around them serves to give them a naive pleasure . . . based entirely on the heightened body consciousness of the animal. When anything moves with our bodies, we feel richer and more stately." In other words, we feel superior.

In addition to the prehistoric hunting and agricultural religious dances with ceremonial clothes of which mention has already been made, the dance has been used from time immemorial to stir up emotions of courage, hatred or fear in which clothing has played an important part. In order to vanquish their enemies, tribal warriors dress in their most frightening clothes, ornaments and war paint and participate in a war dance, the drums working the dancers into a frenzy of excitement. In this way they overcome their fears and rush into battle where they can display their greatest bravery in the face of danger. Other dance ceremonies are often employed in the tribal initiation of the young to educate them in the tribal mores at the time of puberty, and these often involve the use of masks and special costumes to frighten the boys as part of their initiation.

Additional types of dancing among primitive peoples include religious dances, usually involving the use of ceremonial robes and masks; social and tribal dancing such as the Australian Corroboree, in which men and women danced without clothing, their bodies usually decorated with white clay; mimetic dancing, in which the dancers mimic animals, such as the American-Indian buffalo dance; and finally, just dancing for the sheer joy of the physical rhythms and movements, or for the entertainment of others.

From the religious dances of the Greeks developed the high form of Greek tragedy, while down the ages religious ceremonies have usually included rhythmic ritual movement. Peculiarly individual were the dances of the Shakers in which sect the men and women were vowed to celibacy. The women, wearing dark-gray costumes and bonnets, and the men danced together in a common hall, the women on one side and the men on the other, meeting and shaking but never touching one another. The "Holy Rollers" also perform a type of religious prayer rhythm in their churches which may be regarded as the physical if not the spiritual ancestor of the modern "Rock 'n' Roll."

The folk dances of peasants developed from the happier social dances of primitive peoples. Later on the dancers retained their local or national costumes and wore them to celebrate the national holidays or the festivals. Such folk dancing included the English Morris dances of Tudor and Stuart times, and later on square dances. The upper classes danced the more formal dances such as the "Sir Roger de Coverley" and "The Lancers." Square dances, which have never quite gone out of circulation, are now enthusiastically danced all over the United States, where the "calling" of the various steps is a characteristic which has been developed to a minor art.

If someone lavished the same loving care on our native Anglo-American square dancing as has been lavished on American ballet, a European derivative, our native dancers wearing appropriate American costumes could, in my opinion, easily rival the folk dancers of

In folk dances the women in their hampering skirts usually form a background for the antics of the men. Above, dance of Rotorua men, New Zealand. (American Museum of Natural History.) Below, Moiseyev Dance Company, Moscow, in Ukrainian folk dance. (Hurok Artists, Inc.)

Europe, such as the Moiseyev folk dance troupe of Moscow. *In most of these folk dances the differentiation of the sexes by the wearing of skirts by the women and trousers by the men is usually rigorously adhered to. As a result, the men usually win plaudits in the most spectacular feats, being unhampered by their trousers, while the women, handicapped in their ankle-length heavy skirts, form a colorful background for the men.* (It is interesting to note that the best woman dancer of this troupe, Tamara Golovanova, wears men's clothes in her spectacular dances.) The all-women troupe of Beryozka dancers, also from Russia, while charming in a self-conscious girlish way which would have pleased our grandmothers, excelled only in a kind of stately glide in which their long hampering skirts hid the movement of their feet, creating an effect which, but for some shawl waving, can only be described as insipid. *Thus the superiority of the male folk dancer in his trousers over the female in her skirt is affirmed by these two types of Russian dancing.*

About the fourteenth century in Europe, especially in Italy, another form of dancing began to develop which derived from the religious and comedic dances in the festivals of ancient Greece and later on, Rome. In these dances, a story was told dramatically by pantomime, accompanied by music or songs. The Italian form of pantomime dancing was an outgrowth of the entertainment provided by the courtiers in the courts, and court costumes of the day were used by the dancers, who were amateurs. This was the beginning of the Italian ballet.

As in the theatre, so in the dance and ballet the costumes worn contribute to the self-confidence and beauty of the performer. The history of ballet itself includes two important conflicts in which clothing played an important role. *These were the conflicts for superiority between the amateur dancers and the professionals, and later on between the ballerinas and the male dancers.*

Beginning with the amateurs, it is generally thought that ballet was introduced from Italy into France by Catherine de Medici and danced by her courtiers. Under her auspices in the year 1581, a ballet was performed in Paris entitled *Ballet Comique de la Reine*, probably the first complete ballet in the modern sense. According to Lillian Moore, an authority on the subject, Jacques Patin, who designed the costumes for this ballet, "relied very closely on the court fashions of his time; the dresses were extremely long and heavy, rich, even pompous, and laden with embroidered pearls and jewels. It would have been impossible to execute strenuous or complicated dance steps in such costumes, but they were appropriate to the limited technical accomplishments of the courtiers who participated in the spectacle."

Daniel Rabel, a daring innovator, invented extraordinary costumes including those for the Hermaphrodites in *La Dousirière de Billebahaut*. These would be novel even today, for they were divided down the center, and the dancer wore a male costume on one side of the body and female on the other. As ballet became more popular as court entertainment, distinguished dramatists and musicians wrote for it. Among these were Molière, who wrote several ballet interludes as well as ballet comedies such as *The Would-Be Gentleman* which included the famous Turkish ballet. Indeed, when Lully began to write the music for the ballet-plays of the period, ballets had already been danced by the entourage of the French court, with Henry IV and Louis XIV as performers. The combination of Louis XIV, Lully and Molière was irresistible, and *"le Grand Monarque"* danced in several ballet interludes. Lully was the first to insist on the ladies of the court joining in the dances. The ballet written by Molière, *The Dream of Sganarelle,* was reproduced by the Theatre Guild in a version in rhyme of *The School for Husbands* made by Arthur Guiterman and myself, with a ballet interlude staged by Doris Humphrey and Charles Weidman. Our prologue contained the following verse which described somewhat flippantly the goings-on at Versailles:

> "For, in the day when first our play was done—
> To be precise, in sixteen sixty-one—
> Pure drama would have placed too great a strain
> Upon the weary, overburdened brain,
> And so the stage allowed these light incursions,
> These gambols, lyrics, tricks and gay diversions
> Between the acts, which, in the modern way,
> We use as part and parcel of the play.
> And in the ballet-mask that you shall see,
> The King himself appeared, none else but he
> The *Grand Monarque!*—as one of the Egyptians,
> He had both court and players in conniptions,
> And earned—at least, received, as one may guess—
> Resplendent notices from all the press."

When Louis XIV became too fat to dance, the ballet was no longer popular at court. This was not surprising, since the ladies danced in their panniers and hoop skirts and were almost completely covered by full sleeves and ankle-length dresses. Professional dancers then began to replace the amateurs at the opera houses and other places of entertainment. While the innovator Jean Georges Noverre liberated the dance from the full stiffened costumes of his period (*circa* 1760), it was Marie Camargo (1710-1770) who first pioneered in providing costumes specially designed for the dance. However, according to modern standards, her very full skirts and slippers with heels fell far short of solving the problem of the female dancer who wanted to compete with the male.

Dancing, in which the masses originally participated in primitive societies and in Morris dancing and folk dancing, now developed into an entertainment provided by professional dancers, wearing special clothing adapted to ballet. European kings and princes vied with each other in supporting troupes of professional ballet dancers whose training began in early childhood in order to achieve the perfection called for by the great ballet companies. As a result, the enjoyment of ballet dancing became a diversion of the nobility and the upper classes. It is only within the first half of this century in England and the United States, through the unselfish efforts of such leaders as Lincoln Kirstein and George Balanchine of the New York City Ballet, Lucia Chase of Ballet Theatre, and Ninette de Valois of the Sadlers Wells Ballet (now the Royal Ballet of London), and their associates, that ballet has become a popular entertainment for the masses.

The development of point dancing or so-called toe dancing, now so characteristic of ballet, would not have been possible had it not been for the invention and development of special ballet shoes. When ballet dancing was performed completely by the amateurs, as at the Court of Louis XIV, there was a certain amount of rising on the toes by the dancers, but this was only momentarily and did not constitute

Toe dancing was made possible by inventing special ballet shoes. Left, unblocked shoe of 1862 worn by Emma Livry, ballerina of the Paris Opera. Right, Anna Pavlova's ballet shoe with familiar blocked toe strengthened with darning. (The Studio, London.)

Left, *Camargo, who first introduced clothing specially designed for the dance.* Right, *Taglioni, credited as the first to introduce dancing "on point" with specially designed ballet shoes.*

the style of dancing on points which developed later. It is generally believed that to Marie Taglioni is due the credit for introducing ballet or dancing on the points or toe dancing, but Lillian Moore states that Taglioni before her début had admired the strength of the work on points of an earlier Italian dancer, Amalia Brugnoli. Since Taglioni's début was in 1822, this would mean that toe dancing was invented by the Italians in the middle or latter part of the eighteenth century. According to Moore, "The ballet shoes of Taglioni's time were made of soft satin, taffeta, or kidskin, lined with linen or light canvas. They were not blocked at the tip, like the ballet shoes of today, but the ballerinas usually reinforced them with light darning, which made the shoe give a more solid support to the foot. In these light shoes Taglioni and her contemporaries did not do any pirouettes on the points, although they did execute *piques, pas de bourée,* and various positions like arabesques and attitudes, on the full point."

As a greater number of ballets came to be danced on point in the Romantic period, special ballet slippers were designed in order to support the muscles of the foot. These were not only strengthened under the arches, while remaining slightly flexible at the toes, but the dancers reinforced the fabric part of the slipper at the toe by coating it with spirit gum or a varnish which gave it strength.

Toe dancing enabled the dancer to defy the laws of gravity, so to speak, by rising off the ground on the toes and thus to create an illusion of an ethereal being differing from the rest of us earth-bound humans. This also made it possible to perform stories largely peopled by disembodied spirits, as in some of the old Romantic ballets such as *La Sylphide*. It represented another conquest over nature by the dancer. It also affirmed the superiority of the audience, which was not only enthralled by the beauty of the dance, but enjoyed an exclusive form of entertainment which could exist only by the support of the aristocracy and the monied classes. And also inherent in this appreciation of the art of ballet was the male satisfaction that ballerinas were able to perform these feats of motion with a definite impediment to their movements due to the unnatural use of the feet and toes. But though the ballerinas were able to move only in short steps simulating the fettered steps imposed on women by the wearing of French high heels, yet they now managed to make themselves incredibly free by overcoming the limitations imposed on their toes. *As a result they began to excel over the men in the brilliancy of their dancing. But the men still had the advantage costume-wise. So soon the ballerinas began to remove the bulk of their clothes!*

As a result, a revolution took place in the dresses worn by ballerinas which had important repercussions on public ideas of morality during the last century. The ballerinas first shortened the ballet skirt at the beginning of the Romantic period of ballet in Italy. Special bell-shaped dancing skirts thereafter made their appearance. These skirts were just above ankle length and shocked the more sedate members of the audience by their impropriety. But as the ballerinas desired to turn more and more rapidly, and thus rival the male dancers, they began to shorten the skirt and to shock the nineteenth-century audiences still more!

Development of the skirt into the tutu (of which there are many forms) proceeded from shock to shock as the skirts progressed higher and higher up the ballerina's legs. They revealed more and more of what were referred to as "limbs" in order to avoid using the horrifying word "legs," which in Victorian days was regarded as obscene when applied to women. In the step-by-step shortening of the tutu over the years, it first terminated below the knees, then above the

The tutu, or "powder-puff" frock, enabled the ballerinas to compete with the male dancers. Patricia Wilde and Jacques d'Amboise in "Native Dancers," New York City Ballet.

knees, then around the hip and then at the turn of the century it was so shortened that, according to Moore, "the tutu resembled a powder puff."

The purpose of this shortening of the tutu was not, as might be believed, to stimulate erotic interest in the ballerina, but just the opposite, for the more the dancer was clothed, the greater was the mystery, and the more was male curiosity aroused. While the less the dancer was clothed, the more she became an abstract figure with the attention focused on the beauty of the dance and freedom of movement of the dancer.

After reaching the powder-puff stage, this last vestige of female adornment has been removed entirely by many choreographers in recent years, with the result that the girls look almost like the boys, thus abolishing sex as much as possible from the ballets in which they appear so costumed. It will probably never be possible to discard the tutu altogether, since among its other advantages, it transformed the ballerina into a symbol, and made possible many forms of abstract ballet. The tutu was invented solely for the ballet, and sitting or lying down while wearing it is most impractical. The special value of this costume is shown by the fact that after a hundred years, it is still in use. Perhaps it will gradually work its way down around the ankles again, in order to reintroduce erotic interest into ballet from which it has been so largely banished. Indeed, in some ballet circles the female figure with its functional protuberances is looked upon somewhat with disdain, and since these cannot be discarded along with the tutu, the girls who look most like boys are greatest in evidence. To blame this on the dancers themselves is absurd, for it is only within the last few years that the breastless, sexless female ballet dancer has begun to appear.

The artificiality of the Italian ballet, with its dancing on points and its tutu, was to receive a rude shock in its ultimate impact on the less cultured peoples of Russia and the United States. When the great American dancer, Isadora Duncan, who had previously tossed aside her corsets and adopted the clothing and classic movements of the Greeks, reached St. Petersburg in 1907, she met with Fokine, the choreographer attached to the Imperial Russian Ballet. There came about a breaking down of old traditions and a revolution in ballet and costumes which, thanks to Fokine, Duncan and the great designer Leon Bakst, brought a new era of ballet into being in the modern Russian Ballet. Later on under the leadership of Serge Diaghilev this new concept was to spread over the entire world.

Ballet clothes which had followed the Italian form of tutu and leotards for generations took on a new splendor. While tailored for fullest freedom of movement in dancing, they began to represent all kinds of real or mythical figures. Bakst's oriental costumes for *Scheherazade* became classics and influenced the fashions of the day. Many world-famous artists such as Picasso, Roerich, Derain, Matisse and de Chirico designed costumes for Diaghilev's ballets, and their imaginations ran riot. Modern clothes were worn in Bakst's ballet *Jeux* (play) (1911) danced by Nijinsky, and Picasso's *Parade* (1917) was the first to use American modern dress. It remained for such American pioneers as Ted Shawn (*Cowboy Ballet,* 1920),

Masked dancers of New Guinea, Latmul people: Left, *dancer dressed as bird.* Right, *dancer dressed as masked hunter. (American Museum of Natural History.)*

Eugene Loring (*Billy the Kid,* 1938), Lew Christensen (*Filling Station,* 1938), Marc Platoff (*Ghost Town,* 1939), Agnes de Mille (*Rodeo,* 1942), Jerome Robbins (*Fancy Free,* 1944) to popularize contemporary American characters in ballet by using clothes simulating modern reality in these productions. Balanchine introduced modern costumes in musical comedies with *Slaughter on Tenth Avenue* (1936). Agnes de Mille also popularized character-costume ballet in the musical theatre with *Oklahoma!* (1943), and *Carousel* (1945), followed by many other American choreographers. The famous Bolshoi Ballet, after over forty years of Soviet subsidy, provided nothing as original or revolutionary as Bakst's costumes for the old Ballet Russe of Russian capitalist days.

American exponents of the modern dance have tended to use leotards (named after the famous tailor of the French opera), or what has been described as "long underwear," for their dance clothes. Nor has this always been a disadvantage. The dancers often express beauty of movement more effectively when they appear in practice tights or leotards which permit free use of their limbs at rehearsal. Whatever is gained by the use of costume is often lost in

A South Sea Islanders' dance at Waitangi. Native Rarotongans sing and dance for visitors.

impeding freedom of movement. I remember particularly that the main ballet of *Oklahoma* in rehearsal clothes seemed far more effective as dance than when the girls wore the long ungainly dresses which hid their body movements from the view of the audience.

Other forms of dance which could not have developed without special clothes to enhance the pictorial effect and importance of the dancer include the peculiar butterfly dances of Loie Fuller in which special costumes were used to fill space and increase the size and grace of the dancer. On the other hand, the religious dances of the Greeks may be said to have provided the inspiration for the type of plain costumes used by Martha Graham, Mary Wigman and others, whose introverted emotionalism was a rebellion against conventional ballet, and who carried this to the point of wearing sandals or no shoes at all in protest against the ballet toe shoe. They were in direct contrast with such extroverted dancers as Gilda Gray, with her grass skirts simulating a cascading waterfall, whose dancing was related to the rhythms of the South Seas. Ruth St. Denis and Ted Shawn introduced the costumes of the East and the theatre gestures of Del Sarte, thus making a unique contribution to the American dance theatre which still persists in its influence. The rhythm and clothing of African Negro ritual dances finds its modern offspring in the dances and costumes of Katherine Dunham and Pearl Primus. The use of a chorus of women all dressed exactly alike and all moving in precise unison has also created a new type of dance in which costume plays an important role; these originated with the London Tiller girls followed by the American Rockettes.

A peculiar marriage has taken place between the African, Spanish and native American-Indian dances in the various Latin American countries, and given birth to such offspring as the rhumba, the cha-cha and the mambo. The Spanish dances, costumed with the dignity and discretion of a proud and somber race, have given birth to the stately Latin American tango, while the Andalusian gypsy dancers in their long flounced dresses have demonstrated that there is often more sex in a rarely displayed ankle than in the ribald undulations of a vulgar muscle dancer.

Seekers after sensation in the dance, whatever they may find in its superficial aspects, are mystically led to the roots of most of these dance forms, which are either deeply religious or involved in the mysteries of life with its rhythmic pattern of reproduction from generation after generation leading from the remote past into the future. *In all aspects of the dance, clothes perform all their multitudinous functions which distinguish us from the animal world, as well as provide us with the aesthetic pleasures of flowing drapes, billowing skirts, and the colorfully-clad limbs of dancers in motion.*

Leaving the world of dance, we pass to fantasy in art and literature in which man has felt a need to create an imaginary world peopled with supernatural creatures either visible or invisible, friendly or unfriendly. *When these creatures are friendly to us, and therefore obviously superior creatures, we flatter ourselves and them by dressing them more or less in clothes like our own. When they are our enemies, we regard them as our inferiors, and we usually show that they are more like the animals than we are.* Among our imagined friends are the fairies, the pixies, the gnomes, the angels, the elves and the leprechauns. While the fairies and gnomes are divided into good and bad, and the pixies, elves and leprechauns are prone to play tricks on us, we have nevertheless created them in our own image and use them mostly to entertain our children. To preserve their innocent appeal, we have had to dress these little creatures since Victorian times with a full complement of clothes, thus avoiding any embarrassment which might arise if they appeared naked.

However, we usually make an exception with Cupid, whose innocence often comes into question.

While their clothes vary from generation to generation, we tend to attire our fairies in short skirts, and our elves, pixies, gnomes and leprechauns in jackets, knee breeches and little peaked caps. To give our angels dignity, we clothe them in Grecian robes which set off their wings and trail gracefully as they fly through the atmosphere. We rob these good creatures of the visible sexuality which we usually deplore and hide in ourselves, and we thus make ourselves their kin.

On the other hand, we number among our enemies the imps, devils, gremlins and other naughty creatures, and when we depict them, we usually provide them with animal appendages, such as horns, hooves and tails which we ourselves do not possess and do not wish to possess. *Like the creatures of the animal world, they help to build our feeling of superiority as Homo sapiens, the non-animal.*

A new type of mythological creature is being created today by "science fiction." This is the Space-Man and Space-Woman who are usually depicted in aviator's uniform and helmet which are studded with imaginary scientific instruments for seeing, hearing and navigating among the stars. These imaginary persons dwell in the future and are part of the phenomena known as hero-worship, which is in effect the worship of the superior man. Children achieve a vicarious feeling of superiority by wearing the clothes of these imaginary heroes, or even of real heroes of the past who enjoy a transient popularity, such as Davy Crockett, whose coonskin hat was recently reproduced and worn by millions of children in the United States. The happiness conferred on children by wearing these outfits, such as "Hopalong" Cassidy cowboy clothes, again testifies to the effect of clothing in contributing to the feeling of superiority.

It is impossible in the confines of this book to do more than touch upon the functions of clothes to show the superiority of the wearer in paintings and sculptures. The clothing shown in such works of art is not necessarily an authentic depiction of the actual clothes worn. What is carved in marble or painted on canvas may differ from the real garments worn for a number of reasons: (1) the art of the period is nonrealistic, or expressionistic, (2) the clothing depicted in the painting or sculpture is stylized, or (3) the clothing shown is the personal expression of the artist. A full discussion of the subject would involve going far beyond the confines of this examination.

The Radio City Music Hall Rockettes, world-famous precision dancers dressed exactly alike, whose clockwork routines are made more effective by the uniformity of their costumes. (Impact Photos, Inc.)

People show their desire for immortality by having portraits made of themselves, which, together with other works of art, form a valuable source of information about costume for experts. James Laver of the Victoria and Albert Museum, London, owes some of his great knowledge of costume to the fact that part of his career was spent as an art expert which required him to be able to determine the genuineness or date of a painting within a few years by the costumes depicted.

When considering a portrait by such masters as Van Dyck, Rembrandt van Ryn, Gainsborough, Reynolds, and the dozens of other masters of portraiture who might be mentioned, it is important to remember that usually only individuals from the wealthy classes could afford to be portrayed. Consequently the artist with few exceptions painted their subjects dressed in their most impressive clothes. Sometimes when a painter had unattractive subjects, he concerned himself with compensating for the ugliness of the sitter by concentrating on the beauty of the clothing. Goya painted the entire family of Carlos the Fourth of Spain, including an ugly wife, Marie Louisa, and six ugly children. His concentration on the splendor of their costumes makes one forget the lack of beauty in the subject. *In most old portraits, the goal of superiority plays the principal role in the selection of the wearing apparel portrayed, which usually indicates rank and aesthetic beauty, and where the subject warrants, sex appeal.* Some of the exceptions, such as Frans Hals, Breughel, Hogarth and others, gave us some vivid impressions of what the common folk wore. Being realists, their use of clothing is probably as authentic as it is possible to find.

When we consider the religious paintings of the Renaissance, we are struck with the almost universal depiction of rich flowing robes which could not possibly have been worn in Biblical times by the

Greek Maenads depicted in an ecstatic dance. From a 5th-century pyxis. (National Museum, Athens.)

This picture of two women of Ancient Greece putting away their clothes is a masterpiece by the famous vase painter, Douris. From an Attic red-figured cup (kylix), about 470 B.C. (Metropolitan Museum of Art.)

poverty-stricken Apostles and other figures of Bible history. We realize that the artists who painted these pictures have thrown reality to the four winds, and in order to endow their subjects with superior qualities, they have dressed them in superior costumes which would appear ridiculous but for the cloak of reverence these invisibly add to their subjects.

There is little to be said about the use of clothing in the various schools of modern painting except that individual artists use it for their individual purposes. Thus Picasso, in his blue period, dresses his subjects in blue clothes to convey the emotions engendered by his pictures. We learn very little about clothing in abstract art, any more than we do in the stylized art of the Neolithic Age.

The desire to perpetuate oneself by a statue carved in hard stone or marble has existed almost as long as men have worn clothes. Since the dawn of history men have made statues in which clothing has played an important role. From the statues of the Nile gods to the Pharaohs of Egypt, from the gods of Olympus in Greece to the politicians of the Forum in Rome, the sculptors have provided statues in which clothing or drapery is usually present to emphasize the importance or rank of the subject. And while the ancient sculptors of historic times have often made statues of complete nudes, statues or bas-reliefs of people wearing clothing or drapery are far more numerous. This corresponded with the general wearing of clothes by the populace, the gods, and the important peoples of these periods.

The great skill of the Greeks in depicting draped clothing reached a high point in the fifth century B.C. and in the great works of sculpture such as the Symposium of the Gods from the east frieze of the Parthenon (now in the British Museum, London). Some of the finest sculptures of clothing the world has ever known was made in this period by artists such as Phidias and Praxiteles. And the skill in depicting clothing in statuettes also reached a high point in the delicately modelled terra-cotta Tanagra figures in which the flowing drapes made of clay not only have the feeling of clothing but also reveal the body beneath the robes. The exquisite paintings of clothing on pottery also became a great art.

Changes took place in the Greek attitude towards clothes from time to time, as shown by their statues. In the sixth century Greek statuary, other than that depicting the gods and goddesses, was largely devoted to making Temple Virgins which were fully clothed and were placed as votary offerings in the temples; and also to making statues of athletes and boys, all quite naked, which were said to be used to make propaganda for the Olympic games. A successful competitor was sometimes given a statue of himself as a prize. But during the fourth century a few depictions of nude women began to appear in statuary and in the pictures on pottery. The reason that Greek women almost always wore clothing in statues or pictures on pottery prior to this time may be due to the fact that in an essentially male civilization (in which there was considerable homosexuality) women were kept covered and hobbled with freedom of movement sufficient only to permit them to work in the homes and in the fields.

While considering the subject of clothing in art, it is perhaps not
a digression to discuss the reason why so many painters and sculptors
derive creative pleasure in depicting men and women without their
clothes, yet stop at complete nudity. Since their purpose is to portray
the aesthetic beauty of their subject, they usually find that the complete uncovering of the human body is embarrassing because it brings
mankind's lower centers too prominently into view. *Conventional
morality plays a part in this, but more important is the artist's wish
to depict his subject without offending against mankind's desire for
superiority over the animal world.*

Attention has already been drawn to the unwillingness of many
painters to paint nude subjects with pubic hair and hair under the
armpits. In statues of men and women, where the skillful sculptor
was easily able to portray the hair on the head of his subject, the
tuft of pubic hair is often omitted. Why were so many masters of
sculpture, both ancient and modern, so often unwilling to represent
this patch of hair in marble? And in painting, why did such painters
as Michelangelo, Raphael, Botticelli and a host of other artists of the
Renaissance nearly always omit this from their nudes? Or cover it
with a convenient hand, drape or flower? There seems to be a simple
answer. They were idealizing the human body and thought the pubic
hair made it aesthetically unbeautiful and "animal." By omitting it,
they avoided emphasizing our basic inferiority which would become
visible if their nudes were portrayed truthfully. In this matter some
artists in the Middle Ages followed the dictates of the Church. In
ancient Greece, however, there were no such religious restrictions,
yet the same attitude toward pubic hair in female nudes prevailed.
It is believed that women in ancient Greek days habitually shaved
the pubic hair as well as the hair under the armpits. Shaving under
the armpits is a common practice in the United States today for
women in most levels of society.

In partial confirmation of the above, Salvadore Dali, an experi-
menter in every direction in art, assured me recently that a nude
painted with pubic hair as she existed in nature was thought by
many painters to be contrary to art, for the eye of the viewer would
be drawn immediately to her sexual regions instead of to the aesthetic
beauty of her body. Many of our earlier artists idealize the nude as
a revelation of themselves, and usually cannot bear to sully her too
vividly with sex. The nude in such paintings does not actually uncover her body. She hides behind the painter's idealization of it,

Early painters of the nude usually managed to place a hand, a leaf, a drape or a twig over areas which related the subject too closely to the animal world. Giorgione's Venus, Pinakothek, Dresden.

from which he removes the "sexual" qualities, thus fooling himself that mankind alone of all God's creatures, is above sex. However, many of the modern realistic painters who are not interested in beauty deformed by morality depict their models with all the hair in all the places where nature provides it—except on the male chest! And civilization seems to have survived the shock.

The covering of the sexual parts of a nude statue is a popular pastime of puritans of all denominations the world over, and it extends to the Vatican as already noted. The association of our sexual parts with shame and sin constitutes the essential reason for this vandalism, which again confirms our principal thesis, that in our Hebraic-Christian civilization we seek by every means to hide our relationship to the animal world and to relate ourselves to God. A further reason also exists for this suppression in painting and sculptures, and is expressed by Sigmund Freud as follows: "I have no doubt that the concept of 'beauty' is rooted in the soil of sexual stimulation and signified originally that which was sexually exciting. The more remarkable, therefore, is the fact that the genitals, the sight of which provokes the greatest sexual excitement, can really never be considered beautiful." Very different from the artists of the West are the Hindu sculptors of Khatmandu in Nepal. Here the lingam or phallus, symbolizing the god Siva, is a subject of constant worship, and innumerable statues or stones carved to represent lingams are on display in the temples and streets. Possibly there is some connection between this fact and the artistic accomplishments of the Newari people of Nepal whose outstanding artists and sculptors have greatly influenced the art and architecture of China, Tibet and India.

Returning to Western art and our attitude towards nudity, Sir Kenneth Clark, noted British art critic, disagrees with the contention that there is a need to suppress the erotic feelings of the viewer of pictures of the nude. On the contrary, "no nude, however abstract, should fail to arouse in the spectator some vestige of erotic feeling, even though it be only the faintest shadow—and if it does not do so, it is bad art and false morals." We can all agree with Sir Kenneth when he states: "It is widely supposed that the naked human body is in itself an object upon which the eye dwells with pleasure and which we are glad to see depicted. But anyone who has frequented art schools and seen the shapeless, pitiful model that the students are industriously drawing will know this is an illusion. The body is not one of those subjects which can be made into art by direct transcriptions—like a tiger or a snowy landscape. A mass of naked figures does not move us to empathy, but to disillusion and dismay. We do

Modern painters show their revolt against the conventions by painting their nudes as nature made them. Gauguin's "Nevermore."

not wish to imitate; we wish to perfect. We become, in the physical sphere, like Diogenes with his lantern looking for an honest man; and, like him, we may never be rewarded."

John Mason Brown, the drama and art critic, writing on the same occasion, an exhibition of "The Nude in Art" at the Wildenstein Galleries, remarks: "A naked person is merely a person without clothes; a nude is a figure, however naked, in which the artist rather than the model is revealed. The human body is monotonously standard in its equipment. One of the glories of art is how changing is the unchanging human form as seen by different artists in different periods and countries or even in the same period."

While the depiction of nudes will probably continue to be part and parcel of the output of the artist, both now and in the future, it may be noted that the artist follows life in the use of clothing to tell us what he wishes us to know about his subject. And if he wishes only to create an impression, he can make his nude descend a staircase or cut her up into little pieces and mix her clothes into a pastiche along with her features. But whatever may be the vagaries of the individual artist in this field, clothing plays the same kind of role in respect to inferiority, rank or aesthetic beauty as it does in most of the other fields of art and life.

PART VII

CONCLUSIONS

Le vertugadin ainsi appelé par corruption — le véritable terme pour désigner ce jupon, premier et curieux ancêtre de la crinoline — étant « vertu-gardien » (xvıᵉ siècle).

Le grand panier d'apparat décrivant jusqu'à cinq aunes de tour et qui, suivant ses formes, portait des noms multiples : *boute-en-train, gourgandine, criarde*, etc. (1777).

La bétise (deux petits paniers remplaçant le grand) avec un panier postérieur appelé crûment *faux-cul* et, à l'étranger : *cul de Paris*, puisque la mode venait de France (1785).

La crinoline, c'est-à-dire le jupon-ballon à armature d'acier ayant eu pour origine, en 1850, *les polissons* (titre suffisamment indicatif), puis *la tournure*, puis *le jupon empesé* (1856).

Monstrosities of fashion: Extremes of fashion usually make women physically useless for work. Upper left, the 16th-century farthingale; right, the grand pannier of 1777. Lower left, "La Bétise" with side panniers, 1785; right, the crinoline, 1856. Pictures are from the Paris L'Illustration, 1857.

CHAPTER 19

Fashions and Foolishness

Fashion has been attacked for generations as a wasteful frivolity by which men and women, and particularly women, seek to show their social superiority over others by frequently changing the prevailing mode. That this is frivolity is sheer nonsense!

Is fashion actually the useless wasteful hoyden she is so often accused of being by the moralists? Would the world be ever so much better off if we did not tolerate the hussy? Would women become more learned, more accomplished, more useful, more capable and more worthy, without fashion? We do not have to look far for the answer. *Hundreds of millions of women live in the Arab countries where fashions change very slowly, and in India, Indonesia and other parts of Asia, where there are no changing fashions to make them frivolous as in the West. What have the women of these countries, released from the compulsion to spend time and energy in following fashion, accomplished in their countries as compared with ours? They have no equality with men, and practically no participation in any of the professions, nor in politics. They are not enlightened as to the education of their children, nor on sanitation. They have no freedom of expression in the arts and no special laws for their protection. In fact they are, with notable exceptions, almost chattels, and a thousand years behind their sisters of the West.* Blame it on their social or religious systems if you please, but since fashion has played an integral part in Western society for nearly a thousand years, *we may well claim that the feeling of superiority it has engendered in our women has been at least partly responsible for their ultimately achieving equality or near-equality with men in most of the fields in which they work and play together.*

285

Even in Soviet Russia where fashions for women are only just beginning to appear, and women enjoy substantial equality with men, many women are also made to perform heavy manual labor on the roads and in the fields. Conversely, in Persia, Turkey and some other Moslem countries, the wearing of fashionable Western clothes by upper-class women has been accompanied by freedom from age-old traditions. *It may therefore be stated as a general rule that fashion in the modern world is an accompaniment to the higher status of women which is emerging everywhere.*

In addition to enabling the so-called leaders of "Society" to distinguish themselves by their clothes from those whom they regard as their social inferiors, fashion also enables the clothing manufacturers to make clothes obsolete before they are worn out, so that those who can afford to do so will replace them by the new mode. As a result great industries have been made possible in the field of clothing. Fashion also serves to stimulate attraction between the sexes and to satisfy the human need for change. The more rapidly the alleged social inferiors copy the clothes of the "upper crust," the more rapidly do the fashions change, to the delight of those who benefit from it. Fashion is thus an endless game of "follow the leader," with the leader constantly changing her clothes as soon as they no longer distinguish her from those who are following her. *Fashion thus enables men and women to achieve and then maintain the goal of superiority which is one of the chief reasons we wear clothes.*

Who sets the fashions? Formerly it was the monarchy, the aristocracy, persons of prestige, and the so-called dandies, such as Beau Brummel. Today, it is apt to be the eccentric Paris fashion designers aided and abetted by well-dressed Hollywood or Broadway actresses, rather than the leaders of society—especially since society has no fashion leaders in the sense that it once had. Instead, we have our ten best-dressed American women, whose special good taste in clothes lead them to select for themselves what other smartly dressed women would like to copy.

The need of humans for change is one of the most important factors in the phenomenon of fashion. Man's need for change also extends to man-made products, and manufacturers advertise at an immense expense the invention of new and better models to which the customers are exhorted to change.

Due to the stimulus of modern advertising and the rapid improvements in all kinds of goods, we are constantly replacing old models by new at an accelerated speed. We barely install a Hi-Fi record player before we replace it with Stereophonic Sound, which in turn will be replaced by tomorrow's latest gadget, as we rush from change to change. The success of the American automobile industry, with its hundreds of thousands of workers, depends on bringing out a new model each year which is more desirable than the last year's model, so that users may be tempted to change to new cars almost before their old cars are broken in! Alas, one bad guess in American automobile fashions can rock the economy of the entire Western world. This seems to be carrying fashion too far for comfort!

More than in any other field, this desire for change extends to clothes, and the opportunity for change is far greater than with any other product, since there are very few articles of clothing which, if worn constantly, will last more than a short time. All except the poorer classes discard their clothes long before they are worn out. On the surface they do this because they are tired of them and no longer derive the pleasure from wearing them which they originally experienced when the clothes were new. The unconscious reason however, is that the wearer can no longer "see" or be aware of his old clothes, as was the case when they were new, and they no longer contribute to his sense of superiority. This is well illustrated by the fact, as stated in the opening chapter, that a woman commonly remarks, "I was feeling depressed, so I went shopping and bought myself a new hat." By doing this she will not only "see" herself anew, wearing a new hat or dress in which she feels attractive, but she will attract the admiration of others who were so accustomed to seeing her in her older clothes that they no longer particularly noticed her or them. And if her new clothes happen to be "in fashion," her pleasure will be increased by the knowledge that she is participating in the latest mode, along with other fortunate people, thus contributing even more to her feeling of superiority.

Out of these factors has evolved the social phenomenon known as fashion which is the foundation of the gigantic clothing industry which at the present time employs well over two million workers in the United States and, after food and housing, is our third largest industry in terms of the money spent on it. Estimates compiled by the Couture Group of the New York Dress Institute, the major source of fashion news in America, and furnished by its director, Eleanor Lambert, show that women spend eleven billion dollars a year for their clothes—almost half the total of the twenty-two billion dollars spent on apparel for the entire family in 1957. A similarly huge amount is spent on merchandising and other services. Food, housing and clothing are the three largest expenditures of the average American, and in that order. Between 8% to 9% of the American income is spent for apparel. When we add to the above the figures for the rest of the Western world, and remember that with the increase of population the world figures will grow greater and greater as the years go by, we begin to appreciate the enormous importance of the action of those primitive ancestors of ours who were the first to encase their bodies in clothes. If Adam and Eve were the true and first inventors of clothes, as the Bible states, then we must credit them with starting a twenty to thirty billion dollar industry—something not even hinted at in Genesis!

Loud are the laments that fashion plays no such role with men. No less a fashion authority than the Federal Reserve Bank of Philadelphia is quoted in the *New York Times,* Nov. 27, 1958, as stating officially that "The lemming is a small, mousy animal which runs in packs over the Arctic tundra. The American male is more lemming than peacock. It could be that many women like their husbands to be dull dressers as a neutral background for their own finery. What really upsets the men's wear industry is not drabness but penny pinching," the Bank said. "If men spent as much of their income these days for clothing as they did in 1929, sales of men's wear from 1950 through 1957 would have been $20,000,000,000."

Fashion beats but a muffled roll call for the men, but for the women it thunders in waves like the flowing and ebbing of a great seasonal tide. Vast armies of men and women, fabric manufacturers, dress manufacturers, advertising agencies, fashion magazines, department stores and chain dress stores all add their energies to ensure that each wave of fashion design shall be first made select, then made popular, then made obsolete and then be rapidly succeeded by another and different one, so that all the vast machinery of creation, production and distribution shall be kept operating season after season and year after year at high capacity. Man has turned woman's whims in clothing into a vast social and economic machine which functions as a whole with a highly developed seasonal rhythm. Within this general pattern, however, it functions erratically and without control, some fashions remaining in existence for years at a time, and others like comets illuminating the sky for but a brief period. Still others turn back the clock of time and land the women of today into the clothes worn by their mothers and grandmothers. If there is any logic in the direction in which fashion marches, no one seems to have found it, except in the general rule that today's fashion is usually tomorrow's discard.

It has been already stated that once men relinquished the attributes of the flamboyant male birds and animals which made them appear aesthetically superior to their drab females, women were quick to step aggressively into the position of colorful superiority vacated by the men. And since, as Shaw has pointed out in his preface to *Man and Superman,* it is the female who pursues the male, the women of the future are quite unlikely to give up the advantages of fashion, one of the ultimate purposes of which is to aid them in persuading the reluctant male into continuing to play his role in marriage and procreation. *Modern man, who fools himself that he is playing the part of the aggressor, is always ready to retreat, and like the female bird, usually wears drab clothes which make him as inconspicuous as possible.*

The question may well be raised here, is the improved status and freedom of Western women due to the beauty and aesthetic superiority of their clothing over those of the men? Because of the confidence and independence gained by women through wearing beautiful clothes, they have greatly improved their position in life in relation to men. *The feeling of bravura, to use a stage expression, which many women experience when they are well or fashionably dressed, gives them a self-confidence which often urges them to seek positions to which fifty years ago men would have been reluctant to admit them. Thus women, attired flamboyantly like the highwayman or the pirate of old, is already taking a more aggressive attitude in all phases of modern living than her demure grandmother in her hampering crinolines.*

The wearing of fashionable clothes by all classes of society is a modern American phenomenon. In most nations of the past, the poor and the rich have been very sharply divided and as Hurlock points out, "where the rich wear clothing far beyond the reach of the poor, there is little or no imitation, and no necessity for the rich wearer to change to a new fashion until he is ready." Democracy and the new status of the classes has changed all this, and as a result, fashion changes much faster as imitation becomes more rapid and widespread and dress-design piracy more prevalent. (There is still no effective law to prevent such piracy in the United States, although

Monstrosities of fashion: Highly encumbering was the bustle, often combined with the crinoline. Left, fashionable dress with bustle, 1871. Right, unique steel-wire bustle frame worn under dress, 1881. (Metropolitan Museum of Art, Costume Institute.)

I and others worked on a committee of the New York Merchants Association over twenty-five years ago to secure the passage of such legislation despite the continuous opposition of the large department stores.)

Many moralists in the past have expressed strong disapproval of fashion. William Hazlitt, the English philosopher, has expressed the following in his essay, "On Fashion," and no one has ever said it more sourly: "Fashion constantly begins and ends in the two things it abhors most, singularity and vulgarity. It is the perpetual setting up and then disowning of a certain standard of taste, elegance, and refinement, which has no other foundation or authority than that it is the prevailing distraction of the moment, which was yesterday ridiculous from its being new, and tomorrow will be odious from its being common. . . . It is not anything in itself, nor the sign of anything but the folly and vanity of those who rely upon it as their greatest pride and ornament. It takes the firmest hold of weak, flimsy, and narrow minds, of those whose emptiness conceives of nothing excellent but what is thought so by others, and whose self-conceit makes them willing to confine the opinion of all excellence to themselves and those like them."

What can be said in reply to Hazlitt's indictment and in defense of this seasonal tide which every year pours its spring, summer, fall and winter fashions into the retail stores and thence onto the willing backs of the women of the Western world?

First of all, to put it bluntly, fashion whets the sexual appetite. No matter how much we delude ourselves with the belief that man is the sexual animal *par excellence,* he often needs help. Living under

Monstrosities of fashion: Crinoline frames for mother and daughter, advertised as "Improved shapes for summer." M. Freudenthal & Co., London, 1861.

a system of monogamous marriage, when the same woman is expected to perform the role of domestic house manager, mother to her children and mistress to her husband year after year, it is not surprising that the stimulus to sex for the tired businessman or industrial worker needs reactivating from time to time. *Woman can achieve this most readily by changing her appearance by wearing the "latest" in clothes, which gives her a new skin and makes her a new woman, thus arousing her husband's lagging interest and taking some of the monotony out of monogamy! And if fashion helps to hold the home together, shall Hazlitt speak so harshly of it?*

The same purpose achieved by fashion in marriage is also achieved in courtship. Fashion either subtly or blatantly accentuates different sexually exciting parts of the feminine "bag of tricks" and covers them and reveals them at the same time. Some experts claim that there is a cycle in such accentuation, that it is the breasts which come in for the fashion treatment one season, the legs another season, and so on up and down the line, there being seven points in all. Dr. Bergler lists these as follows: "The breasts (neckline), waist (abdomen), hips, buttocks, legs, arms and length (or circumference) of the body itself." (Since women have two of almost everything, I count this as twelve instead of seven.) In the case of a long courtship, with all this accentuation of different parts of her body produced by means of fashion, no girl should ultimately fail in dragging her man to the altar. So should fashion be condemned when it plays so large a part in encouraging marriages and increasing the birth rates of the nations?

It has been pointed out earlier that an important unconscious motive for the design of women's clothes has been to make her movements difficult, and fashion has done a great deal to help men in this sinister purpose. Practically every extreme in fashion has resulted in making women more helpless and uncomfortable. The farthingale (a kind of sausage surrounding the waist under the skirt), the hoop skirt, the crinoline, the bustle, the pannier and the hobble skirt, all effectively hampered the free movement of women and made it difficult for them to engage in the pursuits of men. When the fashion innovators have introduced these extreme gowns from time to time, the men have treated them as hilarious jokes, as witness the cartoons on the subject in the humorous journals of the day. But men have done nothing effective to discourage such fashions, which unconsciously build up their own sense of masculine importance and enable them to remark with chuckles on the antics of "those silly women!"

This male attitude is well illustrated by a "Song of the Hoop" which appeared in *Harper's New Monthly Magazine* in 1857 on the subject of the exaggerated Victorian hoop skirt:

> Sailing down the crowded street,
> Scraping everyone they meet,
> With a rushing whirlwind sound,
> Muffled belles around abound,
>   Hoop! Hoop! Hoop!
> What a vast, expansive swoop!

As to the damage done by such skirts the song continues:

> Hoops that spread out silken skirts,
> Hanging off from silly flirts.
> Sweeping off the public lands,
> Turning over apple-stands;
> Felling children to the ground,
> As they flaunt and whirl around.
>   Hoop! Hoop! Hoop!
> What a vast, expansive swoop!

Are the women really "silly" to adopt such monstrosities and abnormalities in clothes under the guise of fashion? By following fashion a woman can proclaim and maintain her social position, her rank and her sexual attractiveness to her husband (and others), and if unmarried, to her admirers. It also enables her to win the approval and admiration of her women friends, for whom she often dresses even more than for the men. Is she to give all this up simply because a fashionable dress designer has designed an idiotic new mode which has somehow "caught on?" Is she going to continue to wear her dull old clothes which are now *démodé,* and make herself conspicuous and old-fashioned to her husband and her friends by refusing to follow the new fashion? Perish the thought! She is a creature of common sense and knows her values. *She would dress in flags, balloons and bath mats if fashion so decreed, rather than give up the solid foundations on which her home, her husband and her position in society rests.*

Another reason why men have seldom protested too violently against the foolishness of some of women's fashions, is because this flatters them into believing that they belong to the superior sex. And women are usually wise enough to let them delude themselves. But there are more sinister reasons for dressing women in idiotic costumes, and these are due to the idiosyncrasies of some of the men who design them.

It has been shown by recent studies of Dr. Bergler in New York that many of the male dress designers hate women, and take a special pleasure in making fools of them, knowing that the position of these women in their own circles will be threatened if they do not follow the mode, no matter how ridiculous. A couple of fashionable hat designers who led the mode in hats in New York City were heard a few years ago giving vent to bursts of shrill derisive laughter as they decided to introduce women's hats trimmed with bunches of carrots, turnips, radishes and other vegetables. They did, and for one silly season, they were all the rage!

The present fad of dieting, at once so healthful and so harmful, is part of fashion's method of making its votaries uncomfortable in order to attain superiority. The woman of today often tries to fit her body to her clothes rather than her clothes to her body. Thus the wide posterior and pelvis necessary for bearing children, the buxom breasts necessary for feeding them, and the extra layer of subcutaneous tissue which nature has provided women for extra protection are sneered at and in older women are referred to contemptuously as "middle-aged spread."

The ancient desire for slenderness of the waistline existed in the ample bosoms of our mothers and grandmothers, and they obtained it by lacing in their corsets until they achieved the wasp waist. This did not reduce the bust or posterior, but actually increased them, since the laced-in abdomen had to be displaced either up or down. Instances of death caused by foolishly lacing-in too tightly were well known. This was said to be the cause of the death of the wasp-waisted Anna Held, the famous musical-comedy star of Ziegfeld's earliest Follies, who "could not make her eyes behave."

While we may deplore the extremes to which the dress designers' interest in "boyishness" has disfigured the female figure, we must not forget that we have come a long way since the days when Isadora Duncan discarded her corsets. This enabled her to dance on the stage with the freedom of movement which could come only after her mind had been freed from the conventions which shackled women up to that time and made their participation in sports and outdoor exercise almost impossible. By studying the beauty of move-

The whirligig of fashion: Left, a modern balloon skirt designed by Roxane, from the Samuel Winston Fall Collection, 1958. (Photo courtesy of Couture Group of the New York Dress Institute.) Right, a Paris balloon costume of about two hundred years earlier.

ment inherent in the wearing of ancient Greek costumes (which she modified by shortening the skirt) Isadora Duncan started a fashion in the dance which spread to all other activities of women and made the old-fashioned corset not only obsolete but anathema. Modern woman's desire to improve herself by keeping her body trim, healthy, and muscular cannot be laid solely to the effeminate male fashion designer. He has merely accentuated a trend which, in moderation, is more healthful than harmful. But watch him. He is a dangerous fellow and not to be trusted.

One of the most recent tricks played by these prankster designers upon our unsuspecting women was the innovation of the so-called "sack" or "chemise" dress which had the effect of making its wearer appear to be pregnant and almost ready for the delivery room. Millions of women all over the Western world, married and unmarried, appeared to be hovering on the brink of maternity. At first it

Sports in corsets: Left, *shooting costume,* Illustrated London News, *1900.*
Right, *tennis costume, New York, 1902.*

was thought that this fashion had a purpose—to obscure the fact that
the birth rate was rapidly increasing and paradoxically making it
appear that almost every woman from sixteen to seventy was pregnant. However, when virgins and school girls appeared to be in an
interesting condition, the men began to act as though this particular
fashion was not a matter for laughter. Did their disapproval have
any effect? Not a bit of it. The fashion disappeared almost as rapidly
as it began mainly because the shapeless dresses were easy to copy
in cheap materials, and the fashionable wearer could find the counterpart of the dress she was wearing everywhere on the backs of
women she felt to be beneath her. With millions of dollars jangling in
their pockets as the result of this successful prank, one wonders what
these designing fellows and their confrères in the women's clothing
business will think up next!

No one has yet successfully invented a garment by which a stout woman can appear thin, or *vice versa*, although some years ago I handled (in more senses than one) a corset invented in Australia which was intended to enable the wearer to reduce or increase her figure according to the passing fashion. The lady inventor explained it to me in this manner: "This year, Mr. Langner, waists are high, fronts are in, hips are out and backs are flat. First of all, we get the waist high by tying these strings; then we pull the front in by these short strings here. We let the hips out by unlacing here at the sides, and we pull the back in on these cords which tie at the back. That gives the wearer a flat back, which is quite my own idea. No other corset can give it!"

Fashion as it gyrates from pillar to post, plays some mean tricks on women whose bodies do not fit the mode. The extremely short skirts of the twenties which glamorized the girl with beautiful legs, were very hard on the girl who was not so favored by nature. But did the short-legged or bandy-legged girl flinch? She fought the mode by wearing a costume called the *robe de style* which covered her legs and exposed her more beautiful areas of pulchritude. There is recorded the instance in the twenties of a famous young actress whose bandy legs were revealed in the "flapper" costumes of the day, and realizing that this defect would interfere with her career, she had both legs broken and re-set in line again, a stoical remedy which I do not recommend to the fair sex in general.

Isadora Duncan, American dancer who liberated women from mental and physical corsets, 1911. (Photo by Otto, Paris.)

The fickleness of fashion: A fleeting fashion suggesting immanent maternity which arrived and departed within eighteen months. Left, the "trapeze," Suzy Perette, 1958. Right, the "sack," Anne Klein of Junior Sophisticates, 1958. (Photos courtesy Eleanor Lambert Company.)

It is fortunate that some of the best modes stay with us for years and are thus available at all times for the women who for financial, physical or other reasons do not wear the prevailing extremes of fashion. The late Claire McCardell, one of America's most daring fashion innovators, speaking of certain special sensible clothes for women states: "Fashion survives when it deserves to. Fashions somehow earn their right to survive. They prove dateless because they continue to play the same role and consequently reappear again and again. They *stay* becoming and comfortable."

Should we abolish fashion if we could? The alternative to fashion is the uniform, against which humanity eventually tends to rebel. Man has risen from the animal world by his faculty of reason and invention, and has differentiated his clothes from man to man, and from generation to generation. If there is to be a new goal for humanity, the uniform man or robot, then by all means do away with fashion, for it is the enemy of the stereotyped individual, the mass-produced mind and the unthinking human product of the propaganda machine. But since the world progresses by the progress of its individuals, as well as by its masses, there is reason for optimism in believing that fashion, which is the product of individual taste, exercised without compulsion, will continue to exist as it has in the past as a constructive force in the world of the future.

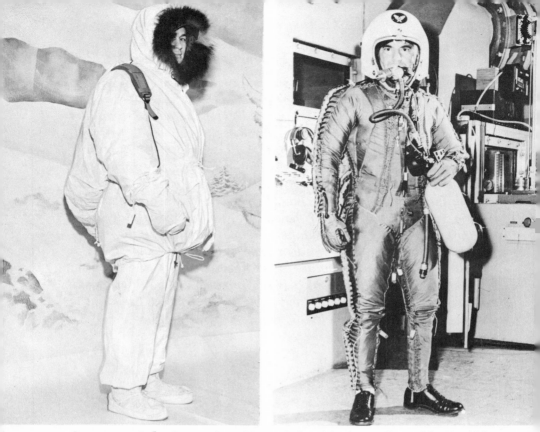

Costumes of the Space Age: Upper left, *U.S. Army dry cold ensemble.*
(U.S. Army photo.) Upper right, *high altitude pressure suit;* lower left,
Air Force fire-fighting wear; lower right, *plastic suit for fueling missiles*
with toxic fuels. (Official U.S. Air Force photos.)

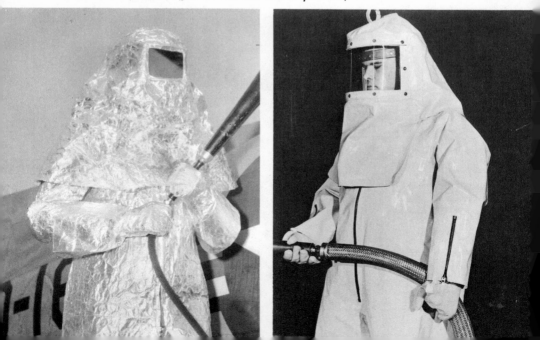

CHAPTER 20

Clothing and the Future

Prophecy is always dangerous, yet in the matter of the future of clothing we have a long past and a vivid present to aid us in arriving at our conclusions. So let us attempt to look into the future, for as a wise man said not so long ago, we shall be spending the rest of our lives in it!

Man's immediate challenge is the conquest of poverty, space and disease. We need have no doubts as to the final outcome. Poverty and its shabby clothing has almost disappeared from many parts of the American scene, and forces are at work to produce the same results everywhere as the problems of atomic power and consumer-goods production are mastered. We are already beginning to live in the space age and are inventing space clothing to explore the other planets or the moon. And with the amazing progress of biochemistry and medicine, we shall soon have a problem of geriatric clothing for extreme old age—bulging, sponge-rubber appurtenances which will enable our hundred-and-fifty-year-old citizens to bounce when they fall. So much for the near present. What of the distant future?

Perhaps, as Bernard Shaw so tellingly states in *Back to Methuselah,* when we live long enough to acquire some real wisdom, we shall partake of the tree of everlasting life which will make us "as gods," to quote Genesis again. *And the next era of civilization may be devoted not to our conquest of the material world, for that will have been already achieved, but to our conquest of ourselves, so that we may become as gods and enjoy to the full the beauties of earth and the brotherhood of man.* When this era arrives, man and his raiment will have come a long, long way on their joint adventure into the ultimate. *These somewhat mystical projections into the far future may be classified by some of my readers under the heading of "wish-ful thinking." Sometimes this is the best kind of thinking, since the wish must precede the event in order for it to come to pass.*

To return to our clothing in a more practical mood, it will be amusing to consider what kind of clothes we shall wear in the near future. For example, up to this time man has been unable to make himself independent of the weather by his clothing. Some brilliant inventor will undoubtedly provide him with an electronic suit equipped with a miniature air conditioner so that on pressing a button, air will flow over his body at the right temperatures to keep him cool in summer and warm in winter. This suit will be made of a material which, on pressing another button, will become transparent to permit the sun's rays to penetrate it, so that the wearer may take a sun bath even though fully dressed. This same material when used for women's clothing (or even men's) will enable them to display such of their charms through the transparency as may be appropriate to the occasion. And of course the push-buttons themselves may be magnetic, and used instead of ordinary buttons or other fasteners. As to our space suits, they are already with us with temperature and radiation control, and look far more convincing than they really are.

The acceleration of invention which is taking place in every field is pouring out a continuous stream of new chemical fibres, plastics, rubbers and a host of other clothing materials. We may even go to a tailor or couturier next year or the year after and have our clothes of hygienic porous plastics sprayed on us with spray guns to save the thousands of hours we spend in dressing and undressing! With the U. S. Army now trying to invent one garment to take the place of over a hundred items of clothing, anything is just around the corner!

But enough of this nonsense—or is it nonsense? As a young man I worked on the patent for a crude electrical selenium device for transmitting pictures through space. "This will probably be perfected in about a hundred years or so" was my wise conjecture at the time. Twenty-five years later it was in actual use as television.

Returning to our crystal ball in a more serious mood, what is the immediate future of clothing, and how will this affect the great problems with which the world is faced today? With this generation witnessing a gigantic rivalry between capitalism and communism, is it possible that clothing could affect this world struggle? The answer is "yes." Both systems are actually part capitalist, part socialist.

In the United States, England and other countries with similar systems, the income tax often results in the governments receiving far more than the profits of individual private businesses, since they collect taxes not only from the businesses, but also from all the workers in them and all the owners who receive dividends. Karl Marx never dreamed of anything as clever! And yet this neat trick takes place in all the so-called capitalist countries of the West, and still leaves enough funds remaining in the hands of the executive class and the working class to purchase clothes of good quality, and often more than a mere minimum.

Under the Soviet system, the capital and all industries, manufactured and agricultural products, etc., are state-owned but are actually controlled and distributed by the Communist party members acting as owners. These form a new governing and administrative class. However, the present policy of putting the major part of production into heavy goods instead of consumer goods has resulted in a working class which is shabbily dressed, with the consequent discontent which follows when a man or woman feels tired of or disgusted with his "skin." John Gunther in *Inside Russia Today* (1958) states: "What contributes most to Moscow's superficial look of drabness is people's clothes. These have certainly improved in the last few years, but they are still revolting. Their positive shabby manginess, as well as cheap quality and lack of color, is beyond description. The black worn by almost everybody is not a shiny, sparkling black, but a doleful black—dead, dreary. Russians are, as a result, acutely conscious of the clothes foreigners wear, particularly their shoes, and people on the street will offer to buy your shoes off your feet. The whole country has a fixation on shoes. Moscow is the city where, if Marilyn Monroe should walk down the street with nothing on but shoes, people would stare at her feet first.

"Some dedicated Russians are, I would say, actually proud of their plainness, even of their poverty. They *like* hardship. That mildewed suit is a badge of honor, because it proves virtue and sacrifice."

This "badge of honor" in relation to shabby, drab clothes is an example of the Soviet puritan mentality which makes a virtue of necessity. Since they cannot win superiority by wearing good clothes, they wear their mildewed clothes instead, and feel superior by so doing. A similar puritan attitude towards clothing existed in England during the Commonwealth of Oliver Cromwell, but it did not last.

There is evidence that the Soviet people will not long continue to be content with shabby bedraggled uniformlike clothes. Small fashion stores and fashion departments in the large department stores are beginning to appear, and indicate an acute desire on the part of the Soviet women of the Communist party upper class to follow fashion. The *New York Times* of May 26, 1957, shows illustrations of a fashion show in Moscow's GOUM, the largest department store in the U.S.S.R. According to the *Times,* "Backed by a five-piece band that blares out dance tunes, six women and two men model the new styles. Women's fashions are highlighted by the décolleté dress, officially recognized in the puritanical Soviet style world for the first time in twenty-five years. . . . The customer must see them modeled to decide whether to order them made in GOUM workrooms or purchase, for fifty kopecks, the patterns to run them up on the sewing machine at home." The sun-suits, décolleté evening dresses and women's sports suits with short bloomers would excite no special attention in this country, as they are all clumsy prototypes inspired by French and American models.

Fashion, with its "capitalist" overtones, is indeed spreading competitively in Russia and the satellite countries. *Since some of the commissars are being paid very large salaries, they and their wives are now spending considerable amounts on clothes which obviously must indicate superior social status.* Dedijer, the Yugoslav journalist who incurred the displeasure of Tito and the Soviets by telling the truth about the workings of communism, states: "The gap between the highest and lowest salaries in the U.S.S.R. is bigger than in many capitalist countries. Employees of the coercive apparatus have especially high salaries." *Since these high salaries are already being translated into better clothes for the Soviet upper class and especially the women, the Communists will ultimately have to yield to the natural desire of the less privileged classes to imitate them, or else face the possibility of greater internal discontent and ultimate hostility. And since nothing emphasizes the difference between classes as much as clothes, the empty dream of the so-called "classless society" of Marx will never be achieved. Instead, with the best clothes for the party members and the "New Class" and cheaper clothes for everyone else, communist society will more and more resemble Western capitalist society in the years to come.*

Khrushchev himself is now reported to have ordered Western-style fashionable clothes made by a tailor in Rome which will slim

Communism and clothing: Fashion show, GOUM department store, Moscow, 1957, with clothing showing Western influence. Left, "daring" haltertop sun dress. Right, man's smart Ivy League business suit. (New York Times, May 26, 1957; photos by Nicholas Tikhomiroff.) In the Soviet exhibition in New York in 1959 the models made up in beauty for what the dresses lacked in style.

his figure. Undoubtedly the other party chiefs will follow suit. Whereas the former Soviet professional proletarian was contemptuous of clothing, and despised a necktie with the disdain of the average American college boy, he is beginning to disrupt the entire Soviet economy by discarding his bell-bottom trousers and top boots and following his wife in becoming fashionable. Khrushchev's recent utterance on the competitive struggle between capitalism and communism was, "We shall see who eats the most and wears the best clothes." We of the West are wearing "the best clothes" at this moment, but we must accept the challenge without being smug, especially since Khrushchev has since stated that by 1970 Soviet Russia will have the highest standard of living in the world. *With over two hundred million people divided into classes by their clothing, and to be kept happy by fashion changes, the Soviets will need mountains of clothes and billions of rubles to buy them and service them. And yet nothing short of another purge will stop it!*

In this connection shall we need radiation-proof asbestos clothing in the years ahead to protect us against the atomic bomb? To many, the future of mankind holds a threat of Armageddon and the end of civilization. To others, including myself, it does not. *This is because in most past wars, man has had a deep-rooted instinct for survival. He stopped fighting when his women and children were threatened with extermination. They carried in them the seeds of the future, and when that was in jeopardy, the wars ended. This same factor which caused the ending of wars in the past, will stop the beginning of wars in the*

Western clothes are rapidly replacing native clothes throughout the world. Women wearing modern dresses in place of their former picturesque costumes, Nigeria, 1956. (Wide World Photos.)

future. Not even a power-crazy dictator could unloose such a war without risking the extinction of his own nation, since no great war can begin today which does not carry with it for both participants the extermination of the women and children and the seeds of the future. Bernard Shaw, in a flash of prophecy, remarked to me over ten years ago that the atomic bomb would put an end to war "because no nation wants to commit suicide." However, this is not time to be complacent on the subject. The constant agitation against the use of these nuclear instruments of wholesale destruction is an ever-present reminder of humanity's instinct for survival which has prevailed for millions of years.

With the rapidly increasing industrialization of the world we may expect to find men's clothing distributed both in capitalist and communist countries in the following ways: (1) The clothes worn by the government and business executives and professionals will probably continue to be derived from our existing drabber sports clothes. (2) The second class, the mechanics, machine operators and so forth, will probably also derive its future clothing from present leisure or sports clothes without collars and ties, but these clothes will undoubtedly be louder and gayer than those of the executives and professional classes—especially now that efficiency experts have informed us that the accident rate in factories will be reduced if the workmen wear brightly colored clothes in order to distinguish them from the machinery! (3) The unskilled laborers, being greatly in demand in an age when everyone wants his physical work to be done by a machine, may well be the best paid individuals of the lot and, together with their wives, may wear the gayest and sportiest clothing!

But who dares to prophesy the trend of women's future fashions? One woman will reflect in her "leisure clothes" her emphasis on independence and sports. Others will reflect feminine fragility and helplessness. They pay their money, and you take their choice. Women's work clothes are a different matter. If her work takes her into the factory, side by side and on the same tasks as men, she will either wear slacks or trousers if the work demands and she has the figure for them, or she will wear simple work dresses suited to the job. Since the wearing of male clothes without feminine trimmings is bad for both the individual and the race, women may be expected when dressed in male trousers or slacks to counteract the effect of these by wearing feminine blouses or tunics over the upper parts of their bodies.

As to college students, both male and female, when they become bored with their self-conscious rebellion against the clothing conventions, which rebellion most of them drop as soon as they leave college, they may again begin to wear conventional clothing while attending the class rooms or dinners. The improving effect of this self-discipline on their studies and examinations may surprise them and amaze their instructors and parents!

With the spread of independence in Asia and Africa, the British and French business clothes and military uniforms formerly worn by the colonial ruling classes are now being imitated in similar Europeanized clothes worn by the new native ruling classes and their followers. *The wearing of Western clothes is already beginning to lead to the emancipation of women in these countries, as well as in a modification of the traditional religions which make for unsanitary living and a lack of interest in science and the material world. When these other races wear Western clothes, they acquire Western ideas along with them. These in turn set a pattern for many advantageous improvements in living.* On the other hand, there are also great disadvantages which we are powerless to prevent, unless the nationalistic movements in these countries retard the spread of Western clothes despite our alluring Western magazine advertisements, salesmen and beautiful fashion models.

The wearing of European dress by many of the ruling classes among the Asians and Africans is a symbol of their feeling of equality with their former colonial administrators. With millions upon millions of these various races of Asia and Africa turning to European and American clothing, the ultimate effect may be to produce among them an unconscious feeling of inferiority to the Europeans and Americans whose clothing they copy. *This is because we of the West sometimes unfortunately tend to regard them as dressed-up imitations of ourselves. And so do some of their own lower classes.*

A tragic example of this latter situation was recounted by Norman Cousins in the *Saturday Review of Literature* of April 20, 1957, under the title "The Man Who Didn't Come to Dinner." William Mondisane, a newspaperman on the staff of *Drum*, a paper published entirely by South African Negroes, informed Cousins that, "an educated African has a hard time inside many of the locations. He is resented because of his knowledge and because he is believed to have an advantage over most of the other non-European people. The same would apply to any well-dressed African. And by well-dressed

Drab Western clothing is replacing picturesque native witch-doctor costumes. A group of Zulu medicine men wearing modern Western dress performing magical rites at Congress of Witch Doctors, Johannesburg, 1957. (Photo by Nickolas Muray, permission from Wenner-Gren Anthropological Foundation.)

I mean any man who wears a tie. According to this standard, it is generally easy to pick out an educated African, for they are better dressed than the others. It is not unusual for educated Africans to be beaten up by gangs." These remarks were made to Cousins in connection with the murder of a young Negro reformer named Henry Nxumalo who was engaged in a fierce journalistic fight for the rights of Negroes in the Union. He had been invited to dinner with Cousins, but was beaten to death on his way there. It was alleged by some that this killing was done by a gang of young Negroes who resent those of their people who are well dressed. Nxumalo was opposed to the gangs and everything about them. He hated to see young boys drawn into these different gangs, each with its own name and dress and habits. One particularly strong gang is known as the Russians. There is no political significance to the name. Another is called the Berliners, still another the Americans. The Russians like to walk around wearing brightly colored blankets. The Americans like to affect zoot suits. How like our New York teen-age gangs, with their special clothing!

Balanced against our misgivings as to the immediate effect of Western clothing on the races of the East and Africa is the ultimate equalizing effect on different races or peoples due to wearing the same kind of clothing. The peoples of Europe, generally speaking, wear somewhat similar clothes (even if they wear their national costumes for special occasion), and we think of them collectively as Europeans, and akin to the English and the Americans. The democratic or levelling effect of wearing the same kind of clothing irrespective of race is nowhere better illustrated than in the British West Indies. In the law courts at Port of Spain, Trinidad, I have seen cases tried before a Negro judge, in which the barristers were mulattos, Negroes, East Indians, Chinese and white British colonials. All were dressed in Western business suits, and the black robes and wigs which they wore symbolized the living truth that all men should be equal before the law. *In this way clothing should play an important part in the future in bringing the peoples of the world closer together, irrespective of race and nationality, and thus produce a new kind of brotherhood of man, based on our common humanity. Thus clothes will emphasize our similarities rather than our differences throughout the world.*

Clothing in the future will also play an important part in contributing to the happiness and self-confidence of the millions upon millions of peoples who are now too poor to afford good clothing. With the dominion which modern invention has given us over the bounties of nature, it is not going too far to prophesy the ultimate dawn of an era when all the peoples of the world will be well dressed and provided with sufficient food and means to change their "skins" from time to time.

Clothing will also contribute to the control of population growth, a most important problem which the world is now facing, for experience shows that the birth rate tends to be regulated when a higher standard of living, which inherently includes clothing, is desired by a populace.

We have seen from the preceding chapters that man, aided by his imagination, his reasoning and inventive powers, and with the help of his clothing, has steadily marched down the ages from civilization to civilization in each of which he has made some major contribution to knowledge and the arts. As he has passed through each era, he has

How Western clothes are replacing picturesque native costumes: Above, African chiefs wearing native costumes take over Executive Council of self-governing Northern Nigeria from the retiring British governor, Sir Gawain Bell (third from left), 1959. Below, members of the traditional "Bunga" or local native parliament wearing Western-style clothes, Transkei, Union of South Africa. (Wide World Photos.)

usually retained the best of its harvest. Thus we still possess the knowledge of law and religion which we garnered from the ancient Israelites, the philosophy, sculpture and architecture of the Greeks, the engineering of the Romans, the credo of the early Christians, the mathematics of the Arabs, the painting and architecture of the Renaissance, and the drama and literature of the Elizabethans, in addition to the science of the present era.

What is the motive power behind this stream of progress but man's desire to be godlike and to achieve as a god? He ever searches to improve his world in one field or another, and his achievements keep adding to the sum of man's knowledge. Little of this progress would have been possible but for the invention of the clothing which originally gave man the feeling of superiority which ever urges him on and on to the conquest of greater heights. It is not beyond the bounds of possibility that the scientists of the future may reach out into space and create new worlds of matter out of the electronic star dust which drifts about the universe. And when this happens, men will indeed be as gods.

In conclusion, we have traced the origins and effects of clothes, and we have noted that modern civilization rests on clothing to a far greater extent than is generally realized. This relationship between clothing and civilization will undoubtedly continue in the future, and emphasizes the importance of clothes to the progress of mankind. *It also emphasizes the fact that since God helps those who help themselves, the future of humanity lies in the hands of man himself, aided by the clothing which has contributed to his belief in his own superiority and his kinship to God. With this aid, it is not over-optimistic to expect that, despite the swing of the pendulum backwards and forwards, men and women the world over will continue humanity's urge towards learning, legal and economic justice, freedom of spirit, the development of the arts, sciences and religions, and the liberation of all the other forces which make for a greater civilization and a happier way of life.*

PART VIII

ADDENDUM

During the past three decades, everyday fashions have become much more democratic and international, giving rise to the possibility of the work of an Australian designer being featured in an Italian magazine that was purchased by an English store buyer while visiting New York. (Photo courtesy Jenny Kee, Sydney, Australia)

CHAPTER 21

Changing Influences and Changing Attitudes

by Julian Robinson DesRCA, FRSA

Since 1959, when this book was first published, the entire Western world has gone through a period of tremendous change that has dramatically affected the way of life at all levels of society —the way we think, the way we live, the way we vote, what we eat, the music we listen to, the cars we drive, the television programs we watch, how we spend our leisure time, our religious and moral beliefs, and the way we dress.

These current changes rival those of five centuries ago, at the beginning of the Age of Discovery, of Expansionism, and of the Protestant Reformation. The underlying dynamics of the fifteenth century were undoubtedly very similar to those of the twentieth: technological revolution, expansion of education, the desire to explore the unknown, a growing and a prosperous middle class. These were further augmented, in 1456, by an innovation that served to revolutionize the current ways of mass communicatión: moveable type.

Replacing the labor-intensive mode of handwriting and illuminating each individual manuscript, the effect of moveable type was to make possible the mass-production of books and other less expensive forms of print communication. This economical method of producing the written page facilitated the development of mass education and the dissemination of knowledge throughout all social stratum of the Western world. The result was the development of a new political consciousness that totally altered traditional political structures and ideological beliefs which had remained unchanged for centuries.

Today, a similar breakthrough in communication has taken place. The introduction of satellite television has spawned a new Age of Information which has not only affected the politics and lifestyles of

315

Western society, but also those of East Europe, Africa, and Asia, and many others in the most remote regions of the earth, regardless of skin color, religious beliefs, or cultural traditions. This electronic mode of mass communication, together with the widespread use of international travel, has helped to create what has become known as the Global Village, the repercussions of which have yet to be fully grasped.

As Langner points out, such changes have always had a universal affect on the way people dress, since the styles they choose to wear symbolize their changing hopes, ambitions, and dreams of a better future as well as many other unvoiced concepts they have regarding themselves and their place in society. In this context, it is important to understand the use of the word "dreams." Our dress changes because it is the most visually conspicuous mechanism available for use as we strive to change ourselves. Thus we find ourselves universally possessed by a common expectation that, by creating a new mode of outward packaging, we will somehow become different people, closer to the ideal we have formulated of ourselves in our "dreams." It is not unusual, then, for individuals attempting self-improvement through this procedure to achieve at least partial success.

Social commentators have noted each era of history has produced a unique body style along with special clothing to fit the time. During periods of dramatic change, alterations in actual physical shape (average weight, height, and posture) of the persons may be altered abruptly, though these modifications may be more subtle.

In the non-industrialized world—where change takes place much slower than in the West, these body changes have been noted recently, apparently effected by a change in clothing. As they encounter and are affected by modern society, many traditional modes of dress are discarded in favor of the ubiquitous blue jeans and T-shirt. It is by wearing these symbols of the American mode of dress that these people hope to become identified with the changes that are taking place. In their "dreams" they are attempting to identify themselves with the American lifestyle as they have seen it portrayed on their village television set.

In my travels I have discovered that many cultural groups, some of whom live in extremely isolated areas, only wear their traditional modes of attire for visiting tourists and anthropologists, since they have learned that these visitors expect and desire to see them so attired. When they are alone, they return to the jeans and T-shirts mentioned above. I have also noted how, even during the most informal occasions, many businessmen from small communities in countries such as Korea and India now wear traditional Western-style business suits. This almost rigid adherence to a dress style they associate with "modern business" serves as symbolic of their new membership in the worldwide community of commerce and of their newly acquired wealth.

In recent years, Western media such as National Geographic, Time-Life and others have, through magazine and video presentations, featured the many traditional modes of beauty found among non-Western peoples. Special television programs and the sensational tabloid press have done much to publicize events such as Miss World and Miss Universe, where the physical attributes of individuals from competing countries around the world are compared and judged. It is interesting to note that until very recent times the inevitable winner

Ethnic modes of dress. Many modes of dress do not conform to Western body covering standards. Unfortunately, these styles are rapidly disappearing, thus decreasing our own sartorial freedoms. (Photos courtesy Maureen Bisilliat and Aubrey Elliott)

was from a Western country. Now, however, this monopoly seems to have changed. Frequent winners of these beauty contests originate from African, Asian and Eastern European countries.

The expansion of influences from "third-world" countries has effected the way post-industrial men and women see themselves. Many Western men, particularly (but certainly not exclusively) those under thirty and/or involved in the arts and entertainment, have, in the past few decades, experimented with non-European modes of attire. They claim the right to wear more decorative clothing than past norms have dictated.

Many women in large Western cities today wear garments which originated in Turkey, Morroco, India or Mexico. Traditionally, the Western mode of dress has concentrated the observer's eyes onto those areas of the female anatomy in which Western women were thought to be superior—face, hair, shoulders, upper areas of their breasts, waist, ankles and hands—with all other areas of the body generally covered. However, due to the rise in world travel this century, and to an ever-increasing interest by the media in the wide variety of ethnic cultures, other important areas of the female anatomy have become available for display in fashionable modes of dress. New styles, particularly in bathing suits, emphasize the legs and buttocks. It would seem that the mere threat of a foreign mode of beauty being more admired than that traditionally accepted in the West has prompted many Western women to expose more of their physical attributes than ever before.

The self-modification evidenced by males and females in Western society no longer has to stop with dress. The latest developments in synthetic hormones and cosmetic surgery have enabled many men and women to completely remodel their physical selves, often blurring the distinct differences between the races and between male and female, thus creating new standards of human beauty.

The influence of surgery and foreign styles of body and dress is superimposed on a pattern that has been with us for centuries. During the past few decades alone, the desire men and women have to be "up-to-date" and stylish has brought about changes which, in themselves, resulted in new body styles as well as new concepts in dress. Each new generation of women and men appears to be more adventurous in its choice of dress styles than the one that came before. New, sexier styles become more widely accepted with each passing year. It is no longer uncommon to find that styles previously found only in adult fetish catalogs and in the private confines of bedrooms have been adapted for normal day wear. The result is inevitable. As the years pass, laws governing the wearing of such styles are gradually relaxed. Today, young people wear as outer garments items of clothing previously considered to be "underwear." This tendency to expose more body in public has contributed to the upsurge in physical fitness.

As recreational dress becomes more revealing, some of the laws relating to nudity have relaxed as they apply to sunbathing and swimming. This is particularly true in Europe. Public beach nudity in America is only beginning to enjoy a limited modicum of freedom, for we still suffer under restrictions more appropriate to the Victorian era. What changes have occurred are due in large to the legal efforts of organizations such as The Naturist Society, the American Sunbathing Association and the Elysium Institute in Los Angeles and to the

New influences: Many men and women now feel free to experiment with a wide variety of sexual and gender roles which they most noticeably express in their manner of dress and physical appearance. (Photographs: Eve, Dan and Yvonne by Mariette Pathy Allen)

existence of a great number of "skinny-dippers" who are joining with these organizations to demand the right to recreate as they wish.

The over-all relaxation of strict dress codes in both business and leisure is reflected in other aspects of human ornamentation. During the twentieth century, there has also been a dramatic change in social attitudes towards the use of facial make-up, perfume, and the wearing of decoratively trimmed lingerie. Now we are accustomed to the use of such items, so it may seem strange to us that decorative lingerie or the use of lipstick or Channel No. 5 should ever have been thought of as immoral. However, such was the case in the very recent past. As late as the early 1920s, the use of pretty forms of under-clothing and beauty aids were relatively new, even among young people. At that time, many of the older generation regarded such items as fit only for use by "courtesans, divorcees, and women of easy virtue."

This change did not come about without conflict. A hotly debated moral issue throughout most of the nineteenth century was whether women had the right to wear any decorative form of underclothes under the traditional plain linen or flannel petticoats. Attention was specifically directed toward bifurcated undergarments on the lower parts of the female anatomy such as knickers or, later, panties. With little biblical text to support them, but with much righteous indignation, ecclesiastics and moralists alike condemned such garments as being "against the laws of God."

This condemnation, however, did not deter the fashionable "demi-mondaine," the elite nineteenth century actress/courtesans under the patronage of Napoleon III (*see color plate* V) from wearing the forbidden items of underclothing. These professional beauties mesmerized many eligible bachelors, wealthy bankers, and influential aristocrats and created much of the high society *haute-couture* fashions of their day. "Decent" women envied the liberties possessed by the actress/courtesans, while only the very wealthy imitated their style.

When writing of this period, the highly respected author Octave Uzanne observed that the demi-mondaine used her expensive array of new fashions, jewels, lingerie, cosmetics and shoes not so much to help her further conquests "as to attract the envy of honest women whose jealousy helped to establish her reputation," adding that, "From the moment that virtuous women say indignantly when speaking of her, 'It is only creatures such as these who can display such scandalous luxury!' her reputation is made."

These fashionable beauties received ecclesiastic and moral criticism. Yet, it was the magical allure of such criticism that added the essential touch of exotic sexuality and sinfulness which made the wearing of such items so appealing. Only the wealthy, who were "above" such condemnation, dared to ignore the standards set by "lower" society. For most women, the old moral standards remained strong. Generations passed before what began as outrageous display finally became common fashion.

Such slow changes occurred in cosmetics, as well. When the 20th century began, "decent" women avoided all forms of cosmetics, considering them fit only for courtesans and women of dubious character. Lipstick, especially, was avoided. Here it is most interesting to note that the lips of a female redden naturally during sexual arousal—becoming engorged with blood and mimicking the change that is taking place in the genitalia. This is why lipstick was and is so sexually appealing to men. Through the turn of the century, only a woman who wished to emphasize her sexual nature (and respectable women never did that!) put any color on her lips.

But new generations of women, particularly in America, refused to accept "archaic" attitudes. The "wild" West had given added dimensions to the feminine character. Women who faced hardships and

Western beauty: Each race has tended to admire and make the most of their more attractive physical attributes. With Western females, this has generally meant making the most of their hair, face and breasts.

worked beside their men as they carved out homes in the wilderness were naturally more relaxed in their behavior than were their mothers. They did not take well to the restrictions still demanded in the Eastern states. So, when they found males in short supply, this new breed of young women considered themselves free to dress as they felt necessary to succeed in their quest for mates.

For a period of time following World War I, American women grew more open in dress and the use of makeup while, in Europe, most "honest" women were still obliged to dress "properly," avoiding the sexy outfits, and the use of cosmetics and perfume which, to them, still denoted a less-than-virtuous professional status. With the arrival of the "flapper girl," developed by the booming film industry, short dresses and cosmetics received a limited acceptance. Movie "stars"adopted the new dress as befitting their exciting lifestyle.

Once the influence of these stars was established, however, women from all strata of American society began modeling themselves after the star of their choice with an almost religious attachment. It became acceptable for virtuous young women, particularly young American women, to wear lipstick, rouge, eyeliner, perfume, nail varnish, or lace-trimmed camisoles or cami-knickers. Many also began wearing the new scanty mode of dress worn by many of the younger group of Hollywood stars.

The influence of this new mode of Hollywood-inspired glamour prompted one social commentator to write that "During the decade that followed the end of World War I (that period we now refer to as the Jazz Age), many young American women were dressed and painted like prostitutes." It must be remembered, however, that in America at that time, there was less of a formal tradition of professional prostitution than in Europe.

During the second half of the 1920s and throughout the 1930s, the American approach to women's dress and the everyday use of cosmetics and perfume spread throughout the Western world, despite the continual condemnation of what was referred to as "Hollywood Glamour" by the clergy and moralists of the time. These same critics condemned much of post-war society: jazz music, the introduction of radio, the use of automobiles, international travel, the airplane, playing sports on the Sabbath, new styles of painting, and many other aspects of the then changing lifestyles of most people. As the years passed, their protests received a diminishing response. More and more women accepted the changes in style as perfectly respectable and acceptable for "decent" society.

Throughout the early 1900s, even when short dresses and facial decoration was acceptable for adult women, children were expected to remain "pure." This standard persisted well into the 1950s. When teen-aged girls, copying popular singers, began to put on lipstick, many older people expressed disgust. Such a display by girls so young seemed inappropriate. Once more the "moral leaders" of the communities roused into action. However they ultimately fought a losing battle. Modern cosmetic firms in search of more customers managed to overcome their objections, and, today, even pre-teeners wear lip color without condemnation. In fact, "play" make-up kits are now available in stores and bought as gifts for young girls who are not yet in kindergarten.

To the end of World War II, *haute-couture* fashion, as promoted by the noted Paris designers and the leading fashion magazines, remained the exclusive province of the wealthy elite of Western society who traveled to Paris twice a year, in the spring and autumn, to see the seasonal collections. Yet even in Paris, the Hollywood influence predominated, with the leading *couturiers*, such as Vionnett, Schiaparelli, Patou and Paquin producing more figure-revealing styles than had been worn since the French Revolution. Each new style that these daring designers produced, whether it emphasized the shape of the buttocks, breasts, legs or waist of the wearer, was subsequently condemned as being more revealing and immodest than its predecessor.

It should be remembered, however, that during the course of Western sartorial history, there have been many other revealing and immodest fashions, such as the tightly laced corsetted styles worn by young unmarried women during the mid-nineteenth century, which emphasized their narrow waists and buttocks and pushed up their breasts which were, except for the nipples, fully displayed in low-cut dresses.

At times such styles were actively promoted by the governments of the day—as in the case of the "immodest style of dress" worn by many unmarried Italian women after the end of the Punic Wars. These women were aided in their quest for mates by a new law which allowed them to display the full rounds of their breasts and the shape of their legs in dresses which were permitted to be slit from the hips downwards. A similar fashion was also popular in Germany after the Thirty-Years War, again condoned by the government, and in England, after the Black Plague had killed more than one-third of her population.

Immodesty in women's dress was also officially sanctioned in France after the Revolution when the extravagancies of the aristocrats of the 1780s were totally abandoned in favor of a very spartan mode of attire that not only displayed the wearers' naked breasts, rouged nipples and bare legs, but also their neatly trimmed and decorated pubic hair—a mode which has so shocked many costume historians that it has been omitted from most books on the subject.

Most fashion historians also omit mentioning many immodest forms of menswear worn during earlier periods, such as that detailed by Chaucer who wrote that many men's garments were "horribly scanty—too short to cover their shameful members." He was, in fact, referring to the continuing fashion for wearing a short tunic, with tight-fitting netherhosen, that was often left unseamed around the underbody line—a fashion first introduced by high-ranking nobles during the reign of Edward IV.

The Hollywood influence: Following World War I, Hollywood films and film magazines greatly influenced young American women to display themselves in a more openly sexual manner, establishing new styles of beauty and glamour throughout the Western world.

If, however, the aristocratic male genitals of the mid-fourteenth century were not of sufficient size to make a distinguished display, they wore a braquette—an explicit glove-like device made of natural skin-colored leather that was tailored to fit a well-padded penis and scrotum. To preserve the exclusivity of this form of explicit sexual display, Edward had a law passed in 1348 prohibiting any person under the rank of a lord "from wearing any gowne, jaket or cloke unless it be of sufficient length on a man standing uprite, to cover his privy member and buttokkes."

During most of the sixteenth century, male genitals were also of fashionable interest when they were neatly packaged in a codpiece which was often decorated with fine embroidery and jewels. Exaggerated padding of the male genital area was also fashionable during the mid-eighteenth century, when it was also the fashion for men of wealth and influence to wear calf and thigh pads under their tightly-fitting garments as a sign of their virility and to excite the female members of society. Lest we assume that such exaggeration of sexual parts is confined to the past, we must note the practice of some 1970s rock

Phallic symbolism: Western men no longer wear the padded codpieces of the Middle Ages, nor do they display their virility in a colored gourd or bound as is still the custom in many areas of New Guinea. Nevertheless, they openly display a distinct phallic echo in the shape of their neckties.

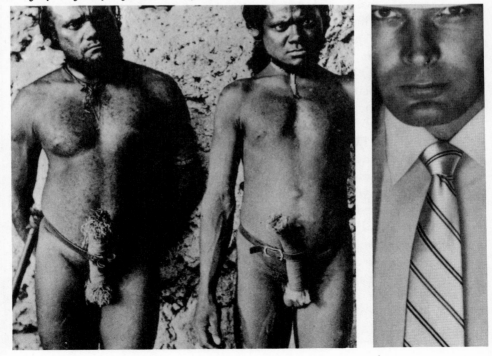

326 The Importance of Wearing Clothes

stars to added padding to their crotch bulge and legs so as to excite their young fans.

From an historic viewpoint, therefore, it would seem that the changes in both male and female modes of dress this century are certainly no more extreme than many worn during earlier periods. The only notable difference is that almost all of the earlier styles were originally introduced by the rich and powerful members of society and then copied by those of lesser rank.

As the Western world has become more egalitarian, so new forms of fashionable clothing become more democratic. This was particularly noted in the period following the end of World War II, when government-imposed rationing was lifted. These restrictions had resulted in a bland, functional, stereotypical mode of dressing which was tossed aside by all classes alike as soon as finances and new designs permitted.

In the spring of 1947, an unknown French designer by the name of Christian Dior, launched his revolutionary "New Look." Though certainly not "new" in the sense of being innovative, it made the most of the alluring feminine features that had been suppressed by government-imposed restrictions during World War II. Using laced-up corsets and padding, Dior put women's waists, breasts and hips once again at the center of fashionable interest. What made his move so innovative was that copies of his styles soom became available in "ready-to-wear." This was, to say the least, a new development. Never before had high-fashion (or copies of it) been so available.

Journalists of the period, reacting in their own way to the new postwar freedom, rushed to publicize this exciting new development. Throughout the war they had been obliged to write dry, repetitive articles praising austerity and make-do-and-mend. Now, with a new fashion innovation unfolding before them, they made the most of it. During the subsequent ten years, these journalists cooed approvingly at each new Dior collection, regularly advising their readers to buy the newest most shapely corset, pantie-girdle, or bra each time the fashionable silhouette changed. They adored each new skirt length, regardless of whether it was longer or shorter, and drooled over the costly lace-edged petticoats which could be glimpsed beneath the shorter hemlines. It was, they claimed, criminal to be seen wearing any of last season's styles. In contrast, changes in men's styles were so miniscule as to warrant little more than a line or two of type with each new season.

For women, however, throughout that entire decade, what Dior created and publicists touted became required dress. But time was passing and things were changing rapidly. By the mid-to-late1950s, a new influence began to dominate the clothing styles of the younger members of society, this time with an assault on the time-honored "business suit," accepted as proper for men with only minor changes since the late 1800s.

In England, Teddy Boys and the embrionic predecessors of the Skinheads, Mods, and Rockers were becoming headline news. In America, the styles worn by Elvis Presley and James Dean, although loudly condemned by those in authority, were beginning to be widely copied. Moralists wrote predicting the end of civilization and portraying this new dress style as "nothing less than a rebellious mood which is undermining our democratic way of life" and as "the clothing of the Devil himself." But these predictors of doom drew little attention. Stores sold cheap copies of each new fitting style of pants that Elvis wore. Men's dress became, for the first time in decades, a matter worthy of the kind of condemnation for so long directed only toward women's garments.

As one would expect, ready-to-wear fashions for the new generation of young women were also beginning to break away from the established mainstream of fashion. Dresses and slacks appeared emphasizing the wearer's nubile charms. This was not surprising. Statistically, the normal male to female ratio was out of balance due to the effects of World War II and the continuing conflicts in Asia and elsewhere. In America, there were nearly five million fewer men than women, while in most European countries, where conscription into the armed forces was still in force, the ratio of available young men to women was far worse.

This shortage had a dramatic effect on the styles worn by teenage girls who were unattached and actively looking for mates. They did not wish to compete with their elder sisters, who, like their mothers were happily wearing copies of the latest Dior fashions. They wanted to express themselves and their femininity in ways more in keeping with the changing times—which were already reflected in the popular styles of music they preferred and the movie stars they idolized.

Television, introduced to Western markets a scant decade earlier, brought into the living rooms of ordinary families pictures of change from around the world. Events were aired as they were happening.

Suddenly, in the mid '50s, TV became not only the new form of amusement, but began, also, to usurp the time-honored way of learning about the world previously held by newspapers and magazines.

Filmmakers in Hollywood changed their products to meet the challenge of this new form of mass communication. A new genre of youth-orientated film such as "The Wild One" and "Jailhouse Rock" captured the rebellious mood of the new generation and in the process made Marlon Brando and Elvis Presley international stars. James Dean also captured this mood in "Rebel Without a Cause" *(See color plate XI)*. His portrayal of sexual proclivity and social disenchantment symbolized teenage revolt and the struggle of the younger generation to free itself from the outdated morés and morals of their elders.

Marilyn Monroe was also greatly admired by the dissenting youth for her disdain of conventional attitudes toward nudity and the flaunting of her sexual charms. Her popularity served in helping break down the middle class ethics that had so bedeviled her mother's generation.

Youthful actresses like Leslie Caron and Audrey Hepburn also enjoyed public esteem for their slender, almost pre-pubescent figures and waifish looks. These two actresses were hailed by the new genre of fashion reporters as "symbols of today's young generation" who had "so captured the young imagination and the mood of our time, that they have established a new kind of beauty—a beauty which many girls are now copying."

As popular as these three stars were, it was the shimmering promiscuity and wayward looks of Brigitte Bardot, as portrayed in Roger Vadim's film "And God Created Woman," which was exactly in tune with the ideas of the new generation. As we look back at the styles of the 1950s, we can see that it was Brigitte Bardot whom many young females imitated.

Incidentally, it was during this period in fashion history that I became active in the field. I was a student at the Royal College of Art (RCA) in central London during the latter half of the 1950s, and saw, first hand, the changes blossoming around me. The young female students at the Royal College were wearing styles which openly displayed their newly acquired nubile charms—short, tight skirts which emphasized the roundness of their bottoms and displayed their knees to advantage. They wore tight, wide patent leather belts to emphasize their narrow waists and shapely sweaters which displayed their conically shaped breasts.

The young male students showed the same disregard for the styles of the past. Like the females, having discarded the conservative mode of attire of their father's generation, they wore thick crepe-soled suede shoes, long square-cut jackets with contrasting velvet collars and cuffs, narrow trousers without up-turned cuffs. They further showed their disdain for conventions of the past by wearing decorative, sometimes frilled, shirts heretofore worn only to the opera or a dress ball. These they topped with narrow ties that matched their velvet collars. Some especially daring youths even sported brocade waistcoats, or vests.

During my final year at the Royal College in 1957, I won a travelling scholarship to Paris to see the major *couture* shows. It was an exciting period in the fashion world. The collections shown by Dior and his great rivals, Balanciaga, Givenchy and Cardin, were, as usual, magnificent, yet they seemed to be lacking in vitality and originality. Following their custom, they targeted their designs toward the rich, aging dowagers who could afford to purchase such items.

It was clear to me that the young salesgirl and secretary would soon be dominating the fashion scene. The rich dowager was a dying breed

Between 1947 and his death in 1957, Christian Dior had an enormous influence on popular dress styles. However, by the early '60s, the young designers of London's Carnaby Street and the Kings Road dictated the newest modes. (Photos courtesy House of Dior, Paris, and Clive, London.)

and the growing fashion industry was demanding larger and larger markets. The vanguard of the post-World War II baby boomer, the young teenager, was already demonstrating a dramatic influence that would grow as their numbers and spending power increased.

On my return to England, I worked for a time with Mary Quant, a shy young Welsh designer who owned a small dress shop called "Bazaar" in the lower Kings Road in Chelsea. I also taught part-time at an East London art school. Among my first group of fashion students were two sixteen-year-old girls—Sally Tuffin and Marion Foale who, a few years later, would become the famous Carnaby Street design team of Tuffin & Foale. There were also two young male students, James Wedge, who would start the famous "Countdown" and "Top Gear" shops before turning his talents towards fashion photography; and Brian Godbold, who would go on to become the driving force behind Marks and Spencer's expansion into the young fashion market.

I also taught two fifteen-year-old students: Sylvia Ayton, who was the original design partner of Zandra Rhodes, before becoming the chief designer for a multi-million-dollar ready-to-wear manufacturer; and Shirley Kingdon; whom I introduced to my flat-mate, fashion photographer Ken Russell, whom she later married. She subsequently

During the 1950s, popular weekly magazines were full of stories about "the dreams of style," " the problems of good taste," and the morality of the new fashions, not realizing that within a few years, the established ideas of fashionable dress were going to change quite dramatically.

persuaded him to turn his talents towards filmmaking and he went on to become a rather infamous off-beat film director. Shirley went on to become an acclaimed Oscar-nominated costume designer.

They and their classmates were a lively bunch of students, always full of questions and always wanting to design and make something that was different from anything they had made before. In them, with the young Carnaby Street fashions as an essential part, I saw a prediction of those changes that would become the benchmark of what became known as the "Swinging London" revolution.

The following year, in 1958, I opened my first ready-to-wear fashion studio in the center of Mayfair. There I designed collections for such prestigious stores as Fortnum and Masons, Lord & Taylor, Harrod's, and for London couturiers Digby Morton, Michael of Lachasse, and Sir Norman Hartnell. I soon realized, however, that expensive up-market styles were not my forté. The emphasis of my work was already geared towards a much younger look.

1958 was also the year when the young twenty-one-year-old Yves Saint Laurent took over as chief designer at the House of Dior following Christian Dior's death from a heart attack several months earlier. Not one to rush headlong into change, St. Laurent offered his

In the late 1950s young fashion photo-journalists like Ken Russell began exploring and promoting alternative forms of dress. This article features young art students in party gear—students destined to create the revolutionary styles of the '60s. (Photos courtesy Ken Russell, Los Angeles.)

first collection in the *couture* tradition. It was hailed as a great success and, for a brief season, the fashion world seem undisturbed. Six months later, however, his next collection outraged the established fashion world.

Through with the past, St. Laurent let his youthful ideas flow. He dared, for example, to create fitted garments and to bare the knees of his established thirty-five to sixty-five-year-old clientel. Shocked, a British Member of Parliament declared, "British women will not take any notice of this nonsense," and in America, numerous "A-Little-Below-the-Knee" clubs were formed to try to prevent such a dramatic change from taking place. The establishment press attacked the new St. Laurent fashions as only suitable "for Left Bank hippies and social drop-outs" but, try as they might, they could not stop the movement for change. Skirts were going to be shorter because the younger generation of women wished to show their knees, and by weight of numbers and their growing spending power, they were destined to take over the fashion scene. Fashion would never be the same again.

The Paris fashion industry in the early 1960s appeared much the same as in the past, despite the obvious changes that were taking place in London and New York. The *couture* houses continued to promote their seasonal collections of desirable, wearable clothes, still primarily aimed at their dwindling clientele. But the press, while happy to support and publicize these collections, was restless. Rumors abounded regarding new, yet untested developments. Occasional articles hinted that many of the young couturiers were considering abandoning *haute-couture* altogether to concentrate on the potentially more profitable ready-to-wear industry.

Certainly some sort of change was inevitable. Many of these Paris-based designers were losing money in exclusive *haute-couture*. The profits from their own worldwide sales of signature cosmetics, lingerie, perfumes, accessories and menswear boutique collections, together with the growing practice of franchising, were propping up their diminishing couture empires. This general change of direction was to develop, in France, into the now influential *pret-a-porter*, a less expensive form of limited-edition but ready-to-wear fashion.

Again, it was St. Laurent who made the first move. He resigned from Dior and came out with his now-famous Rive Gauche *pret-a-porter* collections. Andre Courreges, Balanciaga's former assistant, also left couture to start a *pret-a-porter* range, as did several other young designers of note. Once more Paris appeared to establish itself as the Alpha and the Omega of fashion.

But the move came too late. The center of youthful fashion had already moved to London. Now began the era referred to as "Swinging London," when Kings Road and Carnaby Street were alive with dozens of small dress shops and boutiques owned and operated by young designers fresh from art schools and bursting with new ideas. As *British Vogue* proclaimed, when it eventually seceded from the Establishment fashion camp, "For the first time the young people who work in the rag trade are making and promoting the clothes they naturally like, clothes which are relevant to the way they live—ours is the first generation that can express itself on its own terms."

During this period of change, young American fashion designers were also becoming a major influence on the international fashion scene. Their casual approach of T-shirts, jeans, and over-sized sweaters prompted the noted fashion historian James Laver to write, "Today, almost anywhere in Western Europe and North America, it is possible to walk behind two young people, each of them clad in tight jeans and loose sweater, and each with long hair, and not know whether they are two girls, two boys, or one of each." He suggested that this new approach to dressing might well be androgynous: "For even when the young females are not wearing jeans, they wear miniskirts" which bear "the closest possible resemblance to the late fifteenth century young man in a tunic and tights." The revolutionary nature of this "unisex" development continues to assert itself even today, almost thirty years later.

For almost the whole of recorded history, up until the 1960s, no effort was spared to make the clothes of the two sexes as different as possible. One only has to look back to the mid-1950s and compare a young female wearing a copy of a Dior A-line dress with a young fashionable male wearing a Teddy Boy suit, or just fifty years earlier to compare a woman in a fashionable Gibson Girl dress with a man wearing the then fashionable frock-coat, to see that they are so different in shape and style that they might well be creatures of two quite separate species.

Undoubtedly, this visual emphasis of the difference between the two sexes influenced the way men and women behaved individually and how they dealt with each other, taking into account the relative freedom of male attire and the hobbling effect of women's apparel.

The changing tide: During the 1960s young designers everywhere began to experiment with bold new ideas, while in Paris the couturiers continued to design and market their tradition of controlled "good taste." (Photo courtesy Gina Lollobrigida, Rome)

It is possible that the entire Women's Rights' movement is predicated on the prior achievement of some unisex mode of dress. True, there were individual women in the past who attempted to gain the freedoms previously only afforded to men, but many achieved their goals by hiding their femininity and assuming the garments worn by their brothers. Only when society began to accept unisex dress was it possible for women to retain their feminine identities while still reaching the level of independence heretofore given only to those who denied their gender.

Admittedly, other changes contributed to this important step toward sexual equality. By the 1960s, most male and female children, often from a mixture of races and religions, were being educated together. Apart from traditional educational subjects, they were also being taught what is euphemistically called "the facts of life." They also were learning to compete with each other for career opportunities and well-paying jobs. The sexes began to abandon the idea of gender-related roles and accepted similar goals for their lives.

The new order: Throughout most of the 1960s and '70s, young designers of "Swinging London" dictated the pace of change. New attitudes in photography and advertising design were also developed. (Right illustration: Lightning Striking Coat, *designed by Julian Robinson.)*

Public school in America contributed more to this change. As they shared classrooms and studies, boys and girls found that the rigid divisions between the sexes, races, religions, and cultural traditions were breaking down. As these young people grew up, they demanded new clothes to clarify the new ideas they were learning. They rejected the outdated mores of their parents' generation. Their behavior and their clothing styles represented what was in reality a form of political rebellion. When they disagreed with the political stand taken by their leaders, they were not silent. They joined together in protest, staging college sit-ins and marches in open defiance of authoritarian edicts.

In 1968, when attending a series of lifestyle lectures in London, a group of visiting American university students made it abundantly clear to me that they were quite happy wearing their androgynous styles. They did not want to look as if they belonged to separate species. They had seen the trouble this separation had caused in their parents' generation and they wanted to be friends as well as lovers, sharing their future together—in equality. They did not accept the traditional vision of the submissive wife and dominant husband.

They wished to create a new social equality which they hoped—and expected—would work better than the assigned roles their parents had accepted, and which they had been given when they were children. They believed they knew how to make each other happy. After all, they had played together as young children. They had gone to school and college together. They were planning to work together. They enjoyed each other's company as equals. They found the sex-oriented styles of the past anachronistic. Why, they asked, should male and female have to dress differently to attract a mate.

During their period of growing up, these young people had learned to read each other's body language. They knew the difference between the crotch bulge of the male and the crotch gap of the female, the differences in the posture and walk of each sex and the sexual differences of the male and female hips, waists, shoulders and legs. Many also had a much more intimate knowledge of each other's bodies and sexuality, due to the increasing availability of the birth control pill and other forms of contraception.

These were children of the "Sexual Revolution." They did not feel the need to express their sexual identity all of the time—only when the mood took them. In fact, it became part of their clothing philosophy to customarily dress in a similar manner so that when they changed into their more distinctive male or female styles, the difference in their appearance would have more impact.

As always happens at a time of an important fashion change, the older generation was outraged. Attempts were made to force those in authority to regulate against this growing trend of unisex dress. As usual, such objections and attempts at control failed. Our history shows that, except in times of an external threat such as during World War II, the use of the law to regulate the collective wearing of any new form of clothing is generally counter-productive.

Aware of this, most politicians and lawmakers kept a low profile on this matter while the clergy and professional moralists once again attacked these styles as being "against the laws of God." Now, however, they had a few pertinent passages available to them. They quoted Moses' diatribe against "cross-dressing" in *Deuteronomy* (22:5), and Philip Stubbes' equally narrow vision of gender-appropriate dress in *The Anatomie of Abuses* (1585), both of which can be found on page 61 of this book.

The case in point for this highly vocal and influential moral minority was that the blurring of sexual distinction in unisex clothing was equated with the blurring of sexual distinction in the bedroom. Until a few short years ago, dressing in the garments of the opposite sex was almost exclusively equated with male and female homosexuality, with only rare dispensation given to male actors of the early theatre. Recent research has, however, revealed that cross-dressing behavior has existed from prehistory across a broad spectrum of sexual and gender-based identifications including "normal heterosexuals," bisexuals, transvestites, asexuals, transsexuals *and* homosexuals.

In addition to attacking the fashion of unisex clothing, the growing tendency for men to sport long hair was also attacked. Interestingly, the clergy and moralists overlooked the fact that historically many cultures, including the Western European, have been proud of the long hair of their men. Nevertheless, scattered regulations were enacted which resulted in the initial shortening of some modern male hairstyles. Such controls, however, proved almost impossible to regulate, except in very small communities and government controlled institutions such as prisons and the military.

The eventual result was inevitable. Today men, as well as women, choose their own hairstyles. Though longer hair is still popular among many young people, some young men have returned to the shorter styles. Meanwhile, many men who were youths when males began to let their hair grow, still prefer to keep theirs long. Thus, as with so many such changes, what began as a badge of identification for the young, forward-thinking youth has become common throughout the generations.

With the benefit of hindsight, it is now possible to see that the outrage generated by these young trends was not really about a change in modes of dress, but about the sexual and political beliefs that such styles symbolized. It is also clear that a large portion of older society knew this at the time, else why the angry protests that such dress heralded the end of decent social behavior? These elders objected to the political and social behavior of the young revolutionaries as much as to the clothing they wore and the style of their hair.

Apart from the "Sexual Revolution," the mid-to-late 1960s was also one of political turmoil, with guerrilla groups and freedom fighters everywhere attempting to change the established map of the world. The wars in the Middle East and Vietnam continued to rage, and every evening the television screens of the world were filled with pictures from war zones, civilian riots, college sit-ins, and protest marches against the military draft and the use of indiscriminate bombing. The world as it had been known appeared to be falling apart.

It was at this point of time that the mode of dress of the American college students became of international importance. In as much as it was very different from the clothing of their elders, it represented a sharp break with the past. In its disrespect for high style and fashion, it expressed distrust in the establishment. And in its blending of male and female, rich and poor, dark-skinned and light-skinned into one common pattern, it served as a symbol of dissent against political suppression everywhere. As one journalist later wrote about this mode of dress, "...they were not only clothes; they were clothes/language, instant and eloquent symbols of brotherhood; unity-in-protest clothes that talked body-language."

Television moguls, aware that this band of young people personified the future, no matter how disruptive they might appear, featured the leading pop and rock music groups, many of whom assumed a mode of dress far more unorthodox than that worn by their fans. The lines between male and female grew fine, indeed. Groups like the

The Freedom of the West: By the 1970s and '80s, moral attitudes allowed for extremes in fashions, such as these from popular fetish catalogs, to move from the boudoir to the Discos and into public view. (Photos courtesy Centurian Publishing Company, California.)

Beatles and the Rolling Stones emphasized the breakdown of the traditional masculine role by wearing garments that emphasized the feminine side of their nature. They appeared to deliberately court a bisexual image. Their fans, male and female, followed suit and began to copy these styles. Concerts became social, political and sexual testing grounds with many teenage girls discarding their bras, panty girdles, and other restrictive undergarments as a sign of their new freedom of expression.

As the popularity of these stars grew, so grew the Women's Rights' movement. This was not confined to the very young—to teenagers and those in their early twenties. It was started by adult women who had previously ignored the activities of their younger sisters. They responded to the spirit of protest sweeping the world, and used the enthusiasm it generated to call attention to the subservient position women held in society. It was, they declared, time for women to demand equality. Using the physical confinement fashion had forced on them and the control the male dominated fashion industry had over the feminine form as symbolic of the restrictions masculine society had imposed upon all women, they, too removed their bras, burning these garments in front of T.V. cameras.

The repression of the East: Until the end of the 1980s, the Western press, glorified in its new-found freedom from moral censorships and bigotry, emphasized that any form of repression reflected the uniformity in attitude of most Eastern Block countries under Stalin.

For a brief period, flower children and hippies, inspired by eastern folk religion, psychedelic drugs and Native American culture exemplified a more exotic androgynous trend. The unity they personified was challenged by segments of society who felt they too had reason to demand change but who saw no future in the peaceful "drop-out" from the establishment which the hippies represented.

In the excitement generated by these various groups, attitudes toward public disclosure of the human body without clothes also changed. For those advocates of "nudism" and a return to nature, this appeared to be a natural and admirable development. Once highly controversial, public nudity in the form of nude sunbathing became commonplace on many of the world's most famous beaches. Those "nudist" facilities heretofore hidden dared to open their doors to "outsiders" who experienced, often for the first time, the pleasures of swimming and sunning without clothes.

Others, however, used the disappearance of legal control over dress code to use nakedness as a new form of protest, sometimes with comical results. Nude "streaking," often more for the fun of doing what was once taboo, became, for a brief time, a popular activity. Not since the days of the French Revolution had so much clothing-based symbolism been used in the West to signal the wearer's political, social, and moral beliefs.

Extreme as these changes were, the revolution was not over. As we moved into the 1970s, David Bowie appeared and, with his use of feminine clothing, turned bisexuality into a profitable marketing device. He also led his fans toward a greater acceptance of the dual sexuality we all possess. To this day, with most of the extremes of dress (like Bowie's) a thing of the past for the major populace, the appreciation of human androgyny continues.

During the following two decades, television continued to have a dramatic effect on the fashions of the period and still remains a crucial influence. This, in itself, is not unusual. Since its early beginnings, mass communication has always served as a strong influence on the behavior of society. When story books and magazines first appeared, they served as guides to what was stylish and what was passé. When movies appeared, the younger members of most Western cultures learned the magical power of dress from Hollywood films. Yet, this medium had its weaknesses. Only in the country of their origin were the films truly up to date.

From the 1930s through the early '40s, young people grew up longing to have feet as small as Cinderella's, lips like Clara Bow's, and Veronica Lake's hair. During the years of World War II, every young woman felt she was playing the role of patient, loving wife or sweetheart, dreaming of the day when her man would return. Following the styles of the stars, she dressed in clothes that emphasized her femininity, only putting such frills aside when she took her lover's place in the factory or joined him in the military as a WAC or a WREN.

But the children of the sixties, seventies, and eighties looked to their rock-singer idols for their models. These young people, made pessimistic and untrusting by two major wars and a flurry of smaller (but equally deadly) "police actions," saw clothing more to their liking in a black leather motorcycle jacket worn by Marlon Brando, and duck-tailed hair styled like Elvis Presley's.

What made this period most remarkable was that television brought the same images to young people worldwide—simultaneously. Since the introduction of television, our Western ideals have dramatically changed, as have the ideas and dreams of many other young people throughout the world who see the same television programs as we do via satellite, even in the most remote areas. Now, suddenly, there needs be no "backward" society, as far as being aware of what is happening in the rest of the world.

I remarked earlier that in my travels I saw primitive natives in far-off places dressed in jeans and T-shirts watching the village television set. This is not a rare occurrence today. Television, the world's best means for joining all mankind into a unified global-city, is also the most notorious vehicle through which all differences in culture have been put in jeopardy, seriously limiting the opportunity for individual societies to express and mature their own unique traditions.

Children and young people everywhere now yearn to wear a previously undreamed range of clothing-styles they have seen displayed on television, many worn by their favorite pop stars. Fashion trends toward skimpy black leather outfits, trimmed with metal studs and chains, cut-off tank tops, undergarments worn as outer garments, and an assortment of bondage and fetish styles can be directly traced back to the stage costumes worn by Prince, Madonna, Cher, Queen, Blondie, Suzi Quatro, Cindy Lauper, and the protagonists of Rap music, as featured on television music video programs. And wherever these stars have appeared, the styles follow.

Television, though the most powerful "new media" affecting change, is not alone. The desire for change in clothing-styles has also been fueled over the past few decades by the growing popularity of magazines such as *Penthouse* and *Playboy*. These, and others like them, have helped champion the cause of nudity and sexier modes of dress through their explicit photos of nubile young women, as well as those of the rich and famous.

Travel magazines, too, have helped to widen our clothing spectrum by featuring exotic modes of apparel and body adornments worn by remote cultural groups. They cooperated with television programs like National Geographic to make people aware of the world in a way they never were before. No longer did readers have to be content with simply looking at pictures. Combined, TV and travel publications promoted the growing trend for vacationing in previously inaccessible places, luring tourists to take exotic trips where they purchased unusual ethnic styles of clothing and brought them back home.

This trend opened up an interchange of clothing possibilities that eventually led to a mode of dress which originated in India being copied by a dressmaker in Cairo for a tourist living in London. Soon, the growth of tourism to Asian countries, the Pacific islands, Africa, Brazil and Mexico resulted in a mixing of ideas which greatly influenced the fashion merchandise being sold in most Western cities. Thus, an international style of ethnic-inspired design began to evolve, featuring the use of texture, juxtaposed colors and exotic patterns that had their origins everywhere—and nowhere. Fashion stylists began to share the open attitudes of the people they served. Anything was possible: any combination of colors, textures, and patterns.

Many leading designers, such as Karl Lagerfeld, Zandra Rhodes and Yves Saint Laurent have also helped to widen the spectrum of consumer choice by introducing a sense of theatricality into their designs. St. Laurent in particular has regarded the promotion of his recent collections as a potent mixture of theatre, ballet and opera, that are "full of dreams and phantoms and magic." His seasonal Paris fashion shows of the 1970s and '80s have been described by Alex Madsen, in his book on St. Laurent, as being "the foremost form of modern live entertainment. Ten days of madness...with the big names each wanting to stop the parade...the city of lights became Holly-wood—sur Seine—an extravaganza of color, hysteria and tension, special effects and over-stimulation."

THE OFF-THE-PEG MOULDED BODY TOP

Back to the future: In the mid-1980s, the corset re-emerged as a fashionable item of women's apparel, engineered by modern technology from a plastic molding, thus giving the wearer an idealized shape.

In the late 1980s, this theatricality was further accentuated by the performance clothes worn by rock and pop artists, music video tapes, television commercials, programs featuring Rio-style Mardi Gras, and by many films aimed at the teenage market—all of which has created a very distinctive mode of dress aimed at clothing the wearer's psyche, rather than the wearer's body. In fact, what so many young people became engaged in was not so much the relatively simple process of direct imitation, but the more complex one of total identification.

This concept, though new, can easily be applied to past "copy-cat" clothing styles such as existed in the early days of movies, as well as to the present. The young woman of 1943 felt like a movie star when, dressed in a garment like one she saw on her favorite movie heroine, she waved good-bye to her lover who was, himself, dressed in a uniform that had its own theatrical overtones of heroism and bravery.

Many contemporary commentators believe that clothing style not only delineates the surface of the wearers, but "also projects their soul outside it, revealing their innermost secrets—a vehicle through which we express who we are, where we live, what our age is, what we do for a living, our gender, and often our preferences of what we like doing in bed." As if to prove the point, clothing as a personal art form and as a unique statement of personal expression has increased in recent years.

Yet, despite all of these changes, many people in the Western world are still prisoners of their inherited moral prejudices. We have a tendency, as a cultural group, to claim to be free and to taunt those who believe in a different ideology by calling them conformists. Yet in matters of dress we still reject originality. Many of us still react in horror at the thought of wearing any form of garment which does not fit into our current moral standards.

For example, the very thought of being naked, except in our most intimate moments, so embarrasses most of us that we still call on our lawmakers to protect us from viewing others in such a state. We seem to exhibit a phobia about nakedness that was not present in earlier civilizations—a phobia that serves to keep us from accepting ourselves as we really are. We behave as if only a clothed person is a complete person. A naked person minus his clothes is lacking some important part of himself. Yet, we are all aware that human babies start life completely naked. If a naked child is complete and perfect, then, regardless of the child's sex, education, wealth, race, religion, or cultural inheritance, that child will remain naked for the rest of its life. Those items of clothing or adornment which he or she decides are proper or fit to wear in order to adapt to a socially and/or sexually acceptable norm are added—extra—covering the real person who exists inside them.

Thus, each morning as we prepare ourselves to meet the world, we are performing a time-honored cultural ritual by changing our bodies from their natural, naked state. Depending on our heritage or personal whim, this may mean putting on a printed cotton dress, T-shirts and shorts, a business suit, or simply daubing a few marks of paint onto the face and body, and adjusting a nasal quill.

This desire to change our bodies in some way from their naked state is so prevalent, so pervasive, that many authorities believe such conscious alteration alone sets us apart from the animal world. Recent archeological discoveries have shown that this human desire to adorn and decorate the body is by no means a new phenomenon. The mass of evidence now available from widely scattered excavations indicate that the adorning of the human body is certainly among the oldest of human aesthetic activities, parallel with dancing, chanting, certain forms of music, cave paintings and many ceremonial rituals.

It would seem, therefore, that although our evolution and lineage may be clouded by a certain amount of conjecture, adorning and decorating the human body was undoubtedly among the first of all truly human activities. By adorning themselves, our ancestors not only distinguished their physical bodies more sharply from the animal world which surrounded them, but also added an important psychological cubit to their stature.

All of the recently discovered details about our ancestors' way of life indicate that no aesthetic, religious, food gathering, hunting or lovemaking activity was generally performed without a conscious adjustment to the human psyche—a change that could only be expressed on a social level by a change in their physical appearance. This change in appearance made our ancestors very aware of their physical selves, and it is this same physical awareness which is so important to us today. This, probably far more than for modesty or warmth, is why—in this

The continuing influence: Jet travel, television travelogues, ethnic festivals, international books and magazines, and the growth of new economic powers such as the Middle East and Japan continue to inform our desires and shape our sartorial preferences.

technological age of central heating and air conditioning—we still continue to wear clothes, even on the most informal occasions when it would be more comfortable and far easier for us to go naked.

We are, in fact, addicted to clothing. We use dress to make us look taller, prettier, wealthier, more learned, reliable, younger, more athletic and more desirable than we really are. Garments of some sort or another have become one of our most enthralling indications of social evolution, personal identification, cultural enunciation and artistic expression. It is the medium through which we display our ideas about our social status and gender, and through which each new generation hopes to establish its own identity.

This is why the history of our clothing styles, once the exclusive province of the costume archivist, now receives the rapt attention of political scientists, economists, sociologists, psychologists, anthropologists and art historians. Although the garments we choose to wear today may be more varied than ever before, they may also have become much more personal. One statement modern dress unequivocally makes is this: We are no longer slavishly obedient to the dictates of authority. The "laws" of etiquette and social acceptance previously laid down by the elite members of our society no longer rule our lives and our appearance. Only our own individual inclination matters when we set about choosing whom we should call friend, where we should go, what we should do, what particular garment we will wear, and when we will wear it.

Many of today's styles are deliberately designed to dress our psyche rather than to conceal our bodies. This is fully understood by many of the new designers, whose influence will undoubtedly become increasingly more important as we approach the new century. Their novel ideas are already beginning to reshape our way of thinking about our bodies and the clothing styles we choose to cover ourselves. Having grown up in an industrialized world, these designers are aware that our sexual senses may have become jaded by the constant barrage of sexual signals transmitted through the international media, yet they are nevertheless aware that sexual attractiveness is still very important to the Western clothing tradition.

Sexual attractiveness is just one of the many important messages that Langner made clear earlier in this book, particularly as it related to female clothing. He wrote that woman has "sensibly appropriated all beauty and ornament in clothing to herself, using her clothing to compose an alluring picture of outer manifestations of inner delights. At her best, her clothes supply a discreet invitation to indiscretion. At their worst, they represent a vulgar display of her charms like an over-crowded shop window." He stated that it was the invention of clothing which allowed more emphasis to be placed on man's intellectual quali-ties, rather than his physical ones, thus "becoming an important factor in sexual selection and the later evolution of the human race." He also made it clear that it was the use of clothing that made it possible for governments to obtain obedience, religions reverence, judiciaries a respect for law, and discipline in their armies.

All of Langner's points are still true today, although it is my belief that in the not-too-distant future, people in many parts of the world will wish to liberate themselves of the constraints to their freedoms (which in the past have been imposed by the normative manipulation of clothing styles), as they begin to realize they have a natural birth-right to decide their own mode of bodily presentation: whether to accept fashion for fashion's sake or to display their bodies in a more individualistic way. Freed from the necessity of having to conform to any arbitrarily imposed laws and rules, they will be able to decide by the appearance or "look" alone which style of clothing or adornment suits them best.

I firmly believe, however, that just as our ancestors turned away from total body freedom toward a more concealing mode of dress—as happened during the early nineteenth century after the excesses of the French Revolution—so will our own children or our children's children eventually put at least some aspects of freedom aside. We can hope, though, that such a return will not bring with it all of the un-natural repressive phobias about human nudity that so bedeviled our grandparents' generation, that no decendents of ours will again permit clothing to be used as a method of controlling behavior as it has in the past, and that the garments they wear will be an honest expression of creativity and inventiveness, fully expressing their deepest ambitions, hopes and dreams.

Bibliography

GENERAL

Bergler, Edmund, *Fashion and the Unconscious*, New York, 1953.
Ellis, Havelock, *Studies in the Psychology of Sex*, Philadelphia, 1923.
Flügel, J.C., *The Psychology of Clothes*, London, 1950.
Hammerton, J.A. (ed.), *Peoples of All Nations*, The Fleetway House, London.
Hauser, Arnold, *The Social History of Art*, New York, 1951.
Hiler, Hilaire, *From Nudity to Raiment*, London, 1929.
Hurlock, E.B., *The Psychology of Dress*, New York, 1929.
Langdon-Davies, *The Future of Nakedness*, New York, 1928.
Laver, James, *Clothes*, New York, 1953.
Mead, Margared, *Male and Female*, New York, 1949.
Radin, Paul, *Primitive Religion*, New York, 1957.
Rudofsky, Bernard, *Are Clothes, Modern?*, Chicago, 1947.
Veblen, Thorsten, *The Theory of the Leisure Class*, New York, 1924.
Westermarck, *History of Human Marriage*, New York, 1922.

CHAPTER 1

Adler, Alfred, *Individual Psychology*, New York, 1924.
Carlyle, Thomas, *Sartor Resartus*, London, 1833.
Ellis Havelock, *op. cit.*
Kohler, Woldgang, *The Mentality of Apes*, London, 1925.
Mead, *op. cit.*
Radin, *op. cit.*
Westermarck, *op. cit.*

CHAPTER 2

Allen, Agnes, *The Story of Clothes*, New York, 1958.
Bergler, *op. cit.*
Braidwood, Robert J., *The Near East and Foundations for Civilization*, Eugene, Oregon, 1952.
Crawford, M.D.C., *Philosophy in Clothing*, Brooklyn Museum, New York, 1940.
Davenport, Millia, *The Book of Costume*, New York, 1948.
Gorseline, Douglas, *What People Wore*, New York, 1952.
Hiler, op. cit.
Keller, Werner, *The Bible as History*, New York, 1956.
Kohler, op. cit.

Lewis, Albert, *People of the South Pacific*, Chicago Natural History Museum, 1951.

Maringer, Johannes, and Bandk, Hans-Georg, *Art in the Ice Age*, New York, 1953.

Montagu, Ashley, Man, *His First Million Years*, Cleveland, 1957.

Moore, Ruth, Man, *Time and Fossils*, New York, 1953.

Yerkes, R.A., *The Great Apes*, New Haven, 1929.

CHAPTER 3

Freud, Sigmund, *Basic Writings*, New York, 1938.

Flügel, *op. cit.*

Hurlock, *op. cit.*

Langdon-Davies, *op. cit.*

Moeurs, *Usages et Costumes*, Oceanic, Brussels, 1843.

CHAPTER 4

Chalmers, Helena, *Clothes*, New York and London, 1935.

Coryat's Crudities, Vol. I, Glasgow and New York, 1905.

Hawes, Elizabeth, *It's Still Spinach*, Boston, 1954.

Henry, George W., *All the Sexes*, New York, 1955.

Langner, Lawrence, and Marshall, Armina, *Suzanna and the Elders*, New York, 1937.

Lundberg, F., and Farnham, M., *Modern Woman, the Lost Sex*, New York, 1947.

Richter, Gisela, M.A., *The Sculpture and Sculptors of the Greeks*, New Haven, 1950.

Rudofsky, *op. cit.*

Schweinfurth, *The Heart of Africa*, Vol. I, New York, 1875.

Stubbes, Philip, *The Anatomie of Abuses*, London, 1585.

CHAPTER 5

Cunnington, C. Willett, *Why Women Wear Clothes*, London, 1941.

Huxley, Francis, *The Affable Savages*, New York, 1957.

Langdon-Davies, *op. cit.*

Langner, Lawrence, *The Magic Curtain*, New York, 1951.

Rudofsky, *op. cit.*

CHAPTER 6

Carlyle, op. cit.

Kirk, Ruth B., *American Sunbathing Association*, 1957.

Langdon-Davies, *op. cit.*

Merrill, Frances and Mason, *Among the Nudists*, New York, 1931.

American Sunbather & Nudist Leader, 1957.

Chapter 7

Boas, Franz, *General Anthropology*, New York, 1938.
Coon, Carlton S., *The Races of Europe*, New York, 1939.
Frankfort, Henri, *The Birth of Civilization*, New York, 1956.
Haldane, J.B.S., *Daedalus*, New York, 1924.
Jacobs and Stern, *General Anthropology*, New York, 1955.
Moore, *op. cit.*

Chapter 8

Flugel, *op. cit.*
Guerber, H.A., *Myths of Greece and Rome*, New York, 1893.
Hamilton, Edith, *The Greek Way*, New York, 1942.
Havemeyer, Loomis, *The Drama of Savage Peoples*,
    New Haven, 1916.
Hays, H.R., *From Ape to Angel*, New York, 1957.
Radin, *op. cit.*
Richter, *op. cit.*
Veblen, *op. cit.*

Chapter 9

Nordhoff, Charles, *The Communistic Societies of the United States*,
    New York, 1875.
Webber, Everett, *Escape to Utopia*, New York, 1959.

Chapter 10

New York Times, February 24, 1957.
New York World-Telegram & Sun, January 14, 1957.
New York Times Magazine, January 27, 1957, and January 2, 1957.
Trinidad Humming Bird, Carnival Number, 1957.
Trinidad Sunday Guardian, March 17, 1957.
Variety, November 13, 1957.

Chapter 11

Dictionary of the Bible, Boston, 1863.
Erie, John Dingwell, *The American Women*, New York, 1957.
Hurlock, *op. cit.*
New York Times, July 7, 1957.
Picard-Cambridge, *The Dramatic Festivals of Athens*, Oxford, 1953.
Wylie, Philip, "The Yankee She," *Saturday Review of Literature*,
    New York, 1957.

Chapter 12

Code of Criminal Procedure of New York State, Section 888.
Ibid., Section 710.

Ibid., Section 1140.

Detzer, Karl, "No Clues," *Reader's Digest,* May, 1957.

Ellis Havelock, *op. cit.*

Henry, *op. cit.*

Hurlock, *op. cit.*

Powell, Walter, *The Pilgrims,* Wilmington, 1923.

Sunday Advocate, *Georgetown,* Barbados, March 22, 1957.

Wilcox, R.Turner, *Mode in Furs,* New York, 1951.

CHAPTER 13

Baudelaire, Charles, "The Painter of Modern Life," *The Essence of Laughter,* New York, 1956.

Laver, *op. cit.*

Lynes, Russell, *A Surfeit of Honey,* New York, 1957.

Nystrom, Paul H., *Economics of Fashion,* New York, 1928.

Veblen, *op. cit.*

CHAPTER 14

Hauser, *op. cit.*

Hurlock. *op. cit.*

Kaver, *op. cit.*

Reader's Digest, November, 1956.

Rudofsky, *op. cit.*

Veblen, *op. cit.*

Wilcox, R.Turner, *The Mode in Footwear,* New York, 1948.

CHAPTER 15

Earle, A.M., *Two Centuries of Costume in America,* New York.

Laver, *op. cit.*

CHAPTER 16

Stone, Mrs., *Chronicles of Fashion,* London, 1870.

Willett-Cunnington, C. & P., *The History of Underclothes,* London, 1951.

CHAPTER 17

Beare, W., *The Roman Stage,* Cambridge, Mass., 1951.

Bowers, Faubion, *Theatre in the East,* New York, 1956.

Havemeyer, *op. cit.*

Kuhn, Herbert, *The Rock Pictures of Europe,* Fairlawn, N.J., 1956.

Smith, Winifred, *The Comedia Dell' Arte,* New York, 1912.

Stanislavsky, C., *An Actor Prepares,* New York, 1936.

Stopes, M.C., *The Plays of Old Japan.*

Webster, T.B.L., *Greek Theatre Production,* London, 1956.

351

CHAPTER 18

Clark, Sir Kenneth, *The Nude: A Study in Ideal Form,*
New York, 1956.

Hauser, *op. cit.*

Moliére, *The School for Husbands,* adapted by A. Guiterman and
Lawrence Langner from the original, New York, 1933.

Moore, Lillian, article on ballet costume, *Encyclopedia dello
Spettacolo,* Vol. III, Rome.

Richter, *op. cit.*

CHAPTER 19

Bergler, *op. cit.*

Harper's New Monthly Magazine, "Song of the Hoop,"
New York, 1857.

Hazllitt, William, *On Fashion.*

Hurlock, *op. cit.*

McCardell, Claire, *What Shall I Wear?,* New York, 1956.

CHAPTER 20

Cousins, Norman, "The Man Who Didn't Come to Dinner,"
Saturday Review of Literature, April 20, 1957.

Djilas, Milovan, *The New Class,* New York, 1957.

Hiler, *op. cit.*

New York Herald Tribune, March 15, 1957.

New York Times Magazine, May 26, 1957.

ADDENDUM

CHAPTER 21

Robinson, Julian, *Body Packaging: A Guide to Human Sexual
Display,* Elysium Growth Press, Los Angeles, 1989.

Robinson, Julian,*The Golden Age of Style: The Brilliance of Art
Deco,* London, Paris & New York, 1976.

Allen, Mariette Pathy, *Transformations: Crossdressers and Those
Who Love Them,* E.P. Dutton, New York, 1990.

Index

Back to Methuselah, 301
Bakst, Leon, 270, 271
Balanchine, George, 266, 271
Balanciaga, 329, 332
Bali, 256
Ballet Comique de la Reine, 264
  ballet, American, 260, 262, 266,
  270; English, 266; French, 264,
  265, 266, 266; Italian, 264, 267,
  268, 270; Russian, 270, 271;
  shoes for, 266, 267; Turkish, 265;
  tutu for, 261, 268, 269, 269, 270
Ballets, Africaines, Les, 168, 177
balloon skirt, 295
Barbados Uniforms Act, 170
"Barbudos," Cuban, 188
Barclay, Dorothy, quoted, 142-143
Bardot, Brigitte, 328
Barker, Granville, 242
bath robe, 234
bathing suit, 73, 77, 78, 79, 318
Baudelaire, 190
Bazaar, 330
beach robe, colored, 194
Beare, W., 251
Beatles, 339
beaver hat, 417
Bell, Gawain, 311
bell-shaped skirt, 29, 31
Bells Are Ringing, 244
beret, 195, 335
Bergler, Edmund, 292, 294
Bermuda shorts, 193, 194
Bernhardt, Sarah, 244
Bernstein, Leonard, 133, 134
Beryozka dancers, 264
Bible as History, The, 35
Bible, 277; references in, to use of
  clothing, 165-66, 177, 336;
  symbolism of, 125
bicycle costume, for ladies, 64
bifurcated undergarments, 320
Bikini bathing suit, 73, 78, 78
Billy the Kid, 271

bisexual image of Rock Stars,
  339, 340
bisexuality 340
bisexuals, 337
Bisilliat, Maureen, 317
black plague, 324
Blondie, 341
bloomers, 63, 67
blouse, Cretan, 35
blue jeans, 194, 196; on primitive
  tribesmen, 316; as unisex cloth
  ing, 333
Boas, Franz, 104, 105
Bodbold, Brian, 330
Bolshoi Ballet, 271
"Bond Street Loungers," 190
bonnet, 225
Borneo woman, skirt of, 33
Boston Rational costume, 64
Bow, Clara, 341
Bowers, Faubion, 256
Bowie, David, 340
bowler hat, 223; female, 62
Brando, Marlon, 328, 341
Brassempouy, Venus of, 96, 98
brassiere, 212, 214, 214, 215, 215,
  216
breastplate, 206
bridal costume, 47
"Bride in Breeches, A," 66
bridegroom, suit of, 158
bridesmaid, uniform of, 158
British West Indies, 103
Britons, ancient (frontispiece)
Brittany, trousers worn in 23
Bronze Age, Danish graves in, 29
Brown, John Mason, quoted, 282
Brugnoli, Amalia, 267
Brummel, Beau, 51, 189, 227, 286
Buddha, 112, 125
buffalo dance, 262
bullet-proof vest, 208
bullfight, as costume spectacle,
  162-63

357

students, 338; used to control sex, 339; and Pop music stars, 341; international influence on, 342, future of, 347
Fath, Jacques, 53
feathers, ornamental, worn by aborigines, 7, 10, 216
Federal Reserve Bank of Philadephia, quoted, 288
female impersonation, 173, *174, 175;* in theatre, 247, 248, 256
female styles of dress to blend with males, 338
festivals, Dionysian, 161, 252; seasonal, 160, 161
fetish, adult catalogs, 319
fetishism, 178
fez headdress, 154
Fiji woman, in sarong, *32*
Filling Station, 271
flannel petticoats, 320
flannel suit, gray, 193
"flapper" costume, 297; girl, 322
flight suit, 208
flounced skirt, 31
flower children 339
Flugel, J.C., 44, 72; quoted, 118
Foale, Marion, 330
Fokine, 270
Folies Bergére, 177
footwear, 203-05
Ford, Betty, 137
Forel, H., 82
Fortnum & Mason's 331
fox hunting, clothes worn for, 195
France, ballet in, 264, 265, 266 *266;* high heels in, 205; nudism in, 86; ornamental costumes of royalty in, 188, 189; wigs worn in, 218, immodesty after revolution, 324
Franklin, Benjamin, 78
Freemasonry, 154
French high heels, 205

French Revolution, 179, 187, 188, 220, 221, 340, 347
Freud, Sigmund, 80; quoted, 42, 280
frock coat, 333
full skirt, *49,* 58
Fuller, John G., quoted, 193-94
Fuller, Loie, 272
furs, 316-17, 318, 319
future of clothing, 301-12; equality in, 335, youth and, 338; of hippie styles, 340; predictions of 347
Galileo, 119
Galsworthy, John, 242
Gandhi, Mahatma, 108
Gaugin, "Nevermore" by *281;* quoted, 83
gender-based clothing, 337
Gentlemen Prefer Blondes, quoted, 315
George III of England, 221
George V of England, 320
Germany, nudism in, 86
Ghana dancers, *168,* 177
Ghost Town, 271
Gibson Girl, 333
Gilbert and Sullivan, quoted, 195
Gildersleeve, Birginia, C., 137
girdle of chastity, 207
girdle, invention of, 31, 211; modern, 214; pantie 326
Givenchy, 329
gloves, 326
gnomes, 273, 274
Gogol, 170
golfing tweeds, 195
Golovanova, Tamara, 264
Gorsline, Douglas, 35
GOUM, fashion show in, 304, *305*
government, in relation to clothes, 127-37, *129, 130, 132, 133, 135, 137;* control of male hairstyles, 337; condones style, 324; rationing, controlling, 326

gown, afternoon, 53, 43; décolleté
evening, 166; dressing, 234; of
judge, 135; wedding, 158
Graham, Martha, 272
gray flannel suit, 193
Gray, Gilda, 272
Great God Brown, The, 257, 258
Greek Theater Production, 250
Greek Way, The, 116
Greeks, ancient, clothing, of, 111,
170; creative thinking by, 115;
festivals held by, 161; footwear
of, 204-205; kyulix of, 277;
mantle worn by, 35; pubic hair
omitted by, in female nudes, 279;
religion of, 108, *109, 110,* 111;
sculptures of clothing by, 278;
sense of sin absent in, 89, 90;
theatre of, 250, 251, *251,* 252,
255; underclothing worn by, 229;
view of modesty of, 76; wigs worn
by, on stage, 218
gremlins, animal appendages
of, 274
Grimaldi, Venuses of, 26
Grimble, Arthur, quoted, 41
Guatemalan Indians, *60*
Guiterman, Arthur, 265
Gunther, John, quoted, 303
Gypsy Dancers, 273
Haggin, Ben Ali, 177
Haile Selassie, *129*
hair, in relation to clothes,104,
106; focus on, 318,styles, 337
Hairy Ape, 12
Haldane, J.B.S., 102; quoted, 98
Halloween, 149
Hamilton, Edity, 116
Hamlet, 244, 245, 246
Hand, Learned, 193
hand, importance of, 20
Harlequin, costume of 248
Harper's New Monthly Magazine,
quoted, 293

Harris, Jeff, *color plate X V (lower)*
Harrod's, 331
Hartnell, Sir Norman, 331
hat, bowler, 223; bowler, female,
62; caricatures of, 224; coonskin,
274; felt, 223; flat, 225; high, 222,
223; invention of, 221-22; opera,
222; of Samoan girl, 33; seven
basic shapes of, 225; silk, 222;
straw, female, *62;* ten-gallon, 222
Hauser, Arnold, quoted, 207-08
haute-couture, 320, 323, 332
hippies, 332, 339, 340
Franklin, Benjamin, 78
Havemeyer, Loomis, 253; quoted,
120, 256, 258
Havoc, June, *45*
Hawaiian shirt, 194
Hawes, Elizabeth, 68, 198
Hayes, Helen, 243
Hazlitt, William, quoted, 290-91
headdress, 220, 222, 225
Held, Anna, 294
Henry IV of France, 265
Henry VIII of England, 179
Henry, George W., quoted, 62-
64, 171
Hepburn, Audrey, 328
Hepburn, Katharine, 246;
in *As YouLike It,* 246-47; in
Merchant of Venice, 247
Hera, 109
heraldry, 137
Hercules, 109
Hermes, 112
Herodotus, 35, 77
high hat, 222, 222, 223
high-heeled shoe, 205
Highland kilt, 54
himation, 35
hip extender, *213,* 216
Hippocrates, 78
Hitler, 128, 165
hobble skirt, *52, 53,* 292

269, 270; balloon, 295; bell-shaped, 29, 31; of Borneo woman, 33; Cretan, 35; divided, 67; Egyptian, 35; flounced, 31; full, 49, 58; hobble, 52, 53, 292; hobbling effect of, 53, 54, 55, 58; hoop, 292, 293; invention of 26; male wearing, 60, 61; palm-leaf, 32; reindeer hide, 29; of Samoan girl, 33; sheath, 52, 53
slacks, 46, 67, 70, 327
Slaughter on Tenth Avenue, 271
slipper, ballet, 267-78; evening, with French heels, 205
"slob" costume, 196, 199, 200
smock, 70
smoking jacket, 46
smuggling, 178
soldiers, uniforms of, 131, 132, 133, 134, 135
Solomon Islands, holiday dancers in, 181; palm-leaf skirt worn in, 32
Sons of Freedom, 92, 93
sorcerers, early, clothes of, 27
Soviet Russia, 103, 286; ballet of, 270, 271; dances of 263, 264; drab clothes in, 303-04; juvenile deliquency in, 144; modesty in, 80; nudism in, 87, 90-92 See also Communism.
Space Age costumes, 274, 300
Spain, armor worn in, 206; dances of, 273; Holy Week in, 147; shoe as erotic symbol in, 205
Spanel, A.N., 214
Spanish Levant, 30; rock paintings of, 26, 27, 28, 54
"spivs," 148
sporran, 22
sporting clothes, 194, 195, 296
sports shirt, 194
square dance, 262
St. Laurent, Yves, 331-32

St. Patrick's Day parade, 167
Stalin, 339
Stern, 105
stilts, 55
stockings, 234-37
Stone, M., 229
Stopes, M.S., 255
Strange Interlude, 258
strip-tease, 174, 175, 176
Stubbes, Philip, 336
Stubbes, Philip, quoted, 61-62
Sulu medicine men, 121, 309
Sumerian, male, in robe, 54
sun-bathing, 77, 78, 79, 84
Sunday Advocate, The, 170
Suzanna and the Elders, 70
sweaters and slacks, 46, 328
swimming suit, 73, 77, 78, 79; elimination of, 340
"Swinging London," 331, 132, 335
"T" shirt, 344; on primitives, 316
Taglioni, Marie, 267, 267
Tahiti, 166
Tanganyika, native women of, 11
tango, 273
Tanna, New Hebrides, 22
tannic acid, 29
tanning leather, invention of, 29
Tarascan Indian medicine men, 123
tartan, 137
tattooing, 10, 13, 166
"Teddy boy," clothing of, 143, 148, 327, 333
teen-agers, clothing of, 141-44; makeup, 323, dress for sexual attraction, 327; disenchantment of, 328; fashion designers, 330, 339, 343
ten-gallon hat, 333
tennis costume, 296
Terry, Ellen, in *Merchant of Venice*, 247
Thailand, 256; theatre in, 253